Value Orientations in Counseling and Psychotherapy

The Meanings of Mental Health

❖❖❖❖❖❖❖❖❖❖❖❖❖❖❖❖❖❖❖❖
C. MARSHALL LOWE
University of California, Berkeley
❖❖❖❖❖❖❖❖❖❖❖❖❖❖❖❖❖❖❖❖

 CHANDLER PUBLISHING COMPANY

124 Spear Street, San Francisco, California 94105

Distributed by Science Research Associates, Inc., A Subsidiary of IBM
259 East Erie Street, Chicago, Illinois 60611

*TO MY PARENTS, WHO INSTILLED
IN ME THOSE VALUES WHICH IMPELLED
ME TO WRITE THIS BOOK.*

CONTENTS

PREFACE

The purpose of this book is to relate the theory and practice of counseling and psychotherapy to broad issues of a social, philosophical, and historical nature. Its aim accordingly is to help therapists to ask certain ultimate questions which must inevitably be raised within the context of therapuetic encounter. In other words, this book attempts to bring into sharper focus perceptions of the purpose of therapy which have remained rather myopically blurred.

I believe that it is all too easy for counselors and psychotherapists to be merely behavioral technicians who seek to make changes in their clients without being aware of the moral implications of their therapeutic efforts. The therapist must of course be scientifically knowledgeable so that he can understand why the client behaves as he does. But while therapists have grown increasingly knowledgeable concerning causal links in the client's past, they have not become nearly as sophisticated in charting the directions in which the client should be moving. This unresolved issue of describing the basic goals or values of human existence is the concern of this book.

This book started taking shape in my mind a decade ago when I was still a graduate student. While assembling material for a master's thesis, I discovered that different schools of therapy are guided by contrasting values which appear to be in unavoidable conflict with one another. Although I have communicated this basic discovery through an article in the *American Psychologist* (1959) and through several books of readings which have contained that article, I have known that much more remains to be said on the subject of values. As I have gained professional and academic experience, I have discovered that the ramifications of the value-orientation dilemma extend to additional contemporary issues.

The reader should not expect this book to offer a final answer to the ethical dilemma which has resulted from the conflicting claims of competing value orientations. He will instead be presented with different alternatives from which he can make his own choice.

While my personal biases are not likely to be totally concealed, I have made a conscious effort to avoid being either a polemicist or an evangelist. I still believe that even the well-informed and well-intentioned therapist can not totally escape the horns of the ethical dilemma. I hope, however, that this book will shed light upon the darkened maze of therapeutic morality so that the therapist may more meaningfully and purposefully help others.

This book is addressed to many types of readers, although psychological therapists are likely to be those most directly concerned with the issues discussed here. Whether these practitioners be termed counselors or clinical psychologists (or for that matter psychiatrists or social workers), they must inevitably influence the values of their client or patient. Since the book is constructed on the premise that therapeutic morality is integrally related to broader human concerns, it also discusses issues which touch upon pastoral theology, mental hygiene, and abnormal psychology.

I am indebted to friends, colleagues, and students for stimulation and for helpful advice. I wish again to acknowledge my gratitude to Dr. John R. Kinzer, my graduate adviser at Ohio State University a decade ago, who called my attention to the issue of value orientations in counseling. I am also indebted to those who have offered critical suggestions during the preparation of the manuscript. They include Dr. Robert Dolliver of the University of Missouri; Dr. James Ashbrook of Colgate-Rochester Divinity School; Robert Whiteley of Rutgers University; and colleagues at the University of California, including Professors Theodore Sarbin, Lawrence Stewart, and John Morris.

I wish also to acknowledge the typing assistance of Mrs. Marilyn Smith.

And finally I want to express appreciation to my family for the forebearance they demonstrated in the face of the inattention and preoccupation which were the necessary consequences of writing this book.

C.M.L.

Berkeley, California
November, 1968

Value Orientations in Counseling and Psychotherapy

 *INTRODUCTION*

And the Lord God planted a garden in Eden, in the east; and there he put the man whom he had formed. And out of the ground the Lord God made to grow every tree that is pleasant to the sight and good for food, the tree of life also in the midst of the garden, and the tree of the knowledge of good and evil. . . .

And the Lord God commanded the man, saying, "You may freely eat of every tree of the garden; but of the tree of the knowledge of good and evil you shall not eat, for in the day that you eat of it you shall die. . . .

So when the woman saw that the tree was good for food, and that it was a delight to the eyes, and that the tree was to be desired to make one wise, she took of its fruit and ate; and she also gave some to her husband, and he ate. Then the eyes of both were opened . . . . GENESIS

❖❖❖

Man is an experiencing organism who must learn to master what William James has often described as the "blooming, buzzing confusion" of birth. His nervous system is aroused continually by myriad perceptual stimuli which must be organized into a psychological blueprint or set of attitudes if he is to gain psychological control over his environment. By a coherent process of perceiving and thinking, man learns to differentiate consistently between what he senses to be aversive (and therefore regards as bad) and what he experiences as attractive (and consequently considers good).

The creation of attitudes, however, is merely the halfway point in the development of the process of making choices. Through the use of higher-order cognitive processes, man combines different attitudes into an abstract set of preferences which can be termed a value orientation. Murphy (1947) describes values as canalized drives which provide anchorage for all goal-seeking behavior. A system of values permits man to transcend the momentary pleasure or pain of a particular situation. He can then coordinate a virtually unlimited number of experiences into a unity encompassing the whole of his life experience.

Psychological values are subjective, as no two people experience the world in identical ways. Man, however, is a social animal, and while his system of values must be uniquely his own, his choice of value orientation is limited in its range by the circumstances of time and place. No matter how creative the individual may be, he must inevitably derive values from the ideologies of his particular cultural heritage.

Values, which are created by individuals, must be differentiated from morals, which are produced by the culture. Culture can be seen as a system of consensually validated social expectations deriving from the personal values of diverse individuals. Morals provide the social standard for differentiating between the good and the bad. When the moral code of a particular culture is extremely directive, the individual has only minimal freedom to construct his own values. Such a society is customarily described as moralistic; judgments of good and bad are based on a shared social ideology and any behavior which violates the consensually shared view of the good is likely to be judged immoral. It is difficult for a moralistic culture to tolerate individual differences as they are expressed as personal values. Those outside such a moral system consider it unduly repressive and restrictive. At the other extreme, societies can be highly tolerant, allowing the individual maximum freedom to create personal values that are unique and different. But when standards of conduct become too ambiguous or unstructured, the individual is likely to feel the inner discomfort of bewilderment and anxiety. Without shared moral experiences he also is apt to feel estranged and alienated. When the individual feels uncertain about his personal values and his location in society, it is appropriate to speak of an identity crisis. An identity as defined by Allen Wheelis depends upon "a sense of wholeness, of integration, of knowing what is right and what is wrong and of being able to choose" (1958, p. 19). When a society is at such loose ends that its members typically are unable to achieve a sense of wholeness, constructing a system of personal values can be a bewildering experience.

The social system faces a dilemma. On the one hand it is asked to permit man the freedom to select his own values so that he can experience himself as a distinct individual, but on the other hand it is expected to provide its members with a unifying set of expectations. A culture totally lacking in social control is indeed apt to become the prototype of Thomas Hobbes's classic vision of an amoral society in which life is "nasty, brutish, and short."

THE CHANGING NATURE OF SOCIAL MORALITY

There is a delicate balance between allowing the individual the freedom to choose values which have a personal meaning and at the same time providing him with the stability of a morality shared with others.

Because of the complex nature of such a balance, it is hardly surprising that diverse cultures deal with values and morals in quite different ways. Since morality in contemporary Western society differs quite markedly from moral styles of the recent past, it is instructive to compare these periods in their treatment of the nature of good and evil.

Morality in a Tradition-Oriented Society

In primitive societies, scientific, religious, and moral issues were undifferentiated: Superstitious notions about the physical universe were carried into the area of morality. Judgments of good and evil were so integral to the social fabric that standards of conduct could be questioned only by an outcast of the social system. The world of the savage may not have been a noble one, but it did provide man with a sense of moral security.

Western civilization has shown a gradual differentiation of moral issues from religion, science, and politics, Roscoe Pound (1942) notes that at the time of the Greek city state the same word was used in referring to ethical customs, religious rites, and the legislation of the city, all of these areas being regarded as one. The advent of Christianity separated for the first time theological issues from secular aspects of man's existence. Christians who attempted to divorce religion from cultural traditions were successful for only a short time. After the fall of Rome, theology asserted its dominance over science and politics as well as morality; the result was that bringing together of faith and reason commonly termed the medieval synthesis.

Recently there has been an acceleration in the secularization of society. The medieval synthesis is of course no longer intellectually viable. Bishop J. A. T. Robinson (1963) suggests that it may no longer even be possible to conceive of God as a Supranaturalistic

Being who exists somewhere out beyond the world. We live in what many theologians consider to be a post-Christian era. While much of a traditional morality still exists, society is seen as paying lip service to Christian principles for cultural reasons rather than as a consecration of personal faith.

The attempt of the society as a whole to derive a unifying and uniform morality from institutional religion belongs to what Riesman (1961) describes as a tradition-directed society. Routine, ritual, and religion (and indeed all elements of individual behavior) are encapsulated within the cultural matrix. In such a tradition-directed society, there is scant tolerance for individuals who wish to question the general moral code. So limited is the range of moral choice that there is little need for individualized types of guidance.

Morality in an Inner-Oriented Society

In more recent times the determination of good and evil passed from the churches and other social institutions to the individual. Morality ceased to be a matter of social prescription but instead became based on what was now regarded as the natural right of self-determination. Moral issues became more a matter of philosophy and theology, and reason became the tool for determining good and evil. The source of good which had been mysteriously enveloped in a Supernatural God was taken out of the heavens, and placed within the mind of each individual. The criterion for judging the world ceased being those qualities which man accepted on faith as being part of the nature of God and instead became humanistic virtues which were regarded as being an inherent part of man's nature. If therefore the moral solidarity of feudal society was taken away from man, he possessed in its stead faith in his own rational nature. This faith in reason resulted in the acceptance of certain basic self-evident truths which in their own way were regarded as infallible as their theological directives of an earlier day.

In Riesman's sociological model, periods of tradition direction are succeeded by societies which are inner directed. After the Renaissance, man ceased being beholden to an authoritarian moral code, and instead sought direction from cues emanating from within. The symbol of this inner-directed man is the gyroscope. The individual internalizes the values of his parents at an early age, and throughout later life these inner bearings act as a conscience in such a way that he can act with a sense of moral sureness even when explicit social guidelines are absent. Riesman describes inner-directed modes of social orientation as being present during periods of social expansion. Such a developing society provides each individual with a wide range of opportunities. In such a society the individual needs little help in choosing or attaining such self-selected values which are likely to interfere only rather minimally with the needs of others.

Morality in a Contemporary Society

Just as the tradition-bound values of the Middle Ages gradually gave way to a moral system based on natural law and individualism within the context of a developing society, so the closing of the frontiers marked the end of an era of expansion and called for the creation of new moral standards.

Riesman believes that our times are witnessing the decline of the inner-directed personality and the corresponding rise of the individual who is influenced for the most part by other people. In a complex and crowded urban environment individuals are increasingly dependent upon one another and at the same time find themselves more in each other's way. In an industrially well-developed society, values based on accumulation and production give way to those of distribution and consumption, and the individual can no longer afford to ignore other people as he did in a *laissez-faire* economy.

Because relationships among individuals have become the focus of present-day life, contemporary man can be considered "other directed," in contrast to his independent, inner-directed ancestor. It is misleading, however, to conclude that such an individual is a conformist because he is other directed. While the need for approval may be a dominant value in contemporary society, the nature of behavior which will gain social approval is now more uncertain than in times past. Conforming to the demands and expectations of others has become a highly ambiguous process now when older values have ceased to be believable and there is no new universally accepted system of beliefs.

If the contemporary individual is indeed driven to accept the values of his peers, contemporary morality has become so diffuse that the values of a particular individual can hardly reflect general social attitudes. The contemporary moral situation therefore fails to provide man with the moral focus which tradition or reason once did. As modern man looks to other people for guidance, he can not discover any single authoritative system of morals to which all of his peers give unquestioned ascent. Instead, in a society which has become politically and ideologically open, he perceives contrasting value orientations which compete for his moral allegiance and provide him with a choice which was not available to his forefathers.

MODERN MAN'S CRISIS IN VALUES

In his *Preface to Morals* (1929) Walter Lippmann points out that there is nothing new in man's having ceased to believe in the religion of his fathers. Ours is hardly the first period in history to question old moralities. Lippmann suggests, however, that this is the first time that circumstance has conspired with the intellectual habits of the times to render any fixed and authoritative system of moral beliefs incredible to large masses of men. The corrosive nature of what he terms "the acids of modernity" not only dissolves those usages and sanctions to which man had habitually conformed, but also prevents the crystallization of new ideas which might serve as the basis for a new orthodoxy. Probably the changing times, as Lippmann suggests, have always made the morality of one's forefathers seem uncouth; however, the increasing tempo of change has swept aside the moral anchors of religion and social philosophy which provided security for past generations, leaving man with a growing sense of moral uncertainty.

In this century time's flow has become a flood which renders values anachronistic even within the same generation. Some feel socially dispossessed because they have not had time to attain the latest mode of good living before that vision of the American dream is swept into historical oblivion. Attaining the good in such a society is reminiscent of the circus clown who keeps kicking away an object which he is trying to pick up. The good which our society allows its members to achieve is already outmoded, having been replaced by something better which is not yet attainable. The results are chronic frustration and confusion in a search for moral permanence.

In the agrarian past the consequences of one's actions were predictable. The moral primer placed in the hands of every child consisted of the simplest of fables whose allegorical messages could not be misinterpreted. The sheer complexity of modern society has mottled the black and white nature of the old moral universe, and it has become difficult to decide what is and what is not socially desirable. Building freeways to implement the commercial flow, which results also in a dissection of cities that destroys their natural beauty, is but one example of a complex social problem that defies a simple, unambiguous solution.

In times past the final good was God, who was quite clearly known. But, first for Nietzsche and now for many others, God is dead. If God is the highest good and He can not now be known, then the ultimate nature of good and evil is similarly unknown. Man today, left without clear-cut beliefs of what is good and bad, experiences so-called existential anxiety. With scant comfort from any authority, he must face the moral ambiguities inherent in common social situations. Freed from his moral past, the individual must find what Tillich (1952) terms the *courage to be*. This crisis of values has led theologians to discuss a new morality of situational ethics which would abandon the codified rules of conduct of the past for a new value orientation that could be unique to each social situation.

THE EFFECTS OF MORAL AMBIGUITY

Without an internally integrated system of attitudes and values, the individual can not impose order on experience. As a result he feels that life is chaotic and confused. Contemporary moral diffuseness appears to have much of the vague greyness of the fog which Riesman's psychic radarscope is intended to penetrate. The contemporary individual often feels that the channels of contemporary social morality are inadequately marked. The social space of an urban technocratic society is tightly packed, and only the most morally insensitive individuals are so impervious to the reality of others that they dare to move unfeelingly ahead. The contemporary individual typically feels anxious and uncertain in his social movements as he seeks to maintain a sense of direction in a crowded and fog-enshrouded channel filled with other social objects which are on seemingly changing courses as others also grope for bearings.

When values are too unstructured, clinical symptoms can appear. When the moral world seems chaotic, extreme anxiety and even the derangement of the schizophrenic can result. When moral bewilderment is less severe, the result is that psychological turmoil and confusion which produces character disorders and many types of neurotic conflicts. It is even possible, as Jerome Frank (1961) suggests, that much of the suffering from somatic complaints can be attributed to man's failure to find a convincing source of faith.

Moral ambiguity can also manifest itself in a general philosophical, ideological, and political dissatisfaction. A generation ago Lippmann (1929) describes man's "moments of blank misgiving in which he finds that the civilization of which he is a part leaves a dusty taste in his mouth" (1929, p. 4). Lippmann attributes such discontent to a lost faith that one's life is significant, and that it matters what one does with his life. He concludes that such people "are likely to point to the world about them, and to ask whether the modern man possesses any criterion by which he can measure the value of his own desires" (1929, p. 4). Since Lippmann wrote these words of a decade which in retrospect seems more morally indifferent than our own, his words are prophetic: The new youth has finally begun in a concerted and systematic manner to question the authenticity of the values underlying political, economic, and religious morality.

Counselors and psychotherapists are becoming increasingly aware that the effects of moral ambiguity have created the need for therapeutic services. According to Nicholas Hobbs (1962), therapeutic treatment fills the void left by religion by providing a new orientation to experience which would alleviate much of the uncertainty of contemporary existence. Frank (1961) believes that in earlier times individuals took on new beliefs when their "assumptive" worlds came into conflict with actual experience through religio-magical healing. On that basis he sees psychotherapy as a similar means of modifying the individual's assumptive world so that he can "impose an order and regularity on the welter of experiences impinging upon him" (p. 20). William Schofield notes that the history of therapy has come full circle "from priest-physician to physician to psychiatrist and, finally, to the analyst-priest" (1964, p. 144). In such a normless society as our own he finds that the psychotherapist's role has broadened to include his functioning as emotional tutor, intimate counselor, master philosopher, and guide in the quest for self-realization.

It is unlikely that our society will experience the complete moral breakdown that some alarmists foresee. Many still find direction in traditional morality, while others with sufficient self-possession are secure in a world which some find disordered and turbulent. The morally dispossessed commonly seek the help of a counselor or psychotherapist as a source of moral .direction – often the only available human resource for those outside of the social order. Although the therapist does not usually consider himself a moralist, he is, however, one of the few whose moral authority the typical modern man can still accept.

SUMMARY

This introduction describes some of the problems confronting modern man, who has lost the sources of direction that guided his forebears. No longer able to rely on the guidance of past tradition and unable to provide direction for himself through reason, the contemporary individual is bewildered and seeks help from counselors and psychotherapists, who are for many the most available and acceptable source of guidance.

The problems facing man today have been presented in terms of *values* and *morals.* From a psychological point of view, values are involved. As the world becomes more complicated, man finds it harder to gain cognitive control over the stimuli capable of arousing him emotionally. When the frame of reference is social, however, one speaks of morals, a term defined as a standard of conduct determined by social sanction. A system of morals results when different individuals consensually validate their personal values. Morals in turn influence the creation of systems of personal values.

It is unlikely today that man can be guided by other individuals to standards of belief and conduct which he can accept; therefore he seeks the help of the therapist in finding satisfactory values for himself.

 PART ONE

The Therapist and the Client in a World of Changing Values

Chapter 1

THE THERAPIST AS CONTEMPORARY MORALIST

On the morrow Moses sat to judge the people, and the people stood about Moses from morning till evening. When Moses' father-in-law saw all that he was doing for the people, he said, "What is this that you are doing for the people? Why do you sit alone, and all the people stand about you from morning to evening?" And Moses said to his father-in-law, "Because the people come to me to inquire of God; when they have a dispute, they come to me and I decide between a man and his neighbor, and I make them know the statutes of God and His decisions." Moses' father-in-law said to him, "What you are doing is not good. You and the people with you will wear yourselves out, for the thing is too heavy for you; you are not able to perform it alone...."

So...Moses chose able men out of all Israel, and made them heads over the people,...and they judged the people at all times...EXODUS

❖❖❖

Fashioning a system of personal values can never be done in total isolation. Instead, one assimilates values by interacting with his environment. Through a varied and complex process of imitation and identification, man learns to pattern a system of personal values after the social models which he accepts as reliable and believable. When man wishes to throw off the shackles of inappropriate systems of morality, he must find substitute sources of morality. Henry David Thoreau claimed that the seeming nonconformist is merely marching to the beat of a distant drummer. When modern man is successful in sloughing off traditional morality, it is only because he finds contemporary moral guidelines which seem to be personally more relevant.

THE THERAPIST AS NEW AUTHORITY

When modern man feels that he needs guidance or direction, in his bewilderment he is apt to seek the help of the counselor or psychotherapist. He hopes that the therapist will provide authoritative insights which will enable him to structure the chaotic flow of experience. Even though individuals differ in their attitudes toward therapy and the therapist, many people seem to share certain views.

The Scientific Mystique of the Therapist

As old traditions vanish and reason becomes a less reliable guide, individuals come to rely upon the authority of science, which has replaced those sources of morality rendered obsolete by social change. As the instrument of technology which produced these social changes, it commands the respect necessary to have become the basis of a new morality where what is good is equated with what is up-to-date.

There is no doubt that science has benefited man. It has made possible a physical well-being that the past never knew, and by reducing those contingencies of nature which threatened mankind in earlier times, it has promoted a new sense of security. Science has also helped man to increase his self-esteem. The satisfactions that one era found in mystical contemplation of God and that a later age discovered in reasoning out the enigmas of nature, modern man experiences in his mastery over an increasingly complex environment. If man has been notably unsuccessful in attaining the older virtues, he can find compensation in the achievements of science, which represent the high point of mankind's powers of actualization. As the source of the new good, science has the charisma to lead society to a promised land where what is good is equated with what is recent and modern.

Much of the psychotherapist's appeal seems to derive from his claim to be an expert whose knowledge has been scientifically validated. The exact nature of the therapeutic mystique which allows individuals to reveal hidden aspects of their personalities to a professional stranger when unable or unwilling to confide in intimate friends is unknown. A possible clue is perhaps provided by Jerome Frank in *Persuasion and Healing* (1961). Frank suggests that a man is healed when he has faith in the healer. He is not so unkind as to suggest (as others have) that the psychotherapist is the twentieth century's witch doctor, but nevertheless a number of parallels can be drawn between modern man's faith in the therapist and primitive man's reliance upon the shaman. And just as primitive man believed that the witch doctor exercised special powers over the natural world, many today believe that the therapist possesses special powers which can promote mental healing.

The Therapist as Expert in Human Behavior

In a world where the scientist is master, the behavioral scientist must inevitably be looked to as an important source of moral authority. While the behavioral scientist lacks the mystique of his colleagues in the physical sciences, he has his own kind of charisma. He possesses special skills and knowledge which must be given an ever-higher priority as technological achievements produce an increasing number of unanticipated social problems.

Riesman suggests that our other-directed society is oriented to the reality of other people. If, however, the individual has become dependent upon external direction, he perceives external cues as vague and indefinite. To continue Riesman's metaphor of the radarscope, when the individual's psychic radarscreen fails to provide a definitive image of social reality, he turns to the therapist as an expert in interpersonal relationships.

At one level, the therapist's function may be conceived of as that of a psychic technician whose role is to fix the radar set so that it can properly receive the social signals emanating from the outside other. According to this conception, the therapist's task is to help the client become more sensitive and more empathically involved. Accordingly, therapy is more conceived to be the process of learning to tune in experientially to the presence of others.

At another level, the therapist may be regarded as helping the client to decipher blips on the radarscope which would otherwise remain uninterpreted. The mysterious forms which flit across the radarscreen give only a vague notion of the nature of the external world, so that the anxious client has but an indefinite sense of the nature of the other which stands over against him. The therapist often represents the only tangible reality for clients who have known only a world of depersonalized mass other. Accordingly, the client asks the therapist to translate the symbols of the radarscope into a message that has personal meaning.

The Nondogmatic Nature of Therapeutic Moralism

If the therapist lacks the unquestioned authority of the physical scientist, he has the advantage over other scientists of typically being regarded as possessing a higher degree of human qualities.

While modern man has a profound awe for science, he also treasures his own moral freedom. He is therefore much more apt to
respect the moral authority of therapists who provide direction by
leading rather than by commanding.

A generation ago Walter Lippmann (1929) noted that the
disesteem in which the moralists of the day were held was due to
their failure to comprehend that in an age such as ours the
function of the moralist is to elicit the individual's own conception
of good rather than to exhort him to be good. Lippmann points
out that it has become impossible for the moralist to command.
Instead he must use a form of persuasion more humble than
command and more difficult than exhortation.

Lippmann wrote *Preface to Morals* at a time when counselors
and psychotherapists had less moral influence than they have today;
therefore he does not mention the therapist when discussing the
nondogmatic moralist. Today, however, the therapist appears to
come closer than other professionals in the providing of such a
nondogmatic morality. He is characteristically nondirective. Content
merely to guide, the therapist tries to stimulate the individual to
become his own source of morality by evoking his own values and
feelings.

THE THERAPIST AS SECULAR PRIEST

As a moralist, the modern therapist finds himself performing
many of those professional functions which in the past had been
performed by the minister or priest. The priesthood of Biblical
times occupied a position between God and man, making the
confrontation of the divine less fearful for men. The therapist
functions similarly, mediating between man and society, conveying
the meaning of that social world whose confrontation is so bewildering to modern man. To the therapist belong the keys of a new
kingdom, whose gates are opened not by faith in the supernatural,
but by faith in science as interpreter of social reality.

Since the secularism of contemporary society has blunted the
social thrust of more traditional religions, the theological priesthood
has lost much of its authority, and the social role traditionally
played by the Church has devolved upon science. With the sciences
becoming a sort of secular priesthood, the scientist practicing
counseling and psychotherapy assumes a new moral authority. He is

asked to make moral pronouncements in the name of science in the way the clergy was called upon for religious directives.

The similarity in function and role of these two professions has not totally escaped the new scientists of man. Dicks (1950) finds that the sciences of human behavior are set apart from the physical sciences by having the attributes of a secular priesthood or *therapeutae*. He compares the new ideal of mental health with such concepts as "finding God," "salvation," "perfection," or "progress," all goals which have inspired men in the past. Similarly Lee (1954) compares the professional roles of the new therapeutic practitioner with the more traditional professions, finding that the therapist functions in a broad area spanning the professional spectrum. As Lee describes this new practitioner, he "wears a tunic made from swatches out of ancient robes of shamans, parish clergymen, family physicians, and family solicitors" (1954, p. 519). Describing secular man's need for salvation, London (1964) notes that the psychotherapist who is concerned with moral issues "would fulfill a role more like that of a priest than of any other professional" (1964, p. 163). He would, however, be a secular priest, "whose justifications are not in a theology revealed from heaven, but one discovered or intimated in the laboratory" (1964, p. 163).

This identification of therapist and priest will seem strange to many, and unless the basis for making such a comparison is clear, it will raise needless antagonism and controversy. Indeed, assigning the counselor-psychotherapist a priestly role makes sense only if one discards popular stereotypes—the moralistic bluenose minister, the priest as incanter of magic rites, and the bearded scientist in a long white coat tinkering absentmindedly with exotically complicated equipment—and considers the professional role historically and somewhat abstractly.

The concept of religion in this book is not limited to concern with the supernatural but rather involves in a broader sense faith in what man considers his highest good. The author agrees with Tillich's (1957) definition of religion as ultimate concern and with Fromm's view of religion as "any system of thought and action shared by a group which gives the individual a frame of orientation and an object of devotion" (1950, p. 21). In such a context the common distinction between sacred and profane becomes a matter of personal preference: What is of greatest value to the individual is termed sacred, while everything of lesser value is considered secular.

Accordingly, concern with God within the context of a church is but one example of religious interest. Communism, which exercises the broad functions of a religious system by dictating an ultimate and absolute good that must be accepted on faith, also qualifies as a religion. Capitalism, humanism, ethical culturalism, psychedelicism, atheism, anarchism, and John Birchism are all quasi-religions in that each embodies basic religious attributes in its distinctive credo. If veneration of science is not subordinated to other values, science itself becomes a religion. Faith in the ability of science to achieve a "brave new world" where human misery is irradicated is properly termed scientism. The reliance of an earlier era on God or upon a free-enterprise system is transferred to the scientist, who offers technology to tame the physical world and the scientific method to cope with moral dilemmas.

Religion and the Behavioral Sciences

The clergyman and the mental-health practitioner respond to similar needs in their choice of profession. Each has a sense of calling which combines broad social concern with empathy for others. Traditionally the clergyman's has been a sacred call to serve God. Today, however, those who seek a divinely ordained vocational calling find it increasingly difficult to reconcile the inspired nature of the sacred call with the reality of an institution-bound church whose role and subsequent authority have been taken over by other social groups. Many who forego the clerical calling become behavioral scientists, thereby strengthening the role of science as moral leader.

Why the religiously oriented enter the behavioral sciences varies according to subculture on the one hand and scientific specialty on the other. A rather disproportionate number of Protestant psychologists are children of ministers. They typically come from liberal churches which emphasize education and which allow and even encourage dissent. In the behavioral sciences such people find religious concerns in an intellectual atmosphere whose horizons are much broader than those of the church.

Jews have been drawn to psychotherapy in a somewhat different way. Hollingshead and Redlich (1958) found a disproportionate number of Jews undergoing psychoanalysis. It seems likely that there is a similar situation among psychoanalysts themselves. The most searching analysis of the ideological affinity between Judaism and psychoanalysis is Bakan's *Sigmund Freud and the Jewish Mystical Tradition* (1958). Bakan believed that Freud was more intensely influenced by his Jewish background than he could ever admit because of antisemitic pressures in Victorian Vienna. While Freud remained self-consciously Jewish, he identified not with the orthodox form of the religion which adhered rigidly to the Mosaic code but with the Chassidim, a mystical group. This cult regarded religion as a personal and mystical experience, rather than an experience of ethnic solidarity. Freud developed a messianic consciousness of himself as the new Moses leading mankind out of the social bondage created by the law of the original Moses, whom Freud rather desperately tried to prove was really a non-Jew. Bakan thus sees psychoanalysis as an attempt to free the individual from the continuing restrictive effects of a religiously stringent past.

The Behavioral Sciences as a New Theology

If behavioral scientists often are those who have found it difficult to reconcile their broad social concern with either a socially institutionalized church or a traditional theological doctrine, the expression of their concern results in a new view of man that at times differs substantially from its equivalent theological doctrine. The result is a nontheological theory of man which, because of its immediate social relevance, becomes socially authoritative.

Quite often what the behavioral scientist has to say about the nature of man conforms to the theological definition of a heresy. A partial truth which, removed from its original context, loses perspective and becomes absolute by encapsulating within itself the whole of truth is just such a heresy according to William Temple. Typically heresies are a natural reaction to a theological orthodoxy which has rigidified around an extreme position itself representing much less than the whole truth. But bona fide heresies replace one extreme with quite an opposite one. They can be successful for a time, but often the heretical antidote proves worse than the poisonous orthodoxy it set out to alleviate. However the heresy can be useful if, by Hegelian logic, the two extremes are welded into a synthesis representing a more seasoned approach to truth.

The behavioral sciences have not made such heretical claims for absolute truth, nor have they reacted strongly against orthodox theologies. But as Lowe (1963) points out elsewhere, in other respects the behavioral sciences do closely resemble a theological heresy.

Socioeconomic changes which ended the Victorian pattern of living produced a new concern with the human condition, a subject long neglected by a church rigidified around old orthodoxies. In Europe a new approach to human nature was taken by Sigmund Freud, who reacted quite consciously against the theological orthodoxies of both the dominant Catholic majority and the persecuted Jewish minority of which he was a member. In a soil made fertile by centuries of neglect, the study of man by the behavioral sciences flourished.

In part at least, man's new understanding of himself through science has been a "rediscovery" of certain truths inherent in the Judeo-Christian tradition but almost completely ignored in the history of Christianity. Under the impact of newer ideological currents, theology is becoming more dynamic. In Lowe's view (1963), what has been most significant to theology is man's rediscovery of his social nature. This renewed awareness of the social matrix of existence brought about by the social and behavioral sciences has had an important influence even upon such traditional theological doctrines as sin and salvation. Hence sin is rediscovered as broken relationship and salvation as restored encounter. Thus Buber's description of an I-Thou encounter forms the basis of an entirely new theological model.

Therapy as a Source of Direction

The individual is most apt to seek direction from that source of influence in which he can place the greatest faith. Indeed, Frank in *Persuasion and Healing* (1961) points out that "examination of religious healing in so-called primitive societies and in Western society illuminates certain aspects of human functioning that are relevant to psychotherapy" (1961, p. 36). Both religion and psychotherapy inspire hope. According to Frank, religious healing arouses hope by creating dependency upon the healer, and similarly, as socially sanctioned expert and healer, the psychotherapist can create a sense of security and well-being through the interpersonal therapeutic relationship. Frank believes that when hope is aroused, a shift in what he terms the assumptive form world can effect changes in belief. He believes that the shifts in belief which accompany psychotherapy have their parallels in religious revivalism.

Both revivalism and psychotherapy depend upon a concerned relationship. Frank thus cites General William Booth, the founder of the Salvation Army, as saying "the vital first step in saving out-casts consists in making them feel that some decent human being cares enough for them to take an interest in the question whether they are to rise or to sink" (1961, p. 77). Through this relationship, the evangelist is the catalyst for a religious conversion, which Frank describes as "a change in a person's assumptive world, involving inter-related shifts in his attitudes towards his God, himself, and the people significant to him" (1961, p. 76). Frank notes that when psychotherapy is successful, it also produces a changed outlook in the client towards himself and the world which he cognitively creates.

The point is frequently made that the individual's choice to seek help from a clergyman or from a psychotherapist is somewhat arbitrary. Margolis (1966) points out that both therapists and priests minister to human needs. He describes both professionals not only as advising and counseling about the conduct of life but also as helping the individual better to commit himself to clear and distinct goals. London (1964) similarly finds that it is quite unclear how the roles of the priest and therapist differ from one another. In his view few problems brought to the therapist do not require moral commitments which formerly would have been secured from a more conventional type of priesthood.

Replacing the church with secular psychotherapy appears to have occurred to a greater extent in Europe than in America. (For statistics on English secularization, see Halmos, 1966, Ch. 2). No doubt the reasons for the differences between the Old and New Worlds are complex. Perhaps the influence of the church has declined more in European countries where psychotherapy is now more widely practiced than in America. When European psychotherapists describe how they meet their patients' religious needs, they find their Ameri-can counterparts quite incredulous. Secular psychotherapists in the United States have difficulty understanding statements that European therapists such as Jung, Frankl, and Tournier make about discovering an almost universal need among their patients to find meaning and purpose in life. Carl Jung's statement (1933, p. 264) that all patients past the age of thirty-five who sought psychotherapy from him had a problem he describes as religious seems without parallel in the annals of American psychotherapy.

In America the behavioral sciences seem somewhat slower than their European counterparts in feeling what might be termed an existential crisis. If Americans have not yet reached the point where they seek the help of secular therapists on overtly spiritual problems, nevertheless, the literature of American psychotherapy supports the view that the more sensitive American therapists have become aware of a new role thrust upon them by clients facing a severe conflict in important value choices. Gardner Murphy (1955) has thus noted that the roles of clergy and counselors increasingly overlap. Finding new professions have taken over the traditional roles of clergy and of medical and legal counselors, he believes that counselors must learn to help clients distinguish between good and bad values. This help can not be provided on the basis of scientific skills, which Murphy feels are not adequate for this task, but must be based on the counselor's basic personality resources which transcend scientific training or aptitude. Somewhat similarly Edith Weisskopf (1953) says that the problem of finding one's outlook on life is more acute in our day because of a loss of traditional values. E. G. Williamson (1958) also sees basic adjustment problems arising from the conflict over myriad value choices in the hetero-geneity of modern society. In Williamson's view, a bewildered individual can find help only from other individuals who have greater clarity in their value choices.

Scientific Claims to the Good Life

Counselors and psychotherapists not only make statements about the essential nature of man but also make claims about the final goal or purpose of human life. The therapist must bring man's final goal from the next world into this one. Even though naturalistic terms are used, the scientist's description of a Utopia is still a statement about destiny and purpose.

Ironically many of the scientists who are the most skeptical of theological eschatology are the most dogmatic in their rather grandiose scientific solutions to problems once considered religious. Their terms and promised land are new, but their belief in the power of prediction and control allows them to claim omnipotence and might with an evangelical fervor.

Thus in our day Aldous Huxley can question a *Brave New World* (1946) where the control of man's mind by the scientist is described with a greater immediacy and vividness than the millen-ium formerly depicted by the evangelist. If there is any doubt about the behavioral scientist's willingness to create such a world, one has only to read the description of the Utopian product of social control in B. F. Skinner's *Walden Two* (1948). Here the fondest hope naturalistic science has for man's destiny is a new world of scientific control where the behavioral engineer has become God.

To a social order seeking authority, behavioral scientists can proclaim "We are able." To a society frustrated in its search for the good life it offers hope for realization of a new this-worldly happiness.

THE THERAPIST AS POLITICAL THEORIST
AND SOCIAL PHILOSOPHER

The last five centuries have witnessed a decline in morality based on supernatural sanctions and have increasingly depended on freedom of choice. To a large extent secularized man has turned from formal religious systems to ideologies propounded by social philosophers and political theorists and then to counselors and psychotherapists.

The new political morality, based on faith in the individualized man and in his rational ideas of the good, was expressed in the writings of such influential thinkers as Jean-Jacques Rousseau, Thomas Paine, and John Locke. As the Age of Reason sought to rationalize and to individualize moral values, it found the social-contract theory particularly appealing. The result was a new system of values sanctioned by political conceptions of man's enlightened self-interest.

As a political morality based on such ideas as the social contract and *laissez-faire* individualism ceased to appeal to modern man, the source of moral authority has shifted again. Now the counselor and the psychotherapist have assumed many of the moral functions formerly performed by the minister and the priest as well as the moral authority of the political theorist and the social critic. These new social trends hardly make the lawyer and the politician obsolete, however, any more than the decline of the highly systematized medieval morality deprived the minister and the priest of meaningful social roles. But the shifting nature of public morality does suggest that the therapist and political theorist share an increasingly overlapping authority.

Evidence that the therapist is taking over much of the authority which once belonged to the social philosopher and the political theorist is found in Howard Mumford Jones' *The Pursuit of Happiness* (1953). This book traces the changes in the sources of happiness in American history. Although Jones and Riesman do not appear to have had a direct influence upon one another, the cultural history of Jones and the sociological analysis of Riesman (1961) have a definite parallel.

According to Jones, until the midnineteenth century our nation was guided in its pursuit of happiness by what were essentially political doctrines, given moral sanction by court decisions. The basis of this judicially defined happiness was natural law, based on what seemed at the time a thoroughly reasonable belief that (to quote the Declaration of Independence) "Men are ... endowed by their creator with certain unalienable rights," including the right to the pursuit of happiness. Although the law could be discovered by reason, its ultimate basis was God, the first cause. Since these rights were a part of nature, all men possessed them equally. Although man created civil government to guarantee these rights, Jones makes it plain that goodness itself was regarded as lying beyond man. Quoting from an 1810 court decision, civil government must "derive assistance from some superior power, whose laws extend to the temper and disposition of the human heart" (1953, p. 34).

For Jones, midnineteenth century represents a transition from divinely sanctioned natural laws to a more individualistic good. Happiness was defined in increasingly vague and contradictory ways by the courts but with new clarity in literature. The patron saint of the age was Ralph Waldo Emerson, who is perhaps the culmination of the inner-directed man. The new happiness was the opportunity to do the work one was born to do, and Jones quotes a characteristically Emersonian phrase: "Every man has this call of the power to do somewhat unique, and no man has any other call" (1953, p. 117). And perhaps even more revealing from a Riesmanesque standpoint, Jones also quotes Emerson as saying, "I look on that man as happy, who when there is a question of success, looks into his work for a reply, not into the market, not into opinion, not to patronage" (1953, p. 118).

Significantly Jones marks the transition to our current stage of the pursuit of happiness not by court decisions or by essays but by the publication of William James' *Principles of Psychology* in 1890. James, along with Freud and Jung, form a watershed in the pursuit of happiness between public achievement in politics and economics and the personal concern of psychology. Jones notes that since the time of William James there has been a "steady transplanting of the roots of happiness out of the world of Adam Smith and Benjamin Franklin into the world of the doctor, the psychiatrist, the personnel director, and the social psychologist" (1953, p. 146). He concludes that the ancient doctrine of happiness as living in accordance with nature has been transformed. Happiness now requires man to bridge the outer and inner worlds of nature, and as a result, candidly examine the relationship between inner feelings and external facts. Jones suggests that this connection appropriately takes place with the help of a new expert in interpersonal and intrapersonal affairs.

Howard Mumford Jones limits his discussion to the rather unique events of American history, although signs indicate that similar changes have been taking place in other countries. In a recent book entitled *The Faith of the Counsellors* (1966), Paul Halmos describes a decline in the influence of political ideology in Great Britain due to what is termed "the politics of antipolitics." Because the modern Englishman feels that political solutions to pressing moral problems have been unsuccessful, he now turns to that general mental-health practitioner whom Halmos terms the "counsellor." He believes the public expects to find in the "counsellor" the individualistic values and professional expertise that it feels the politician lacks.

Halmos describes a number of factors which he believes have contributed to general political apathy, two of which seem particularly relevant here. Halmos believes that modern man has become disillusioned with politics first of all because of the complicated nature of modern life. Social problems in the thermonuclear age seem more serious than ever, and man is constantly aware of the hazards in almost any political action. He also attributes political apathy to an increased skepticism toward the values which underlie political interest. Indeed, Halmos believes man is becoming skeptical of spiritual solutions to problems at the same time that he is becoming disillusioned with political activity. Halmos says that the individual has lost his respect for politics because political actions have become wasteful of human sympathy, and harden and depersonalize one's concern for others.

The same factors which cause the modern citizen to turn from the politician do, however, motivate him to seek the "counsellor's" guidance. In a complicated age fraught with moral peril, it may even be, as Halmos suggests, politically immoral to be unscientific. The respectable politician must therefore have science rather continually at his elbow. Halmos concludes that "One might say that today's ideology demands that ideology be replaced by social science and that politics be made all but unnecessary by scientific and technological planning" (1966, p. 13).

Halmos describes a new basis for political morality in an individualistic solution to social problems requiring a therapist. Halmos notes that "the man with a 'full-time social conscience' today is a professional man who does a service for a 'client' and whose service is centered on the individual" (1966, p. 16). The basic moral credo of the "faith of the counsellors" is that human happiness is found in the autonomous condition of an individual, rather than in political programing.

Much of the disenchantment with political solutions to social problems which Halmos has observed in Great Britain can also be seen in America. A new type of political liberal resents governmental attempts to create a good society because he believes that government action increasingly submerges man's individuality beneath the bureaucratic structure of a massive political establishment.

Moral disillusionment with the political establishments is most marked among members of the so-called New Left. New Leftists, who are likely to distrust any organized group, are as skeptical of the professional activities of the counselor and psychotherapist as they are of the political establishment. Distrust of bureaucracy is hardly limited to the far left, however. The political right also dislikes government intervention, and more significant still, so do an increasing number of moderates. Many citizens who are less extreme in their political views may well turn to therapists and to other behavioral professionals to solve social problems when political programs have failed.

The overlapping moral concerns of the therapist and politician would seem to impinge when individuals are faced with social, and therefore political, problems. Attempts to personalize the political process must involve the therapist in a wide variety of sociopolitical activities extending from a concern for individual social welfare to a general attempt to embody the society's moral concerns in comprehensive jurisprudence or social justice.

The Individualization of Social Welfare

Traditional charity and social welfare are increasingly regarded as moral and economic failures when they are not relevant to the unique needs of individuals. Indeed, the soup kitchen, the dole, and the condescending or "do-gooder" charity can themselves be regarded as social evils when their depersonalization deprive the recipient of his personal dignity and his sense of responsibility for his own destiny. Awareness is growing that worthwhile charitable and social programs should seek to increase man's sense of individuality.

Responsibility for the care of the needy, which once lay with individual benefactors or with voluntary charitable social institutions, resulted in a chance approach which failed to meet a rising moral concern. Since an urban industrialized society requires comprehensive social planning, the responsibility for the well-being of others has been placed upon the so-called welfare state. However, suspicion is growing, particularly among the welfare recipients themselves, that political attempts to solve pressing social problems will not succeed. Welfare recipients are often repelled by governmental aid because of the impersonal and bureaucratic procedures involved in its administration. Politicians and taxpayers are dissatisfied because they are discovering that existing welfare systems are self-perpetuating, forcing the recipient into a humiliating and supplicating role which significantly retards his efforts to become independent.

In *The Faith of the Counsellors* (1966) Halmos describes the contributions which "counsellors" and psychotherapists may appropriately make to social welfare. Through his nonjudgmental attitudes the "counsellor" can offer the recipient a respect which provides him with an incentive to become the type of human being who is valued by his culture. Halmos notes that in England politicians increasingly recognize the helpful role which "counsellors" can play. While he notes that conservative politicians still believe that any individual can solve life's basic problems if the right appeal is made to him, he observes that more typically the politician is enlightened about the welfare recipient's need for therapeutic assistance. He reports that more of England's resources are devoted to providing services which can be rendered only by professionals, and positions in social work, social casework, clinical psychology, and psychiatry are increasingly subsidized. While the massive involvement of the United States in world affairs has made the discovery of trends in domestic politics more difficult, the same long-term trends appear to be operating in this country.

The Therapist's Role in Social Reform

The fact is all too obvious that the counselor's or psychotherapist's work is frustrated when the values which the client has developed during therapy are thwarted by noxious elements in his extratherapeutic environment. Therapists therefore often become highly motivated to reform the social forces in the culture which, from a therapeutic standpoint, are immoral. Trained counselors and psychotherapists frequently become active in various types of social planning and in implementing such planning through more humane and personal administrative procedures.

Concern for the client's welfare may stimulate the therapist to seek social reforms in specific institutions with a significant impact upon the individual. Thus psychological counselors are constantly seeking to improve the schools and colleges so that learning becomes a personal experience more closely tailored to the specific needs of each student. Stewart and Warnath in *The Counselor and Society* (1965) call upon the guidance counselor to make significant changes in the social climate of the school system. The clinical psychologist has attempted to reduce the monolithic impersonality of the mental hospital by transforming it into what Maxwell Jones (1953) calls the "therapeutic community," The therapeutic community mobilizes the whole hospital staff to resocialize and rehabilitate patients whose development has been thwarted by cold and insensitive attitudes in the larger outside community. The pastoral counselor is also to be enlisted to make therapeutic changes in the institutional church. The church itself can be analogously considered a therapeutic community (see Lowe, in press) in which interpersonal relationships become transformed into a "communion of saints" which provides fellowship and acceptance for its members.

An important emphasis in community mental-health programs is the establishment of a general social welfare by educating society about the nature of attitudes and practices which harm the individual psychologically. Community mental-health therapists generally do not wish to be identified with general social reform. However, so many aspects of community life are related to psychological functioning that the distinction between community mental health and broad social action will become increasingly blurred.

Concern for Social Justice

Both the therapist and the social philosopher must be concerned with the abstract and exceedingly general concept of social justice. The therapist with vision finds himself looking beyond the welfare of the individual client to the abstract ideals which guide the political commonwealth. This perspective permits him to visualize the values which guide therapy to become in an enlarged form the ideals of Western democracy. Thus he dreams of a world in which the values which provide the criterion for therapeutic improvement are engraved upon the whole of the social structure.

A philosophical search for social justice has traditionally been the concern of jurisprudence, although the attempt to define social justice in legal principles may seem rather alien to the professional concerns of the counselor and the psychotherapist. The same social changes which have produced a need for the therapist also require him to exercise new political and legal functions. Legislators and jurists have not lost the ability to make and apply laws, but they have lost a comprehensive schemata for the social life of man within the body politic. To some observers this loss threatens the maintenance of law and order. As in the case of religion, the older traditions which are no longer respected are apparently being replaced with new truths supplied by the sciences of man. To an increasing extent the behavioral scientist provides a new social philosophy for those who operate the scales of justice.

The politician and the jurist share with the theologian a concern with good and evil. Law can in fact be regarded as the culture's attempt to translate its values and ideals into a social order which can maintain them. Monolithic social conditions have a homogeneity of religious and social ideals that blur the distinction between theology and jurisprudence. Within the Judeo-Christian tradition, religious and political power have not successfully rested in the same hands for three thousand years.

The day when laws could be engraved on tablets of stone or written in the human heart are certainly long past. Lawmaking, however, still attempts to translate the abstract and general religious ideals of justice and right into a social reality. The politician and the jurist today depend upon a social view of the good life as a common denominator of the individual values of citizens. The craft of the politician, therefore, is to fashion a social commonwealth from the extremely abstract ideals of freedom, justice, and equality, which are in fact but the broad generalizations of ideals unique with each individual.

In our day new laws are written to ease points of social abrasion between individuals and groups with different ideals and values. As other social forces change in the transition from an inner-directed to an other-directed society, so does law. Law ceases to provide the greatest possible opportunity for the individual to exploit a material environment and instead minimizes the social collisions that are inevitable when too many individuals compete within a crowded social space. In this new situation, law must somehow strike a medium among different value systems, balancing the continuing desire of the individual to be free against the needs of a commonwealth which subordinates individual demands to the general welfare. This new society must weigh the accelerating pressures of technological change against the stabilizing counterforces of tradition and social habit.

As the older law built on theological and philosophical principles passes into disuse, a new basis for law must be found. In the present situation where older philosophical assumptions are unacceptable, a new law is required to reconcile man's individuality with his social nature.

In a situation in which older ideals have disappeared, the social and behavioral sciences have a new relevance for law. At the height of rationalism Blackstone is reported (Boorstin, 1941) to have found it expedient to justify current legal practices with elaborate appeals to social history and to primitive cultures. Today it is even more necessary that politics and jurisprudence are aware of man's social nature. Increasingly, therefore, jurisprudence is aware of the implications that social science and law have for each other. In a number of books, such as *Social Control through Law* (1942), *Law and Morals* (1926), and *Spirit of the Common Law* (1921), Roscoe Pound seeks a new cultural basis for legal definitions of justice. More recently Eugene Rostow (1962) describes a need for law to be guided by the changing ideals of the culture which it serves, so that law in turn can raise the level of social behavior. For Rostow, the social concerns of law are so far reaching that law itself becomes an all-embracing social institution. Because it is so closely concerned with all aspects of man's social behavior, Rostow sees law becoming the universal social science, although this role plainly can not belong to law alone. The lawyer must join with all others dealing with the human condition to find an ideal for law that will raise the standards of existing law and the modal level of all social behavior.

Both the lawyer and the behavioral scientist must accept the fact that as social conditions change more rapidly, so must the basis for maintaining social control and order. The social bedrocks of tradition and reason are gone. The ideals of justice and equality which remain need new meaning in an evolving system of law and order. Justice must find a way to reconcile individual integrity with social interdependence in a way that includes all the significant aspects of man's existence.

The key to social control through law lies in integrating the therapist's knowledge of the individual with the jurist's and the social philosopher's comprehensive ideals for a commonwealth.

THE THERAPIST'S MORAL AUTHORITY

Counselors and psychotherapists find themselves in a unique new social role that combines the objective professional stance of the scientist with the highly personal and subjective concern of a therapeutic practitioner to whom modern man confides his bewilderment with morals and values. As older moral authorities find it more difficult to provide leadership, the individual turns to those among his fellow man who seem wise enough in their knowledge of human behavior to provide contemporary, and therefore relevant, answers to moral issues.

Because the therapist is an expert in the social and the behavioral sciences, he is called upon to direct man's moral quest. The spiritual man, who was replaced by a rational individual, is in turn replaced by the social self. This new interpersonal being is to be evaluated, not by conformity to the will of God or by economic achievement, but by his ability to adjust to the contemporary social customs defined as congruent with mental health and with other social values.

The counselor and the psychotherapist have a pervasive impact upon the new, general social good. They grade variations of social mores as good or evil, applying their yardstick of mental health to an ever-wider range of human behavior. In his early years, the child's parents seek instruction from the psychologist about new social customs in child rearing. In the schools, educational psychologists help educate the young to live in a democracy interpreted by sociology. On the job, where capitalistic independence once reigned supreme, organizational machinery is tuned by industrial consultants who mold industrial might into the new social image of man. And in politics the pollster, with his expert finger on the public pulse, helps create a new meaning for democratic living: He and the new political image maker create a political leadership where leading and following are so tangled that a new political science emerges.

Although the behavioral sciences have had a profound effect upon man's experience of the good life through their far-reaching effect on social mores, the therapist has had a direct and highly specific effect upon social morals themselves. Therapists have seldom hesitated to speak out on issues involving sexual morality, either as individuals (see Ellis, 1966) or as professional organizations (see Group for the Advancement of Psychiatry, 1965). Therapists have generally advocated a more permissive approach to sex than traditional standards of morality tolerated. Their influence can be seen in a more tolerant attitude towards the homosexual. The British Wolfenden report reveals insight into the nature of homosexuality gained from the psychotherapist (C. Berg, 1958). Finally, an increased reliance upon the therapist's moral authority is seen in new opinions concerning the nature of alcoholism. The alcoholic is regarded less as a moral derelict, due to the therapist's urging, than as a patient who suffers from a disease or a person who satisfies his needs through a distinctive pattern of life.

As therapists become more comprehensively involved in modern living, their moral influence must inevitably increase. In a recent American Psychiatric Association Presidential Address, Howard P. Rome noted a new revolution which rides the crest of a "long-brewing discontent with the traditional, established order of many of our social institutions" (1965, p. 296). Rome interprets this discontent with old authorities as a clarion call for psychiatry to move from the consulting room and the mental hospital to greater community involvement. Indeed, Rome notes that already "ideas and values that derive from psychiatry have spread on every level, from educational philosophy to child-rearing practices, from opinions about the causes of deviance and delinquency to the desirability of traditional attitudes" (1965, p. 296).

SUMMARY

Having destroyed its old masters, science now finds itself supreme in a world in which man is no longer directed by the faith of his forefathers. But in a world that seems off balance, he can no longer find the inner stability of the self-directed man. The self-possessed man of the gyroscope has been replaced by the other-directed person of the radarscope, who must seek the therapist's help to find from his environment some social other to direct him.

The therapist who is called upon to provide social and moral direction is not accustomed to his new duties. He can not immerse himself in the study of pure truth, nor can he hide behind the folds of his academic gown. For the first time, he must come to grips with the necessity of social responsibility because his task is to integrate all knowledge into a social system that meets every essential human need. The therapist must start to play roles which are an anathema to the scientific tradition. He must give up his cherished role of objective observer and take sides in complex issues of social planning. As a practitioner of a new way of life, he sees his own personal tastes become social values affecting the lives of others.

The therapist now finds himself doing the things which he had for so long condemned other professions. If he formerly condemned the social judgments of others as moralism and do-goodism or as Utopian pipe dreams, he now finds he must propose social solutions so bold that he seems a radical to many. If he once dismissed as theological any value judgment of good or bad, he suddenly finds that ethical evaluations are an integral part of social prescriptions. If previously he considered the definition of happiness as philosophic, he must evaluate it as a scientist.

Although in many cases the therapist still aspires to be a scientist, he finds himself increasingly performing functions which seem inappropriate for a professional whose ideal is objectivity and impartiality. Even though the therapist may wish to continue his morally neutral identification with science, this desire is not likely to keep him from becoming involved in the controversial issues of religion and politics. As he provides the new authority and the direction to life, the therapist finds that he has become far more than a scientist.

Chapter 2

MORAL OVERTONES IN COUNSELING AND PSYCHOTHERAPY

Then Jephthah gathered all the men of Gilead and fought with Ephraim; and the men of Gilead smote Ephraim, . . . and the Gileadites took the fords of the Jordan against the Ephraimites. And when any of the fugitives of Ephraim said, "Let me go over," the men of Gilead said to him, "Are you an Ephraimite?" When he said, "No," they said to him, "Then say Shibboleth," and he said "Sibboleth," for he could not pronounce it right; then they seized him and slew him at the fords of the Jordan. And there fell at that time forty-two thousand of the Ephraimites. . . . JUDGES

❖❖❖

Although the counselor and the psychotherapist increasingly function as moralists in contemporary society, it is unlikely that either regards himself primarily as a moralist, unless he is a pastoral counselor. Counseling psychologists often view their professional function as facilitating vocational and educational choices. Therapists with a medical orientation customarily view their professional role as the treating of neuroses and other types of psychopathology. Therapists whose professional interests involve personal adjustment counseling or nonmedically oriented psychotherapy typically see themselves as helping the client to implement a self-concept, release growth potential, or facilitate self-actualization.

Counselors and psychotherapists generally regard their professional conduct as guided by theoretical orientations derived from the study of personality. They typically interpret psychotherapy in terms of learning theory, a phenomenological view of the self, and the like. Because the processes and purposes of therapy can be interpreted in many ways, it is certainly not wrong for the therapist to identify himself as an expert in behavioral modification, interpersonal relationships, or ontological analysis, but it is a mistake to delineate his professional role so narrowly that he preempts the possibility of making alternative interpretations. No matter how explicit the therapist may try to be in describing his professional identity, ambiguities inherent in the social definition of his role prevent a clear-cut professional identity like that of the surgeon or the tax accountant.

Because counselors and psychotherapists are professionally concerned with human behavior, their professional actions have inevitable moral overtones. Perry London has written that "at some level of abstraction, it is probably correct to declare that every aspect of psychotherapy presupposes some implicit moral doctrine" (1964, p. 6). Counseling and psychotherapy both seek to produce change, either by modifying behavior or by changing attitudes. If one attempts to change the client's behavior, moral issues intrude because the resulting behavioral change will almost inevitably have social consequences affecting other people for good or bad. If, on the other hand, one tries to modify the client's internal frame of reference, his values inevitably change. Insight therapies, which seek to change the client's attitudes, must also influence those values which determine his view of the world.

No single major system of psychotherapy views its primary purpose as that of changing the client's values. The terms used to describe these changes—such as symptom removal, improved interpersonal relationships, and existential courage—appear to be morally neutral, but they nevertheless do imply their own distinctive cosmologies. Every system of psychotherapy must have as its goal the improvement of the client's personality and behavior, and value judgments determine how this improvement is defined.

Values are related to many aspects of the therapeutic process, and inevitably they are hard to separate from other constructs quite legitimately used to interpret the therapeutic process (Lowe, 1964). While it would be wrong to regard counseling and psychotherapy as a process of value modification in every case, nevertheless, values have a variety of impacts upon therapy. The therapist himself is not always aware of the extent of interaction between values and the therapeutic process.

THE CLIENT'S FAITH IN THE THERAPIST'S MORAL AUTHORITY

Chapter One discussed how the counselor and the therapist have assumed many social roles formerly performed by the clergyman and by the social philosopher. As man loses faith in older solutions to moral problems, he often turns to more contemporary sources.

When he feels that the older values and moral standards are of little personal benefit to him, he is particularly apt to turn to the therapist. He may feel that the therapist can provide a special type of help because he has the valued characteristics of both the contemporary and the scientific.

A client is not likely to come to a secularly oriented therapist complaining of bewilderment at the loss of values and moral standards. He is much more apt to speak of a general dysphoria and a vague sense of anxiety. Because the emotional discomfort is so vague and diffuse, the symptoms of what Schofield (1964) terms a philosophical neurosis may include such varied manifestations as obsessions, feelings of guilt, and somatic complaints.

The vague nature of the client's complaints, which can be variously described as personal-adjustment problems or anxiety neurosis, may be interpreted in a number of ways. The trend in recent years has been toward interpreting typical client problems as a general cognitive failure to construct attitudes enabling one to integrate his experiences in meaningful and personally satisfying ways. Schofield (1964) describes the typical problem as a philosophical neurosis; Hobbs (1962) writes of a client's inability to discover a meaningful personal cosmology; and Frank (1961) speaks of the patient's inability to fashion the appropriate assumptive world.

Many times the client whom these writers describe experiences significant improvement when he enters a therapeutic relationship because he respects the therapist's moral authority. Frank (1961) has suggested that much of the effectiveness of psychotherapy is due to the patient's expectation of help. Frank draws an analogy between psychotherapy and medical treatment, noting the medical truism that all forms of treatment work best just after they are introduced. In Frank's opinion this improvement is largely due to the "ability of something new and untried, *especially when recommended by an authority*, to arouse the patient's hopes" (1961, p. 144; italics added). He compares the effectiveness of psychotherapy with the placebo effect and concludes that certain symptoms will be equally relieved by the placebo or by psychotherapy. He also draws a parallel between faith healing and psychotherapy. Noting that "the core of the effectiveness of methods of religious and magical healing seems to lie in their ability to arouse hope by capitalizing on the patient's dependency on others" (1961, p. 62), he concludes that faith healing and psychotherapy have important elements in common.

Unfortunately, rather little is known about the motives that cause clients to seek the help of the counselor and the psychotherapist. Frank cites an abundance of experimental evidence to justify his claim that placebo treatment not only changes attitudes but also produces noticeable physiological effects. The motivation of clients who seek the help of nonmedical therapists, however, may be entirely different from that of patients who visit physicians.

Nevertheless, it seems reasonable to suppose that clients form a general class of dependent individuals in their having given up attempts to be completely self-directing and having expressed the desire to be guided or helped by another person. Although it would be presumptuous to suggest that clients display all the characteristics of other-directed individuals, apparently many do display some of these attributes. Some clients feel bewildered and alienated because they fail to perceive a social structure or to construct a system of personal values. In such a situation they can become highly suggestible and are likely to be influenced in some-what irrational ways by their perception of moral authority. Through this series of reactions, a client can be influenced in highly subtle ways to adopt the therapist's system of personal values.

Landfield and Nawas (1964) conducted an empirical investigation of the relationship between improvement in counseling and adoption of the therapist's values. They suggest that the client is more apt to adopt the therapist's values when he perceives the therapist to have a higher status. Although some research studies (Rosenthal, 1955; Landfield and Nawas, 1964; Welkowitz, Cohen, and Ortmeyer, 1967) indicate a statistically significant tendency for patients and clients to adopt the therapist's values when they improve in therapy, attempts to replicate these results suggest that the relationship between therapeutic improvement and adoption of the therapist's values may be neither simple nor straightforward. Various studies (Farson, 1961; Nawas and Landfield, 1963; Cook, 1966) indicate that the effect of the therapist's values varies with different types of clients and with different types of therapists.

THE THERAPIST'S VALUES AND CLIENT SELECTION

Therapists differ from other professionals in their rather arbitrarily selectivity of clients. Few therapists pretend that they can help every person who seeks their treatment. Since therapists are generally fairly sophisticated in sensing the client's motives in seeking treatment, they are apt to screen out potential clients who are too obviously naive and incredulous in their expectations and direct them elsewhere. The criteria that therapists use in selecting clients are typically highly personal and require value judgments by the therapist.

In choosing his clients the therapist first judges whether they will be able to relate and to communicate meaningfully. Counselors and therapists typically require that clients meet such objective criteria as having above-average intelligence and being between adolescence and early middle age. In addition they are likely to make more subjective judgments of client suitability, and they often insist that clients possess a working conscience, a tendency to introspection, and motivation for self-improvement.

Therapists obviously have sound reasons for preferring clients who seem to be verbally facile and who appear to want to better themselves. It may not be entirely coincidental that the characteristics regarded as implying a good prognosis for psychotherapy also tend to be the cardinal virtues of middle-class morality. Counseling and psychotherapy are obviously middle-class occupations. Thus when Hollingshead and Redlich (1958) discovered a strong tendency for therapists to treat patients of the same socioeconomic status as themselves, they also found that depth-oriented psychotherapy was almost entirely limited to members of the middle class.

The therapists' preference for clients who share their own cultural heritage is not always irrationally prejudicial. When differences in social background are too great, therapists are likely to distort their perception of the client's life because they use a different moral standard to evaluate behavior. Differences in moral heritages may also produce a conflict between the personal values of the client and those of the therapist. When this friction occurs the therapist is less likely to be able to comprehend the client's description of his basic inner experiences and become empathically involved with him. When congruence is lacking between the values and aspirations of the client and therapist, they find it difficult to agree on therapeutic goals.

The therapist's selection of clients is also guided by what he judges to be the purpose of treatment. As originally practiced by Sigmund Freud, psychotherapy was intended to treat patients diagnosed as psychoneurotic. (The next chapter discusses the somewhat involved and complicated history of the concept of neurosis.) In our day the term neurosis often describes a person who is regarded as a suitable candidate for psychotherapy. As a diagnostic term, neurosis may be contrasted with other psychiatric labels, notably psychosis and character disorder, which often have negative implications for therapy.

The neurotic is often described as a person who has been unable to fashion for himself a system of satisfying personal values or who has discovered a meaningful personal identity but is unable to attain his personal goals because he seems inefficient and inept in his acts, thoughts, or feelings. The resulting behavior may therefore be regarded as neurotic because the patient's symptoms impede him from realizing his values. Even though the neurotic may have difficulty in constructing an attainable system of values for himself; nevertheless, he is an individual who possesses what the therapist calls a working conscience. Put another way, the therapist perceives the patient reacts to the same general moral standards that he does. (Typically the neurotic's pangs of conscience stem from middle-class morality, a fact that provides a logical explanation for the association among one's being middle class, being neurotic, and being in psychotherapy, which Hollingshead and Redlich [1958] uncovered). Because the therapist and the patient share so many assumptions about the purpose and meaning of life, the patient is likely to express goals for therapy that seem quite appropriate to the therapist. These expressed goals, in addition to moral virtues held in common, easily establish a therapeutic relationship. The therapist has little difficulty in providing the patient with the necessary warmth and unconditional positive regard which many therapists believe are essential to success.

The same considerations which motivate the therapist to accept the neurotic as a client cause him to reject those he judges to be psychotic or psychopathic. The diagnostician tends to regard as psychotic (and therefore as unsuitable for psychotherapy) a "patient" whose values appear bizarre, unorganized, and unpredictable when compared to his own. The therapist senses only a limited likelihood of success with such an individual. Because he is unable to comprehend the organizing core of the patient's values, he is unlikely to understand the significance of what the person is saying, and he may therefore find it impossible to empathize with him.

Psychotherapy with a psychopath is also given a poor prognosis. Although the therapist typically finds the psychopath's internal frame of reference is easier to understand than the psychotic's, he is likely to perceive that the patient's values are rather diametrically opposed to his own. Therefore he interprets the behavior of the so-called psychopath as a flagrant disregard of the basic canons of morality and finds it difficult to develop a positive regard for the patient. Therapy with a psychopath is likely to become prolonged and involved because of a basic clash of wills.

Are counselors and psychotherapists justified in seeking to limit therapy to clients with whom they are morally compatible? Donald Glad in *Operational Values in Psychotherapy* (1959) develops a theoretical rationale that sharing the therapist's values greatly enhances the patient's chances for success in psychotherapy. He suggests by way of example that patients who are democratic in their attitudes are likely to respond rapidly and positively to democratic attitudes that Glad believes the client-centered therapist typically displays. He also argues that clients who are unafraid to venture into creative pathways and therefore to struggle against social belongingness will respond best to a Rankian therapeutic philosophy. On the other hand, Glad cites as reasons for failure the difficulty that the democratically oriented therapist is likely to experience when confronted by a client who values artistic creativity.

Unfortunately only limited research has investigated the possible interaction between the therapeutic value orientation and the benefit which the client derives from therapy. Mendelsohn and Geller (1963, 1965, 1967; Mendelsohn, 1966) have conducted a series of investigations to determine the effect on counseling of the similarity between counselor and client on the Myers-Briggs Type Indicator, a self-reporting measure of personality attributes closely related to what this book describes as values. These studies have related client-counselor similarity to attitudes toward counseling, to the number of missed sessions, and to early termination. The results of these studies suggest that the effect of a similarity of values is not the same in all counseling situations but that it is an important therapeutic variable.

Values Prescribe Therapeutic Aims

If therapy is apt to fail when the values of therapist and the client are too dissimilar, it often does so because the goals which the therapist sets for therapy do not provide the type of help which the client wishes to receive. The bulk of Glad's *Operational Values in Psychotherapy* (1959) relates different types of what he terms operational values to the methods and goals of corresponding types of psychotherapy.

Glad describes four families of psychotherapy, each with its own value orientation: the psychoanalytic, which centers its attention on unconscious-thought processes; the interpersonal psychiatric, which emphasizes security seeking and the reduction of anxiety generated by faulty interpersonal relationships; the dynamic-relationship approach, which focuses upon those feelings experienced in the immediate therapeutic situation; and the phenomenological, which stresses the personal reality of the client as he experiences his private self.

As Glad describes them, the goals of these psychotherapies are guided by different sets of operational values to achieve distinctive types of personality integration. He describes the therapeutic outcomes in terms of psychoanalytic paternalism, interpersonal-psychiatric socialization, dynamic-relationship creativity, and phenomenological-empathetic individuality.

> The psychoanalytic patient is likely to become an internally organized, emotionally controlled, parentlike person.
> The interpersonal patient will apparently become a socially integrated, accepting, and accepted part of his society.
> The dynamic-relationship client should become an intensely individual, creative "island unto himself" with an artistic bridge to the mainland.
> The client-centered counselee will develop an internally articulated, comfortable selfhood, prizing his own individuality, and democratically understanding the individuality of another (1959, p. 62).

Therapists describe the goals or value orientations of therapy in different ways. Lowe (1959) has described four different value orientations as setting different goals for therapy. Charlotte Buhler (1962) describes four basic tendencies in life which she relates to therapeutic goals, three of which are similar to those set forth earlier by Lowe. Buhler's goals, paired with the similar values of Lowe, are: need satisfaction (naturalism), self-limiting adaptation (culturalism), and expansive creativity (humanism). The two writers clearly differ on the fourth value orientation. Buhler speaks of an "upholding of the internal order," while Lowe describes a theistic value orientation that directs the individual towards God.

The fact that theorists arrange therapeutic goals into different value orientations should not obscure the basic point which all these writers are trying to make. The purpose or goal of therapy is an expression of one's personal value orientation, which may be stated in various ways. (Chapters Five through Eight of this book describe what seem to be the four most popular goals among contemporary therapists.)

Values Determine Therapeutic Methods

Attempts to maintain distinctions between goals and the methods or means used to reach them are often somewhat arbitrary and artificial. Glad (1959) describes the different therapies guided by contrasting operational values. These values influence treatment by directing the therapist's attention to topics closely related to the values he regards as important. Indeed, Glad suggests that when the therapist makes interpretations and the patient develops insights, each is merely expressing a preference for a particular type of operational value.

Glad cites by way of example how various operational values guide therapists in responding to a patient who kept daydreaming that she was a queen like Cleopatra, surrounded by a harem of big handsome men enchained as her slaves. He notes that the psychoanalyst would typically respond by making an inquiry to elicit the description of a transference relationship. Thus he might ask the patient if any of the men in the dream reminded her of her father. The interpersonal therapist, who would be more likely to notice the patient's security operations, might ask her if she were trying to control the therapist by thinking of him as her slave. The dynamic-relationship therapist would probably be concerned with the emotional meaning of the dream and might attempt to elicit her feelings about the relationship. The client-centered therapist might respond to the dream by discussing with the patient her ability to talk about her fantasies without feeling threatened.

Values enter therapy in different ways, depending upon the orientation and style of the therapist. In analytic and depth-oriented psychotherapy, an exploration of personal values is typically part of a general reconstituting of personality. Thus a depth-oriented approach requires the client to examine rather critically those basic moral standards which he internalized at an early age. Nicholas Hobbs (1959) points out that the psychoanalyst is tacitly forced to accept John Locke's classic observation that self-evident values are simply reflections of early childhood indoctrination. This influence has been described in more modern terms by Lewis Feuer, who writes: "The moral faculty is too often the unconscious residue of our nursemaid's admonitions" (1955, p. 7). Since the psychoanalyst seeks to free the patient from the moral control of his distant past, he uses psychotherapeutic methods to help the patient develop "insights" into the parts of his value orientation dominated by unconscious determinants and therefore "irrational" in nature.

Values, which are exposed in depth psychotherapy, are also integrally involved in short-term counseling concerned with decision making. E. G. Williamson sees values as permeating the whole of the counseling process. Defining a value as an idea on which people act or a principle by which they judge how to act, he argues that the conduct of counseling must be affected by values "because every choice and every action must be based upon explicit or implicit acceptance of a value" (1958, p. 524). Williamson describes the intrusion of values into counseling in the following way.

> If we agree that value judgments are implicit in every action we take, we should also agree that counselors cannot fully escape introducing their own value systems into the counseling interview. While the counselor's moral and ethical standards may not be made clear to clients or even to the counselor himself, they are influential in his reactions to the client's story, his emphases, his choice of objectives and counseling method, and in the techniques he uses to carry out the chosen method of interviewing (1958, p. 524).

Counselors and psychotherapists have rather carefully attempted to nurture the belief that nondirective treatment allows the therapist to divorce his personal biases from therapy. Skepticism appears to be growing, however, about the prevalent assumption that the therapist can maintain his moral neutrality merely by not giving advice. Halmos (1966) discusses the fiction of a nondirectiveness which states as its ideal that "the counselor must do his work without ever violating the personal initiative, uniqueness, and freedom of the patient or client" (1966, p. 90). He points out that no matter how much care is taken to allow spontaneous growth in personal directions, one can not assume that arbitrary influence can be avoided.

Patterson (1959) describes how values can influence therapeutic methods in ways so subtle that neither the therapist nor the client detects them. Patterson points out that patients commonly conform in their words, their thoughts, and even their dreams to the theories and the terms of the therapist: "If therapists value dreams, patients dream; if therapists value sexual material, patients produce it, etc." (1959, p. 67). He cites experiments by Verplanck and Greenspoon in which the experimenters were able to control the subjects' verbal behavior by means of operant conditioning, without any apparent awareness by the subjects that their conversations were being shaped. These experiments differ from an actual therapeutic situation because the experimenter deliberately and rather artificially attempted to manipulate the subject's verbal behavior along predetermined lines. The safeguards which the experimenter's conscious control may provide are likely to be absent in the more typical therapeutic situation. Therapists can hardly be expected to be conscious of the myriad reinforcements which they constantly provide the client. Confirmation for much of Patterson's concern seems to be provided by the analysis of a therapeutic interview conducted by Carl Rogers (Truax, 1966). Truax argues that client-centered therapists such as Rogers may unwittingly shape the client's conversation by providing positive reinforcement for verbal responses such as those that describe feeling and refer to the self in positive terms.

Pepinsky and Karst (1964) call the general way in which clients learn to accept the values of the therapist *convergence*, drawing upon the experimenter effect of Robert Rosenthal, the autokinetic effect of Sherif, and studies of conformity behavior by Asch. When convergence of these types occurs in therapy, the client's behavior becomes more like the therapist's. Pepinsky and Karst believe that therapists consider this similarity to mean that the therapy is a success. They also believe that convergence explains the results of the previously cited study of David Rosenthal (1955), which describes an increasing resemblance of the patient's values to the therapist's. They note that the process of "inducing 'desirable' value change in the client as a therapeutic goal" (1964, p. 335) is a common element in what would otherwise appear to be highly dissimilar types of psychotherapy.

THE INFLUENCE OF THE THERAPIST'S PERSONALITY

As counselors and psychotherapists increasingly believe that moral nondirectiveness is an impossible ideal for the therapist, they tend to place greater emphasis upon the therapeutic benefit of the mere presence of the therapist in the therapeutic relationship. They see the therapist helping the client not merely because of his knowledge or his interpersonal skillfulness, but also because of who he is as a person. The therapist influences the client's values simply because he is a man whose distinctly human qualities are easily perceived by the client.

E. G. Williamson (1958) notes that the counselor's values are an essential part of his personality and can not be hidden. He observes that the history of Western civilization indicates an individual often desperately needs the help of others if he is to develop fully. Williamson believes that one person can help another to develop only when he provides him with a structured personality with which he can identify. Thus Williamson decries counselors' attempts at self-effacement because he believes that the counselor's own mature development should provide inspiration for the client.

Gardner Murphy (1955) also emphasizes the importance of moral encounter for counseling. He objects to the loss of what he terms the sense of human nature because of an overspecialization in counseling techniques and methods. He emphasizes the differences between treatment based upon techniques and therapy centered upon personality, believing that only the latter is genuine. Murphy realizes the danger of a directive counselor becoming an arrogant meddler who (figuratively) beats the client with the whiplash of his own values. He feels, however, that an even greater degree of arrogance is implied by the counseling technician who believes his technical skills can sufficiently guide clients in a complicated and shifting world.

Murphy is more concerned with the values which the counselor himself has learned to accept than he is with those which he tries to teach the client. He believes that certain values must be basic for both the counselor and the client: "Some values, such as those of sympathy, tenderness, generosity, and self-control resonate to the deeper chords of human nature, and ... they are for that reason intensely practical and dependable, [while] other values work badly, either because they cannot be solidly built into human nature or because they involve profound internal contradictions" (1955, p. 8).

Murphy believes that the client can attain these values by following a guide who has already found the way. Only when the counselor himself is a "whole person" who has "real roots in human nature" can the client sense either directly or indirectly the helping perspective of the guide's life.

> The point that I would stress is that self-realization on the part of the person guided is likely to be feasible only if there is a lot of self-realization on the part of the guide. This means, of course, ego involvement; it means feeling deeply and fully absorbed in the tremendous human importance of what one is doing (1955, p. 9).

Client-centered therapy currently stresses the need for the therapist to present himself to the client as a human being with a distinctive set of personality attributes. While early formulations of the client-centered therapy of Carl Rogers seemed to limit the therapist to a largely passive reflection of the client's feelings, Rogers and his associates increasingly recognize the need for a genuine encounter between client and therapist in which each learns to communicate his inner feelings to the other. In their many writings Truax and Carkhuff stress that the helpful therapist must be transparent or genuine because only when he becomes open can the client explore his feelings. Eugene Gendlin (1967) describes the client's discovery of his personal values as occurring through an experiential process which takes place only in an open relationship.

Truax and Carkhuff have found in a wide variety of empirical studies that the ability to be genuine or transparent is closely related to the accurate empathy and nonpossessive warmth which the Rogerian believes are additional prerequisites for successful therapeutic outcome. They report that the occurrence of these therapeutic qualities together is related to a variety of outcome measures. In a recent review of their own and their colleagues' work they reached the following conclusion about the personal qualities of the therapist.

> That the therapist, within the relationship, be himself integrated, genuine, and authentic seems most basic to therapeutic outcome. Without such genuineness, a trusting relationship could scarcely exist. The counselor or therapist must be a real person

in the encounter, presenting himself without defensive phoniness, without hiding behind the facade of the professional role. The current conceptualization of genuineness (or authenticity or congruence) requires the therapist's personal involvement; he is not simply "doing his job" as a technician. The therapist's capacity for openness and personal freedom in the therapeutic encounter offers, in part, a model for the client to follow in moving toward openness and freedom to be oneself (1967, p. 329).

Signs indicate psychoanalysts are loosening their formerly insistent attitude that the therapist be completely asceptic in regard to his personal values. Halmos (1966) summarizes a rather impressive number of writings from psychoanalytic sources to support his assertion that those values which are basic to the "faith of the counsellors" have become commonplace even in the practice of traditional psychoanalysis. Halmos cites references which justify countertransference on the part of the analyst because it is a sign that he cares. While the practice of psychoanalysis was once guided by the Victorian values of restraint and emotional detachment, the new psychoanalytic virtues are flexibility, reliability, and strength—traits regarded as prerequisites for therapeutic effectiveness. Halmos concludes that the psychoanalyst is no longer required to betray his kindness, concern, and idealism about man because of his desire to help the patient attain the competing values of insight and rationality.

COUNSELING AND PSYCHOTHERAPY AS MORAL GUIDANCE

One might conclude from this discussion that values intrude into therapy in ways so subtle and all-pervasive that the therapist has little control over his moral influence upon the client. When therapists are unaware of the moral implications of counseling and psychotherapy, they often unwittingly project their values upon the client. Fortunately recognition is growing of the different effects which the therapist's personal values have upon the conduct of psychological treatment. As counselors and psychotherapists become aware of the degree to which values are inextricably entwined within the therapeutic relationship, they seek to direct the moral concerns inherent in therapy to the client's personal need to discover his own values.

E. G. Williamson (1958) notes that counselors typically deal with problems arising from processes of growth and development, many of which arise from conflicts among the different life choices open to the patient. Williamson points out that the counselor in vocational and educational counseling must also help the client select a moral life style in which the choice of goals becomes an expression of the client's personal values. Joseph Samler (1960) somewhat similarly doubts that the counselor can divorce his personal values from his professional concern with helping clients develop and understand their own characteristic life patterns. He believes that in the past counselors have too often assumed values to be self-evident. The typical counselor has accepted as a matter of course that choice of occupation should reflect the individual's optimum potential, that interests should be capitalized upon, that university training is the highest good, and that job stability is to be preferred to job hopping. He suggests instead that counselors should question these tacit assumptions and help the client to find his personal values from the counselor's attempts to help the client articulate an integrated and articulate picture of himself and of his various social roles.

More depth-oriented psychotherapy also seems to be accepting the fact that therapists must actively confront the issues raised by values and by morals. This trend can be found even in discussions of psychotherapy from a psychoanalytic perspective.

A discussion of various strategies which psychoanalytically inclined therapists have adopted for dealing with values is found in Charlotte Buhler's *Values in Psychotherapy* (1962). Buhler believes that a psychotherapy which seeks only to free and strengthen the ego is incomplete.

Although psychotherapy may help the patient develop an increased capacity for identification, she doubts that even the person with a fully developed sense of self can be morally self-sufficient. Indeed, she sees the indecision of the contemporary individual as a sign not so much of failure in ego functioning as an indication of the ambiguities and uncertainties inherent in contemporary value systems. She concludes that "in a culture that to a great extent has lost its unifying beliefs and convictions, even persons with stronger egos and better judgment than some of our patients could ever muster may feel stymied when it comes to certain basic decisions, decisions about right and wrong" (1962, p. 6). She cites the bewilderment the individual confronts in deciding among conflicting values inherent in such typical contemporary problems as sex, authority, and discipline.

In Buhler's view, the essence of a depth psychotherapy is to "lead the patient to think about his motivation on a deeper level in a new way" (1962, p. 20). She sites as an example the puzzlement of a young psychologist to whom a very capable student-patient complained because he could not make A's. For Buhler the basic question to ask the patient was not "Why can't you make A's?" or "Why should you make A's?" but, "Why is it important for you to make A's?" Because Buhler believes that a person requires goals, she urges the therapist not only to examine those wrong values which block the patient's development but also to help him formulate new values to provide direction towards future goals.

THE MORALITY OF MENTAL HEALTH

The usual defense of the counselor or psychotherapist to the charge that he interferes with the client's choice of values is that he is treating a condition that is psychologically or psychiatrically abnormal. The therapist thus defends himself against the charge that he is moralistic by stating that the purpose of therapy is to eliminate anxiety and other bothersome symptoms which make the patient unhappy and interfere with his efficient functioning. In short, the therapist is apt to say that the goal of therapy is simply to make the patient or client mentally healthy.

The concept of mental health is little more than a therapist's or a personality theorist's description of the ideal person (Lowe, 1964), and in large measure is therefore a projection of the therapist's own highly personal values. Earlier this chapter noted that therapists frequently use psychiatric categories to rationalize their choice of clients, which in practice is greatly influenced by their values. Similarly the concept of mental health provides the mental-health practitioner with the false sense of security that his therapeutic activities are in fact geared to some objective standard detached from philosophical or moral considerations.

Halmos (1966) notes that even though the therapist generally aspires to be nondirective, nevertheless he quite intentionally tries to direct the client toward mental health. He concludes that although the therapist sees himself as remaining neutral and uninvolved in the client's personal affairs, he "*means* to direct the patient towards health and will include in his direction his own personal and idiosyncratic version of health" (1966, p. 94). Ginsberg and Herma (1953) similarly suggest that when the therapist defines therapeutic goals in terms of mental health, he is merely reflecting personal and social values. Arthur Burton (1960a) notes that the so-called clinical judgment of the therapist is often as moral as it is clinical. He concludes that "in the absence of a specific criterion for 'cure' or for mental health itself, he may project his own inner conceptions as to how he believes that patient should be" (1960a, p. 211).

The next chapter has more to say about the moral myths and the moral meanings of mental health. The present chapter merely suggests that using the concept of mental health (or mental illness) to justify the therapeutic orientation of the therapist is little more than a shibboleth. Therapists find safety and security when they can describe the purpose of their activities in technical terms such as anxiety reduction, symptom removal, or positive mental health. Using impressive terms makes the therapist seem professional and may give him some claim to scientific expertise, which in turn justifies his high fees. The counselor or the psychotherapist has found it too easy to deceive himself (and others) into believing that psychiatry and applied psychology have little to do with morals and values. This deception imposes upon the client a highly arbitrary morality which has little to do with health as it is conceived medically and even less to do with science.

SUMMARY

The previous chapter examined the therapist from a social or external frame of reference and discovered that he plays many of the roles of the moralist for the larger society. This chapter views what the therapist does from an internal frame of reference and discusses the therapeutic role which he plays in his consulting room or office. The therapist usually regards himself as an expert in the behavioral or health sciences. He believes that the services he provides result in such objective benefits as anxiety reduction, insight, or the alleviation of symptoms. Personal values and social morals do become involved in his therapeutic efforts in many different ways however, although he often rationalizes his moral involvement with mental-health concepts. The moral implications of mental health are discussed further in the next chapter.

Chapter 3

MORAL MYTHS AND THEIR MEANING

Then the Lord God said, "Behold, the man has become like one of us, knowing good and evil; and now, lest he put forth his hand and take also of the tree of life, and eat, and live for ever"—therefore the Lord God sent him forth from the Garden of Eden, to till the ground from which he was taken. He drove out the man; and at the east of the Garden of Eden he placed the cherubim, and a flaming sword which turned every way, to guard the way to the tree of life. . . . GENESIS

Contemporary man prides himself that as he becomes more civilized, he becomes less reliant upon superstition and myth. As natural explanations have been found for an increasing number of the riddles, man has become less fearful of his world. He is no longer afraid that a dragon will swallow the sun when a solar eclipse occurs. He has stopped fearing evil spirits since he found that medical hygiene is much more effective in controlling disease. Against even grosser aspects of nature which man can not control directly—such as the weather—he has largely learned to guarantee his physical preservation by means of weather forecasting, flood control, and similar measures.

Modern science has been of inestimable help to man in gaining whatever intellectual mastery he has over his physical environment. The contrast between our technological interpretation of physical events and the primitive ways our ancestors dealt with their environment is striking. Primitive peoples were forced to rely upon ideological beliefs from another area of life to explain physical reality. Lacking any other way to anticipate coming events, primitive man was superstitious in much the same way that laboratory animals become "superstitious" in an otherwise unstructured Skinner box, although man has a greater capacity to be systematic about his beliefs. Verbalized in a systematic fashion, superstition can properly be termed a myth, which is perhaps best defined as the "natural product of a primitive imagination in its endeavor to explain the wonder-compelling world" (Buttrick, 1928, p. xv).

The workings of myth are easier to see in cultures which are ideologically removed from our own, and easiest to see in primitive cultures. Bronislaw Malinowski (1948) describes certain indispensable functions of myths in primitive culture as facilitating belief, strengthening morality, and providing practical rules of guidance. Mythology is for Malinowski far more than savage speculation about the philosophical origins of things: It is a "pragmatic charter of primitive faith and moral wisdom" (1948, p. 101); and thus it "is not merely a story told but a reality lived" (1948, p. 100), or again it "is not an idle tale, but a hard-worked active force" (1948, p. 101). Malinowski's argument that myth provides a sociological charter appears to be a general truth applicable to all cultures.

We popularly relegate the mythological to primitive cultures or to our less-enlightened past. In areas of life where scientific method has been effective, superstitions and myths obviously become less necessary. While contemporary society has its own stresses, at least it has been spared most of the stark terror that exists when natural and supernatural phenomena fuse into an amorphous mass of uncertainty from which come such basic physical threats as plagues, uncertain food supply, and sudden attacks by enemies and wild animals.

Superstitions and myths persist in areas of man's environment where prediction and control of future events are less effective. Remnants of the primitive past are even seen in those scientific areas which are still on the frontiers of knowledge. As a comparatively young field of knowledge, behavioral science is still clearly afflicted with certain of these nonlogical aspects of understanding. Cook (1963) speaks of "superstitious" behavior on the part of the Skinnerian learning theorist who attempts to understand learning in the rat, and Kiesler (1966) lists certain "myths" which persist in psychotherapy.

In one area of man's life, however, scientific method has been of comparatively little use to him. Science has been unable to resolve the ambiguities in human behavior when man must judge between good and evil. While consensual agreement has been obtained in physical and biological sciences, marked differences in values and ideals persist in the study of social behavior. Indeed, the changing basis of the good has in fact destroyed the traditional views to which social man could generally assent and has left only fragmented notions into which man is apt to project superstitions and myths.

If Malinowski is correct about the function of myth in primitive society, mythology must be understood as a realm where science gives contemporary civilized man scant advantage over the primitive. For Malinowski, the live myth "is not an explanation in satisfaction of a scientific interest, but a narrative resurrection of a primeval reality, told in satisfaction of deep religious wants, moral cravings, social submissions, assertions, even practical requirements" (1948, p. 101). Being a pragmatic chart of primitive faith and moral wisdom, mythology deals with an area where technology seems to be totally irrelevant. If the myth is the cultural universal that Malinowski claims it to be, then its role may be as active in our culture as it is in the most primitive society.

We can rather easily expose as superstition the ideals and beliefs of those who are historically remote from us and whose culture is technologically more primitive than our own, but it is much more difficult to see the fallacies in our own thinking. While it is popular, a myth is recognized for what it is only by those whose public exposure of it causes them to be branded as heretics or subversives. Everyone else accepts the myth unquestioningly, finding authority for his belief in common sense, self-evidence, or a similar semantic device. Only the light of history or the eyes of some other culture see the myth as irrational. Thus modern man must wait for history to expose fully his patterns of value.

THE MYTH OF MENTAL ILLNESS

As cultural change takes place, a new value orientation replaces a particular system of social values and older moral views which no longer seem credible or useful are relegated to the realm of mythology. The most recent belief to be exposed as myth is that of mental illness.

Mental-health practitioners have become increasingly dissatisfied with the medical mental-illness model. Their growing disillusionment with disease-entity thinking has appropriately found its most vocal outlet in a psychiatrist, Thomas Szasz. Because he has titled both a widely circulated article (1960) and a book (1961) *The Myth of Mental Illness*, Szasz has made this phrase a slogan that may well come to represent a radically different viewpoint in psychiatry and in related disciplines.

Szasz discusses two aspects of the mental-illness concept which have the characteristics of a myth. First, mental illness is a myth because it implies the existence of an organic disorder, when in reality it deals with a person's beliefs. He reasons that "a person's *belief*—whether this be a belief in Christianity, in Communism, or in the idea that his internal organs are 'rotting' and that his body is in fact already 'dead'—cannot be explained by a defect or disease of the nervous system" (1960, p. 113). He finds that these beliefs have no real medical significance and result in diagnoses without locus in the brain or in any other part of the body as do conditions which are more specifically neurological, such as skin eruptions and fractures. Although the concept of mental illness was once supported by such phenomena as syphilitic involvement of the brain and delerium-producing toxic conditions, a particular set of beliefs can not easily be grounded neurologically. Instead, Szasz finds that it is much more useful to regard such deviant beliefs as problems in living.

The second reason Szasz calls mental illness a myth is that the diagnosis is subjective and requires a judgment of the propriety of another's conduct. The psychiatrist applies the mental-illness label because of differences in beliefs with the patient, differences that he uses to judge what is and what is not a mental symptom. Such a judgment "entails . . . a covert comparison or matching of the patient's ideas, concepts, or beliefs with those of the observer and the society in which they live" (1960, p. 114).

The behavior that other psychiatrists diagnose on the basis of certain categories Szasz would evaluate as matching or not matching psychosocial, ethical, and legal norms. The basis for these behavioral norms must ultimately be a subjective idea of the good. Thus for Szasz such notions as "excessive repression" or "acting out" or "unconscious impulse" illustrate the use of psychological concepts to judge mental health or mental illness. The "idea that chronic hostility, vengefulness, or divorce are indicative of mental illness would be illustrious of the use of ethical norms (that is the desirability of love, kindness, and a stable marriage relationship)" (1960, p. 114). Szasz finds psychiatry much more closely tied to ethics than to medicine, and he prefers the term "problems of living" to that of mental illness. He believes that the concept of mental illness obscures the basic fact that for most people life is a continuous struggle, not for biological survival, but for a "place in the sun," "peace of mind," or some other human value which provides a "harmonious, satisfying, and secure basis of a 'good life.' "

Szasz's discussion of mental illness as myth is somewhat pejorative in its emotional tone. He clearly uses the term myth disparagingly to create dislike for the mental-illness concept and to convey strong feelings of moral dismay. Szasz does not develop the anthropological detachment which characterizes Malinowski's discussion of myth, although his use of mental illness conforms to Malinowski's description of the functional utility of myth in several important respects.

Szasz regards mental illness as involving human beliefs. These beliefs are important because they rather directly represent problems in living that also involve morals. Indeed, in Szasz's thinking, a diagnosis provides strong social sanctions for a moral condemnation of a given behavior. Thus mental illness functions anthropologically as a myth by providing suitable moral guidelines and at the same time enforcing sanctions against behavior of which the society disapproves.

Szasz seems to enjoy being controversial and obviously not everyone agrees with his viewpoint, although others have made carefully reasoned support for it. Indeed, other writers have significantly extended an understanding of the ways mental illness functions as myth for modern man. Sarbin (1967) describes the "illicit" transformation of mental illness from a metaphorical concept to a literal one and he lists a number of logical fallacies involved in current uses of the term. Both Nicholas Hobbs (1964) and William Schofield (1964) compare the relinquishment of a physical explanation for mental illness in our day to the liberation from a belief in possession by "foreign powers" and the Devil at the end of the Middle Ages. As a result of what he terms mental health's third revolution, Hobbs believes that "a perhaps even greater stride forward may result from the growing recognition that mental illness is not the private organic misery of an individual but a social, ethical, and moral problem . . ." (1964, p. 824). Schofield also believes that it is impossible to imagine mental health or mental illness without reference to some basic social value. The healing mode for mind that once passed from priest to physician now replaces the healing touch with the healing word in a third enlightenment.

Schofield holds that today man uses the concept of psycho-pathology to refer to either of two ideas. More benign are the "philosophical" neuroses, the product of the "Western myth that a state of happiness is both a primary and achievable goal of life" (1964, pp. 149-150). Man becomes so upset when he is unable to define the nature of happiness philosophically that he decides that he is neurotic and needs psychotherapeutic treatment. A second basis for judging a person maladjusted is his failure to be optimally productive. Schofield describes modern man as living in an efficiency-oriented value system. Because of the general social emphasis upon economic values, Schofield detects a connection between judgments of mental abnormality and judgments of social loss when an individual is regarded as socially deviant because he fails to achieve his full productive capacity.

Perry London notes "students of mental health find that it is difficult even to define such terms as 'health,' 'illness,' and 'normality,' without some reference to morals" (1964, p. 5). London extends this reasoning to the moral implications involved when science tries to help individuals with their personal problems. The new need to provide man with moral answers to personal problems has transformed psychotherapy as a profession into what he terms a secular priesthood. However much the therapist may try to remain scientific, he finds himself implicitly called upon to provide moral direction for his client's life.

It takes little presumption to deduce from Schofield, Hobbs, and London that certain psychological doctrines occupy the role in our society that myth had in more primitive cultures, but it is unfair to claim that the psychotherapist is the twentieth-century witch doctor. It does seem necessary, however, to recognize the parallels between the moral function of myth in the primitive cultures which Malinowski describes and the role of the diagnostician and psychotherapist in our society which other authors depict. Thus the behavioral scientist provides a psychological structure for our society in which the satisfaction of religious wants and moral cravings has become highly ambiguous.

EXPOSURE OF THE MENTAL-ILLNESS MYTH

This decade has seen a startlingly rapid defection from the once nearly unanimous belief in the value of the mental-illness concept.

Without seeking to minimize the creativity of such men as Szasz, Hobbs, Schofield, and London, the way in which each independently seems to reinforce the ideas of the others suggests that the intellectual climate of our times has changed and that the concepts of mental health and mental illness no longer have social meaning.

While Szasz has been the first to publicly decry mental illness as a myth, a handful of the more farsighted have described limitations in the model for some time. A generation ago Ruth Benedict (1934), writing from an anthropological standpoint, claims that so-called abnormality is merely an expression of cultural values. In an important article which has not been sufficiently appreciated, she points out that those whom our society regards as distinctly "abnormal" function with ease in other cultures. In some of those cultures, behavior we regard as blatantly psychotic is honored as a desirable mystical experience. On the other hand, Benedict regards the "successful" aggressive businessman who typifies current Western ideals as demonstrating what any other culture would regard as a serious deviancy.

At approximately the same time Kingsley Davis (1938) discusses the mental-hygiene movement from a sociological point of view. He sees it as basically a social movement which set standards of conduct based not on "scientific" analysis but upon the values of the so-called Protestant ethic. He notes that mental-health professionals use psychiatry as a scientific rationalization for their conventional middle-class values of private initiative, personal responsibility, and individual achievement. He finds the practitioners of his day going beyond the illusory goal of mental health to judge the whole social system by practicing morality in a scientifically mobile world under the "aegis of [a] medical authoritarian mantle".

Benedict and Davis were lone critics, however, who now seem to have been a generation before their time. The concept of mental illness was a self-evident truth in the nineteen-thirties because its social function as a myth was still too meaningful. The broader assumptions which were the basis for the mental-illness model have slowly been eroding away and are being replaced by newer ideological foundations.

Time and a transition to new values offer the chance to explore the basis of old myths. As our ways of conceptualizing good and bad change from health and illness to some other model, we can gain historical perspective and chart the broad social and cultural influences which culminated in the myth of mental illness.

One can describe the general cultural differences separating the present from pre-World War II Western society (and even more sharply from the nineteenth century) in many different ways. The Introduction discussed Riesman's characterization (1961) of the transition from an inner-directed to an other-directed society as the most piquant way of describing the social changes many observers have noted. This transition has not been sudden or uniform throughout the society. (Riesman finds inner-directed values still represented in rural and small-town America, which has been less affected by social change.)

The author believes that the gradual breakup of a rational inner-oriented culture and the likely demise of the mental-illness myth are related. While direct links between such abstractions are impossible to find, historical and circumstantial evidence supports the view that mental illness has been socially conditioned to an era which is now passing. While man has previously lacked the temporal perspective to examine the past basis for the mental-illness model, the transition to a postrational period permits an examination of how the traditional and inner-directed past dealt with the problem of defining good and evil. Although this book can not present a detailed historical analysis of philosophy or sociology, it will summarize man's ideological concern with good and evil in earlier sociological periods.

MORAL MYTHS IN TRADITION-ORIENTED CULTURE

In the traditional past, undesirable behavior was believed to result from demonic possession or witchcraft. The Old and the New Testaments provide historical evidence for the belief in demons that seems to have been a general moral myth of Biblical times. This myth can be understood as the way prerational people most naturally thought of the origin of evil. A belief in demons and a companion belief in a supernatural Deity, both of whom were directly involved in man's daily life, form a consistent part of an overriding belief in control by forces external to man. Biblical scholarship describes the demonism of the Old Testament as an externalization of human experiences in which "feelings and sensations, moods and impulses, even physical conditions, which might otherwise be described as obtaining autonomously *within* a man are portrayed on this basis, as outer forces working *upon* him" (Gaster, 1962, p. 818; italics in original).

While belief in demons is not infrequently alluded to in the Bible, the writers of that narrative were themselves relatively unconcerned about the nature of demons. Having postulated direct control over historical events by an omnipotent Deity, they were only tangentially concerned with demonology. Indeed, one of their main concerns was judging their more "superstitious" contemporaries who appeared to lack faith in direct divine control. However, as God's direct intervention in human affairs became less apparent, the influence of demonism was seen as increasingly malevolent. A dour social reality forced belief in a far more sardonic source of social control. As God seemed less in control, the demons myth made an understandable world out of grim mystery, and through rites and incantations provided a suitable outlet for the frustrations of life in a world that seemed overpoweringly evil.

By medieval times a belief in witches possessed by the devil was added to a belief in demons. The classic exposition of witchcraft is the notorious *Malleus Malleficarum*, which according to Zilboorg (1941) represents the "fusion of insanity, witchcraft, and heresy into one concept" (1941, p. 155). The book is currently regarded with horror and amusement at its quaintness, a response that obscures its real meaning. The usual psychiatric interpretation is that the book is the diabolic scheme of two monks to impose fascistic thought control on a society whom the Church deliberately terrified. This attitude is perhaps best typified by Zilboorg, who charges the two monks with brushing aside almost casually and with stunning simplicity "the whole mass of psychiatric knowledge which had been so carefully collected and preserved by almost two thousand years of medical and psychiatric investigation" (1941, p. 155).

Szasz (1961) points out several difficulties in this viewpoint, however. As one might expect, he attacks the view that witches were simply "unfortunate" persons who "fell ill" with "mental illness." Despite Zilboorg's protestations to the contrary, the "two thousand years of medical and psychiatric investigation" that preceded the persecution of witches had produced ideas that are scarcely less appalling to the modern mind than the superstitions about demons and witches. Furthermore, Szasz deduces from Zilboorg himself that the classification of witches was scarcely limited to the "mentally ill," but included what we would call the criminal and the theological heretic.

Szasz's view is that witchcraft is better regarded as deviation from a dominant social norm that was predominantly theological in nature. Thus he regards witches as those who violated dominant social values, not as unrecognized mental patients. Witchcraft is no longer considered to be the peculiar province of the fiendish malevolent, but as part of the fabric of medieval life. Szasz thus concludes: "If sainthood and salvation formed one part of the Christian game of life, witchcraft and damnation formed another" (1961, p. 216). However much contemporary society may regard the apparent cruelty of witch-hunting, it belonged integrally to more positive social values, just as military decorations for bravery and punishments for desertion belong together.

While Szasz seems correct in regarding witchcraft as part of a rather precarious social system whose only unity was theologic, nevertheless the persecution of witches did not begin until the old medieval ideas were being challenged and it reached its height during a period of great social change. Zilboorg himself recognized that "The *Malleus* was a reaction against the disquieting signs of growing instability of the established order" (1941, p. 153). This social and political restlessness in Christian Europe produced a "persecution mania" from the controlling social institutions now threatened by change. The Church and the State found it all too easy to oppose and curse as the devil these "new social forces and new spiritual ideals [which] were about to rise and to threaten the very heart of the regime which ruled medieval Europe" (Zilboorg, 1941, p. 153).

Riesman describes the time when witch-hunting reached its peak as a period of transition from a tradition-directed to an inner-directed culture. In the context of cultural transition, the victims of the witchcraft persecutions can be regarded as heretics who no longer conformed to the older traditions. In the face of impending social dissolution, a witchcraft which had been sanctified by traditional values provided a last desperate rationalization for feudal values which Renaissance individualism was judging.

MORAL MYTHS IN INNER-ORIENTED CULTURE

Individualism was not reborn without travail. The Renaissance, with all the disorders of its transition, did create less restrictive moral standards. The individual who emerged from closed feudal society was an inner-oriented man whose like had not been seen in the Western world for a thousand years.

The Renaissance was more tolerant of personal values; man was his own highest good. Free now to regard medieval ideas as myth and superstition, the individual turned from faith in the old moral standards and looked to his own reason to dispel the primitive illogical past. As his mind opened to new ideas, so his physical world also broadened. Unlimited new economic horizons beckoned the individual to try his self-confidence in the marketplace and later in the factory. Such new achievements poured upon man a wealth which justified the new values. The ideological hallmark of the Middle Ages, synthesis of faith and reason, was replaced by the Protestant ethic, which sanctified the new middle-class values of frugality and achievement.

Not until 1782, according to Zilboorg (1941), was the last witch decapitated; remnants of a traditional social order persisted a long time. Nevertheless, demons and witches had obviously long ceased to explain deviances from the social order. The individual was increasingly free from the arbitrary despotic control of social institutions over his mind and would seem to be free in mind, body, and spirit.

By the time belief in demons and witches had been abandoned, the new mythology of mental illness was already in its ascendancy, however. Just as the myth of demons and witches died slowly, so the belief in mental illness grew gradually from virtually imperceptible beginnings. Probably the first use of the concept was merely metaphorical. In a search for the origin of the mental-illness concept, T. R. Sarbin (1967) finds its first use in the sixteenth century by a prominent churchwoman, Teresa of Avila. During the Counter-Reformation she attempted to save some nuns from the Inquisition by suggesting that their deviancy had a natural cause, and therefore she declared that the nuns were not evil but *comas enfermas* (as if sick). Teresa implied that practitioners of physic, rather than the clergy, should be the responsible social specialists.

From Metaphor to Myth

From such simple origins the belief in mental illness slowly grew from a metaphor to a reality that held the same terror as the old demons and witches. The Age of Reason developed its own superstitions. It did, however, subject the deviant individual who rejected its values to what in some ways was a more abject fate than that of the witch. The irony that a supposedly urbane and reasoning age created its own form of intolerance has been underscored by Michael Foucault in *Madness and Civilization: A History of Insanity in the Age of Reason* (1965). Foucault gives a detailed chronicle of the Age of Reason, describing the various ways in which the so-called enlightened society dealt with a deviant few.

Foucault begins his narrative at the close of the fifteenth century when the pall of leprosy was lifted from the countryside only to be replaced by a sudden disquiet which soon took the form of fear of madness. He notes a morbid fascination with a "ship of fools" which plied its strange journey as a means of extraditing those whom society could not tolerate. The new age saw the boat of the socially derelict as a symbol of its quest for that reason which had heretofore been forbidden fruit. The air of mystery surrounding reason did not remain long. Foucault notes that by the seventeenth century a very practical need for mass confinement had arisen that had never previously been necessary. The new mass "madness" was based on the fear of economic chaos. The author traces the need for confinement to an achievement-oriented society which feared mendicancy and idleness as the source of all disorders. This need to confine became especially acute during times of economic recession, when society saw the unemployed as a likely source of vagabonds and tramps. He notes that places of confinement served a useful purpose even in times of prosperity by providing cheap labor to help level off the economic cycle.

The confinement of the social misfit was but the beginning. Not until the eighteenth century, according to Foucault's narrative, did the fear of madness itself reach the social scene. The individual who saw reason as the essential aspect of his nature now dreaded to be reminded of that other part of him which contained inner furies. Being unable to ignore this other part of himself, he chose to detach it from him by making it part of an animal. Foucault writes that the image of madness borrowed its face from the beast, and the asylum became a menagerie with those chained to the cell walls "no longer men whose minds had wandered, but beasts preyed on by a natural frenzy" (1965, p. 72). If the seventeenth century had justified confining deviants and misfits because they threatened the economic order, the eighteenth century was hardly more enlightened: If the madman was not sick or even demon possessed, he was an animal whose savage nature could be tamed only by discipline and brutalizing. The madman who was considered an animal, however, could not yet be seen as a sick human being.

Foucault notes a change in the eighteenth-century attitude that touches the unreason of the time. The inmate of the asylum was no longer hated; now he was feared. "In the anxiety of the second half of the eighteenth century, the fear of madness grew at the same time as the dread of unreason; and thereby the two forms of obsession, leaning upon each other, continued to reinforce each other" (1965, p. 211). Suddenly the fear was of becoming ill, and the new myth was that suffocating and noxious disease spread abroad on the city air from the houses of the sick. Citizens were now afraid that the contagions would spread through disease-tainted air to the residential quarters, threatening entire cities with malevolent vapors impregnated with rottenness and taint. The devil had taken another form.

This displacement of fear from a fallible mind to a tainted and noxious body made madness an illness. The physical basis for the troubles of the "mind" which Hippocrates had "discovered" in the golden age of Greece was "rediscovered" in the next age, the rational and inner-directed Enlightenment. Perhaps inner orientation and mental illness go together coincidentally in these two instances; however, at the apex of his pride in reason, man finds he must still deal with that other side of his nature which he could no longer give to the demons and witches or, as he became more humane, to the animals. The individual newly emancipated from the control of traditions needed a new explanation for what he felt still bound him to the furies of an inner emotional unrest.

Demons were regarded by the rational man as being, like reason itself, within man. If the good in man was surely his reason, the bad must also be within him; if not in his mind, then in his body. Insanity thus became a sickness for which the age turned for diagnosis and cure to the physician. Zilboorg observes (1941, p. 297) that the physician found it completely natural to approach so-called mental diseases with the same preconceptions which had proven so realistic and useful in treating physical diseases. The new psychiatrist was scarcely able to differentiate his practice from general medicine. Zilboorg writes of him, "Whatever psychological labels he attached to mental diseases, he considered them physical"

(1941, p. 297). As Zilboorg notes, the intense struggles of the preceding centuries against demonology only served to accentuate the physician's natural propensities to shun his own psychology and turn to a physical, corporeal, and organic viewpoint. Based on social needs, one form of superstition was replaced by another myth.

At this point a transformation occurred in the metaphorical "as if" sick (the *comas enfermas* of Saint Teresa). Man began to drop the qualifying "as if" phrase and forgot its earlier use. Saint Teresa's suggestion that practitioners of physic, rather than of religion, aid the socially deviant had been heeded. As Sarbin (1967) points out, it became awkward for the post-Renaissance physician who revived Galenic classifications to talk about both "real" illness and "as if" illness. Sarbin suggests further that the decline of the power of church authorities to diagnose extraordinary imaginings and perplexing conduct was paralleled by the rise of science. He notes that "the prestige of the scientist helped in establishing the model of Galen for both kinds of 'illness'—those with somatic complaints and observable somatic symptoms and those without somatic complaints but with unusual behavior standing for somatic symptoms" (1967, pp. 448-449). In this way, the concept of mental illness was gradually transformed from metaphor to myth.

From Myth to Myth

In the nineteenth century, everything that had been so rationally and logically put together during the preceding four hundred years began to come apart. The logical compartmentalization of men's lives into separate, thought-tight compartments had been carried so far that it became more difficult to separate the reason from the emotion, the mind from the body, and the social from the economic. Accelerating technological progress put rationalism on an intellectual treadmill which required that thinking adapt rapidly to a constantly changing idea of the good life. The rational basis for social norms and individual expectations was increasingly questioned by changes which made even the recent good seem uncouth. As the nineteenth century neared its close, a significant number of the socially anomic were left in the backwaters of the industrial revolution. While most men tried harder to keep up with the rational view of man, for the first time a few heretics were questioning the whole logical basis of the social order. Kierkegaard and Nietzsche stand out as the first to foresee the impending breakup of the old order.

At the close of the nineteenth century cultural strains which had not existed since the breakup of the Middle Ages some four hundred years before reappeared. The sudden increase in demonology and witchcraft during the Middle Ages has been cited as a last desperate attempt of a traditional society to maintain itself. Similarly, at the end of the nineteenth century a new myth of sickness arose as an inner-directed society struggled to maintain itself against new social forces which threatened to end man's rational self-sufficiency.

The eighteenth century classified only the severe forms of mental disturbance as medical ills, but the nineteenth century extended the behavior termed sickness, calling the milder forms of social deviancy neuroses. The discovery (or invention) of the neurosis resulted from a protracted sociomedical dilemma that culminated in psychoanalysis with the controversial figure of Sigmund Freud.

The history of psychoanalysis in a sense begins with the neurologist Charcot. Like other neurologists of his day, he was constantly called upon to treat the hysteric, typically a difficult patient to cure because he represented an impossible therapeutic situation. Before Charcot, medicine had treated the hysteric as a malingerer, rejecting his complaints when a physical basis for his disability could not be confirmed. The hysteric had therefore lacked the same dignified status accorded to patients suffering from tangible and treatable physical maladies.

Szasz blames Charcot for converting hysteria into a sickness and bestowing upon the hysteric the full dignities of a patient. By removing the previous stigma attached to hysteria, Charcot unwittingly made it far too easy to be sick. Szasz does in fact compare Charcot with Guillotin, who made it less painful for those condemned by the French Revolution to die and thus unwittingly increased the death rate when he invented the device which bears his name. In a similar way, Charcot made it easier for sufferers to pretend to be physically sick when in fact they had no objective basis for illness. The prestige of a famous neurologist could hardly have a negligible effect on how medicine defined illness, in Szasz's view, and he bases his case upon subsequent events.

By merely claiming that the elusive complaints of the hysteric were a fit subject for the neurologist's study, Charcot began a movement logically concluded by Breuer and Freud. They compounded an already serious medical error by regarding hysterical symptoms as disorders in the physiochemical machinery of the body. Indeed, Freud built the entire superstructure of psychoanalysis upon the assumption that neurosis is but the psychological manifestation of dislocated libidinal impulses which derive their biological energy from a disequilibrium in mucous membranes.

While Breuer and Freud were diligently seeking the physiological ramifications of hysteria (to tap the current high level of medical prestige, according to Szasz), they were obscuring the real bases of hysteria, which Szasz claims have been psychological, social, and ethical. Mental illness has increasingly been used "chiefly to obscure and 'explain away' problems in personal and social relationships" (1961, p. 205), just as witchcraft had been used for a similar purpose a few centuries earlier. The result is what Szasz terms the medical game, which effectively allows man to deny the nature of social, moral, and personal controversies. In this situation "virtually every human event—from personal unhappiness and marital infidelity at one end of the spectrum to political misbehavior and deviant moral conviction at the other—is regarded as a facet of the problem of mental illness" (Szasz, 1961, p. 71). If mental illness is but the reflection of general social norms, it must reflect moral and ethical judgments of good and bad. Beginning with a modest approach to the isolated physical malaise of hysteria, the medical model becomes even more inclusive, covering a wide range of personal and social problems until it provides a complete plan for the good life.

The reasons that Szasz gives for placing the hysteric under psychiatric aegis may be correct, but one must still consider carefully why medicine did so at the end of the nineteenth century, rather than a generation before or after. Fortunately J. H. van den Berg (1961) has attempted to place the origin of the neurosis in its proper social perspective.

Van den Berg traces the origin of the neurosis to the summer of 1882, when it appeared in the conclusions that Breuer reached after treating a young woman with a sudden inability to drink water. Van den Berg claims that the type of neurosis which Freud described had not existed before 1882. In the last quarter of the nineteenth century the individual was suddenly losing a firm connection with the body social, a state van den Berg describes as anomie. As the nineteenth century progressed, society began to deprive the individual of strong and stable social connections so that he lost a sense of belonging to other individuals and even to clearly defined groups. This social diffuseness gave the individual a self that could function within a group but which was deprived of the social intimacy that gave him a sense of self-solidarity. The superficial selves produced by conflicting group identifications created the double life of Dr. Jekyll and Mr. Hyde, and at times even plural lives. Van den Berg concludes that "what Breuer and Freud saw was the first manifestation of an exceptionally extensive occurrence: The manifestation of the effect of a disintegration of society on the individual" (1961, p. 170).

While the Victorian became dislocated from people in general, one particular form of estrangement became crucial—the emptiness of sex for the Victorian woman. Indeed, the sexual situation caused women to faint because the emptiness of this social encounter resulted in a social atmosphere too rarified to sustain consciousness.

Sex was something which even the Victorian women could not ignore forever, even by fainting. In psychoanalytic terms, sex was repressed and became part of the unconscious. Freud noted the symptoms of the hysterical neurotic and, finding their genesis in *la chose sexuelle*, wrongly (in van den Berg's view) considered it a pathological condition involving conflict between ego and superego. In reality what he saw was but the social dislocation of an individual detached from a meaningful other.

Freud saw the symptoms of a particular neurosis, even if no one before him did. For van den Berg "It is clear why nobody ever described or treated neurotics before Janet, Breuer, and Freud: There were no neurotics; they also appeared in the nineteenth century" (1961, p. 185). Hysteria had been known since antiquity but it had never before been considered a psychiatric disorder. In fact, hysterical signs such as the stigmata had been venerated as signs of extreme religiosity. Although the symptoms themselves were no different in Freud's day, the people who had them were: The so-called neurotic could no longer cohere to a social group. Finding himself psychologically rendered asunder by conflict among different groups, he turned to the psychoanalyst to unravel his tangled identity.

If indeed no "neurotics" existed before Freud's time, none have existed since. For van den Berg, however, the term neurotic is not correct because the defect was not in the neurons or even in the individual. The individual becomes "neurotic" only because of a state that exists in society, and because causes are external, van den Berg prefers to speak of *communicoses* or *socioses*.

Szasz would appear to be unduly critical of his medical colleagues. The myth of mental illness is far more than a synthetic fabrication which allows the psychiatrist to preempt that authority to judge human behavior which once belonged to the churchman. The myth has been popular because it has been socially so useful. The medical model is hardly a nefarious psychiatric plot to subject the world to a new autocracy; instead it is a natural social response to the needs of an inner-directed man for a suitable explanation of what he finds to be bad within himself. When rational man looks within himself for his failings, he finds the inner reality too hard to face without defenses against the full measure of truth about himself. His defense is an illness with its symptoms.

Just as the need to believe in demons and witches became greatly intensified when tradition-bound society gave way to inner-oriented man, so also man suddenly became neurotic when inner-oriented society started to disintegrate. The individual troubled because self-directing values were failing him found solace in blaming neuroses and other psychiatric manifestations for his failure. The characteristic symptoms of the hysteric mounted to a climax when man found his inner-directed individuality in conflict with a new, postrational self. When hysteric dissociation failed to keep these two contradictory aspects of the self apart, the result was neurosis.

Freud's work gains new meaning when it is regarded as a bridge between the rational and postrational ages of man. Seen in this light, Freud is among the first to behold the so-called other-directed man emerging from his cultural cocoon. Because this man had not existed before the end of the nineteenth century, van den Berg is correct in concluding that the neurotic of Freud's day had not existed before.

Although he attempted to treat individuals who were becoming other directed, apparently Freud himself was anchored to the old individualistic values. While he could not miss observing the newly important social nature of man, he saw it not as an adaptive, evolving set of directional antennae but as an encapsulated super-ego, which he regarded as a rather anachronistic residual from primeval society. Although Freud was the first to realize that man's social nature was the source of his problems, he hardly envisioned the dynamic aspects of culture. Thus he blamed man's social difficulties not on a decaying Victorian society but on the earlier traditional state in which man lived in small groups under the domination of a tribal chieftain.

In a sense Freud was the culmination of an inner-oriented age which had now overreached itself. True to his cultural heritage, he looked backward to blame social ills on the last vestiges of tradition orientation still enshrined in Victorian morality, which was particularly oppressive in Roman Catholic Vienna. He sought to free man from his social nexus by releasing a highly individualistic libido, but society was already rapidly changing in ways he did not anticipate. Although Freud gave man more sexual freedom, he solved the wrong social problem. The problem was not one of an inner-directed man in a tradition-directed society but of what Riesman would describe as an inner-directed man in an other-directed society.

REALITY IN CONTEMPORARY CULTURE

The traditional man and the rational man each had his distinctive myth which enabled him to make value judgments in a consistent and an understandable way. Postrational man also needs a cognitive process which will enable him to differentiate between good and bad.

We can not get the same perspective about the way our age distinguishes good from evil that we can about past ages. We must leave to our descendents the amusing task of finding the illogic in what we feel is sacred and unquestionable, assumptions that will seem as mythical to them as the medieval belief in witches and demons does to us.

Perhaps this postrational society is still too new to have developed a satisfying mythology. If our age is insecure and vaguely unsure of itself, our lack of myths may also deprive us of the convenient rationalizations that enabled our forebears to be so certain about their values. Indeed, what some philosophers call an existential crisis may be but another way of saying that we lack the ideological tools to fashion a moral cosmology.

Although it would be fatuously premature to depict our ideological idiosyncracies, two facts stand out concerning the present situation. The ways we deal with good and evil express current life as well as the demons and witches represented an earlier age and as sickness symbolized a more recent period. Newer terms already have the semantic flavoring of a world of social relationships. Terms such as *adjustment, problems in living,* and *behavioral modification* assume that the good life takes an outward direction.

The second fact of modern life is that if man has not yet found new moral and ethical guidelines, he will not cease looking until he has. Probably he will invent new constructs with the same definitiveness that sin and salvation had during the Middle Ages, or that diagnostic entities had during the inner-directed past. One can hardly foresee the emerging ideological framework for the new good and the new evil, but one can predict that man will inevitably look to the behavioral sciences for a new social understanding of himself. Theories of personality offer new definitions of good and evil, of mental health and mental illness.

SUMMARY

This chapter places morals in a sociohistoric perspective and deals with what man has judged to be undesirable or abnormal behavior. Tradition-oriented man often explained social deviancy as demon possession or witchcraft threatening him from without. Later, inner-oriented man attempted to explain what he preferred to regard as natural occurrences by projecting the evil inward, within his mind. Contemporary man, who is again in transition, can no longer accept the diagnosis of unwanted behavior as psychopathic or mentally ill.

The failure of the mental-illness model heightens modern man's crisis in choosing values and moral standards. He can no longer believe that his difficulties are due to evil spirits or to defective neurons. He must find new concepts of morality that are meaningful, culturally relevant, and logically satisfying to increasingly sophisticated individuals.

 *Chapter 4*

THE MORAL MESSAGES OF PSYCHOTHERAPY

And Moses went up from the plains of Moab to Mount Nebo, to the top of Pisgah, which is opposite Jericho. And the Lord showed him all the land, Gilead as far as Dan, all Naphtali, the land of Ephraim and Manasseh, all the land of Judah as far as the Western Sea, the Negeb, and the Plain, that is, the valley of Jericho the city of palm trees, as far as Zoar. And the Lord said to him, "This is the land of which I swore to Abraham, to Isaac, and to Jacob, 'I will give it to your descendants.' I have let you see it with your eyes, but you shall not go over there." So Moses the servant of the Lord died there in the land of Moab, according to the word of the Lord . . . DEUTERONOMY

❖❖❖

Because he is a contemporary moralist, the therapist finds himself called upon for many of the guidelines once supplied by the priest and the social philosopher. If the therapist is called upon to be a moral herald, however, his trumpet gives forth an uncertain sound. Chapter Two discussed a significant number of moral overtones to counseling and psychotherapy; however, the moral tone of contemporary therapy does lack clarity because it has not been brought into tune.

As the therapist is sought as a new moral authority, if he is to avoid becoming completely arbitrary in his judgments, he must find a basis for his pronouncements. He can no longer call upon the sanctions which the church once invoked, nor appeal to reason, nor invoke the metaphors of illness and of health. Because he can no longer conceal from himself the moral implications of these illness concepts, he can not expect society to continue to accept them either.

The client asks the counselor and the psychotherapist for help in imposing a new cognitive order on the moral chaos caused by the decline of old authorities. Just what structure the therapist should provide, however, is totally unclear. Science has done much to destroy moral beliefs based on divine precepts as well as man's faith in his own reason. Although science has found older systems of values easy to destroy, it has had much more difficulty creating new standards that are universally acceptable in a society whose values are so diverse.

As old myths lose belief, the behavioral sciences are called upon to provide modern man with new and more acceptable cognitive structures. Like the mythology they replace, they must have the social reality to perform the same integrating functions as the older beliefs, providing a cognitive certainty and the social security of knowing that one's values are morally acceptable. These new beliefs must rejoin sundered cultural ties and in the process describe a grand way of life to provide contrapuntal unity for all man's social endeavors.

If the therapist is to fulfill a socially meaningful role, he must become an authority in areas which contemporary society experiences as most subjectively real.

REPLACING OLD MYTHS WITH NEW REALITY

Each period in man's history has had its distinctive conception of reality. Primitive cultures see various animistic forces in nature, the Judeo-Christian tradition focuses reality in a monotheistic God, and traditional periods locate the highest reality outside of the self and the social system. At the end of the Middle Ages, the locus of subjective reality gradually shifted from witches and demons, which were external to man, to human reason, which was within him. Thus metaphysical reality advanced from the hereafter to man's immediate life as divine reality was placed within the mind of man, a person Riesman fittingly describes as inner directed. The powers of the mind and the penetration of rational thought now had the most basic reality.

In our day the location of what seems ontologically most basic to man is shifting again. Now man's powers of reason are not as apparent to him as is a new, externally imposed reality. This new reality is man's inner feeling of having his identity threatened by what he regards as the pressures of other directedness. External reality thus becomes other people over whom man feels he has no control. As social contacts increase in number, they also become more superficial. When the individual enters a social encounter, he finds the real "you" increasingly hard to embrace. Reality has become diffuse.

If an older reality studied man in a theological perspective as a child of God and if a newer reality placed man's mind at the center of his existence, the modern view projects reality outside man and requires that he be studied as a creature who is subject to the same prediction and control as the other subject matter of human knowledge.

It can hardly be coincidental that man first experienced this new reality at precisely that time when authoritative definitions of happiness were in transition from the law courts and the literary philosophers to the new practitioners of what Howard Mumford Jones terms the technique of happiness.

In his history of American culture, Jones implies strongly that before 1890 man had no need for psychology. He states that "for the Age of Reason man was equipped with rational faculties to keep his passions in order, in a universe of clear design and mechanical perfection" (1953, p. 128). The eighteenth century guaranteed man the right to happiness from God, basic truths were self-evident, and man's right to know them was assured by the metaphysical reality of natural law. If the courts somewhat vaguely interpreted the nature of happiness, the transcendental philosopher Ralph Waldo Emerson clarified new definitions with metaphysical fluency.

Although William James was spiritually akin to Ralph Waldo Emerson in many ways, the generation between them spanned an age in human thought. Post-Civil War America was becoming industrialized. As Jones notes, court decisions reflected the new economic reality in which the right to happiness became the right to property. Industrialization brought urbanization, and closing the frontier restricted the social space. As the opportunities for individual expansion became limited, the dominant mode of outward movement changed from the physical to the psychological.

By 1890 a definite shift in man's perception of his nature had occurred. Psychological solipsism had ended and man sought new meaning for his life. William James believed that nineteenth-century psychology needed to become a science, and he saw that it might do so by discarding its metaphysical and theological clothing. James thus became a part of a new intellectual ferment which severely jolted the metaphysical and theological interpretations of reality: By the late nineteenth century, man saw himself as a creature of nature. The body extended the mind downward by a theory that whatever man experiences as emotion is determined by physiological processes in the body. Even the self was extended by James' belief that it should be defined to include all that man called his own. Man was no longer exalted by nature to a lofty perch where he could be solitarily self-determining but was forced to enter a functional encounter with his social environment. As Jones notes, happiness became an adjustment between an inner self and an outer world.

While James was describing changing New World values, a much more violent ideological upheaval was taking place in Europe. Two years after James published *Principles of Psychology* in 1890, Freud and Breuer published their famous work on hysteria. If one believes in the significance of historical process, one must attach great significance to the fact that the two works which completely overturned a system of values over five hundred years old were written within two years of each other by men who were culturally, ideologically, and professionally remote from each other.

Chapter Three discussed the accusation that Freud popularized the neurosis form of the mental-health myth. The fact that he did so, whether he was right or wrong, does not matter for our purposes. No single figure in the behavioral sciences has been so influential for the disciplines involved in the study of man, and the effects of his work extend far beyond the scientific community. Freud has influenced man's thinking about himself so extensively that he may even be described as the symbol or the myth of our times.

Freud stands accused of perpetuating the mental-illness myth by treating hysteria and later other so-called neurotic conditions as medical ailments. Discussing the implications of psychoanalysis from different angles, both van den Berg (1961) and Szasz (1961) expose him as one who somewhat unwittingly gave the solace of medicine to alienated and isolated individuals. The Victorians who sought help in hospitals and doctors' offices for imaginary ills found they were diagnosed medically as if they had physical significance. In different ways Szasz and van den Berg charge Freud with failing to be aware of the cultural significance of the symptoms he observed. To use Riesman's terms, Freud was treating the inner-directed individual under such strain that his ability to be self-sustaining was starting to break down.

Szasz and van den Berg are not alone in implying that Freud was a social conservative who looked to the past in his view of human behavior. David Bakan (1958) describes the influence of Jewish mystical traditions on Freud's thought. Erich Fromm (1959) finds Freud's theory of need satisfaction had its sources in nineteenth-century economic theory. Many trace the origin of the theory of needs to the principles of physics of Freud's day. Jerome Bruner (1962) finds that Freud inherited from Charles Darwin the belief that man's origin was in nature.

Freud could hardly have had so great an effect upon the twentieth century merely by drawing upon old ideologies, however. In significant respects he is a revolutionary who parted company with the values of his time. As Whyte (1960) points out, man had been aware of the irrational aspects of his personality for some time, but Freud was the first to see how sorely beset individualism had become. Man was threatened not only with rumblings from his libidinal unconscious below but also from pressures without, internalized pressures within the superego that could also act directly upon him. (Though Freud seems to have been the first to appreciate the extent to which the human will must bend to internalized social pressure, he was not aware of the changing nature of the other that sorely besets the frail ego. Indeed, Freud's social absolutes were so rigid that he could represent social reality with the primeval scene in *Totem and Taboo* [1938].)

Freud did largely part company with an inner-oriented age when he posited the doctrine of psychic determinism. Before his time, thinking was a free act, pure and unsullied, which could not be reduced to prior cause. Freud's claim that thought is not its own master, but ultimately is the servant of the body demolished the self-sufficiency of human reason. The freedom which the Renaissance had given man to advance toward rationally chosen goals was now withdrawn. Psychic processes could no longer be thought of as the mythical homunculus of thought trapped within the skull, as the Age of Reason appears to have supposed. Even the sanctity of human progress and individual achievement was taken away from man. Psychoanalysis scarcely cared to measure human progress by the amount of economic advancement, since the march of civilization was but a more elaborate way of protecting man from his own true nature.

Freud was in large part true to both his professional and cultural heritage in presupposing that if man was bound to the irrational, the forces within his own body must be ultimately physiological in nature. But psychoanalysis did not limit man's inner conflict to a struggle between id and ego. Rather the ego was seen as desperately striving to maintain control amidst a struggle between the internal forces of man's physiological nature and the external control of social forces. If man was ultimately dependent upon civilization for security and even more immediately beholden to the basic libidinal needs of the body, he had scant chance for freedom.

Thus Freud became aware that the individual was so tightly bound by civilization that he hardly had a chance to freely satisfy his desires. Although Freud may not have been aware of it, he was in large part tolling the knell of the inner-oriented man. From then on, man was considered to be controlled from without by immutable social forces. While Freud's thinking contains much of the mythological past, psychoanalysis has been man's pervasive way of thinking about himself in this century because it presents a new social determinism resonating with the experience of the other-oriented man. This new man no longer feels free to move outward in all directions because he is constricted by an overcrowded social space. No longer his own master, post-Freudian man enters another age which regards civilization, not as man's most rational achievement, but as a necessary evil to protect the individual from the uncontrolled emotions of primal man.

The limitations of psychoanalysis are due to Sigmund Freud's legacy of the diagnostic tradition in medicine and many late-nineteenth-century ideas of normal and abnormal. The broader significance of psychoanalysis lies in the fact that Freud enabled man to find a new basis for conceptualizing the aberrant behavior of his fellow man. Freud was the first to look for psychogenic origins of what had so manifestly seemed to be behavioral deviancies. What others took to be symptoms of behavior so warped and distorted that they could but indicate a diseased mind, Freud placed in a cause-effect sequence where they were regarded as lawful reactions to frustration. If Szasz (1961) is justified in his charge that Freud helped compound Charcot's error of diagnosing the hysteric as sick, he did at least redeem himself in part by interpreting the seemingly incomprehensible symptoms of the hysteric as functional attempts to deal with frustration. From this starting point Freud opened to science the analysis of seemingly commonplace behavior, which was now given new significance by the motives it was designed to serve.

The study of man's behavior in society, which had seemed so irrelevant before Freud, has gained new meaning. The new reality lies in social relationships, and if the new good is to meet the social expectations of others successfully, its nature, no longer self-evident, must be interpreted by the new experts in social relationships. At this time (the late nineteenth century) rational man had been able to rely on the self-evidence of reason for his values.

THERAPY AND ITS SOCIAL SIGNIFICANCE

The task of completely and accurately relating counseling and psychotherapy to their time must be left to the future historian. Today we are just gaining a perspective on the significance of events which occurred near the turn of the century when therapy first became a profession. The growth of the profession appears to be associated with a radical shift in the way man experiences his world.

Rollo May describes a shift in values in Western culture within the last three or four decades.

It is, of course, not at all an accident that these are also exactly the decades when counseling, psychotherapy and psychoanalysis have come to play such important roles in our society. For it is precisely the breakdown and radical transition of values in a society, causing the individuals in that society to founder in storm-shaken seas without solid mooring posts or even buoys and lighthouses which can be depended upon, which makes the professions of helping individuals so necessary (1962b, p. 1).

When man was no longer willing to consider the mind a homunculus with the little man "making the wheels turn," he had to find an intellectually more acceptable and a behaviorally more tangible way to describe his inner world. The old reality saw man as free, yet chained to his animal past through a state of unreason called mental illness; the new reality believes man's thoughts and behavior can be understood and explained by certain general principles or laws. Thinking, feeling, and striving are not to be interpreted as resulting from an abstract act of will but as part of a link between antecedent conditions and predictable conclusions.

Counseling and psychotherapy have become professions as practitioners have brought the assumptions which the behavioral sciences make about the causal reality underlying human behavior to a guiding, interpersonal relationship. Since the therapist assumes that man does not behave in a whimsical or a random manner, he typically seeks insight and understanding into the client's behavior. Insight therapists assume the existence of certain regularities in the client, and they therefore regard the essence of therapy as the communication of these perceived regularities to the client. Action therapists, on the other hand, perceive regularities in human behavior as due to habits established by patterns of reinforcement. Their purpose in therapy is to interrupt behavioral habits through shaping and relearning.

Because Freud is considered the father of psychoanalysis, he must also be regarded as the father of psychotherapy and even of counseling. He does not appear to have been the first to observe the reality of what he termed "psychic determinism," however. Whyte (1960) cites an impressive number of European thinkers who had been aware of the irrational; such contemporaries of Freud as James and Watson in America had also interpreted thinking in functional and behavioral terms. Freud was the first, however, to apply the knowledge of this new reality to an intensive and systematic attempt to change another person. Because psychoanalysis and its offshoots were the only therapies practiced for well over a generation, psychoanalysis becomes the reference point in discussing the social and moral significance of counseling and psychotherapy. Howard Mumford Jones (1953) notes a transfer of authority to the scientist, who gave new meaning to the pursuit of happiness previously sought in natural law and individual rights.

Needs

Freudian theory starts with motivation. Freud has done more than any other individual has to destroy the concept of inner-directed reason. He did so by claiming that thinking is motivated; thought processes are not pure acts of rational will. Thinking is a physiologically driven mechanism for providing the most efficient discharge of certain prurient tensions in the body.

Because Freud came to psychiatry after being trained in the medical sciences, he used various physiological principles to explain (directly and analogously) how the mind functions. The scientific thinking of Freud's day was still rather mechanistic in its orientation and thus sought a fixed source of energy for psychic functions. Because the results were never allowed to stray very far from their cause, the most convenient proximal source of energy was perceived to be within the body. As a physiologist, Freud was aware that certain areas of the body have more nerve endings than others and therefore are more prone to stimulation. Because mucous membranes are rich in sensory nerves, Freud concentrated his attention upon what he regarded as the most neurologically sensitive parts of the body—the mouth, anus, and phallus—as areas progressively important in maturation. Stimulation of these sensitive areas produces tensions or disequilibrium which in effect directly causes cognitive events in the mind, the tensions acting as a mechanical force upon a watchspring. Freud needed to link the mental and the physiological because his contemporaries had regarded these two parts of man as very dissimilar. From his medical training, Freud used the term *instinct,* which he defined as the mental representative of stimuli emanating from within the organism and penetrating to the mind. The rather intricate elaboration of ego function develops later because of the complicated intrusion of social demands. The ego postpones instinct gratification, but it can hardly be denied forever in Freud's view, since all psychic life is ultimately reduced to the pleasure principle. Freud wrote that "any given process originates in an unpleasant state of tension and thereupon determines for itself such a path that its ultimate issue coincides with a relaxation of this tension" (1922, p. 1). If tensions in the mind have come from tensions in the body, all seek a reequilibrium with nature.

Freud is so controversial that he is criticized from a number of vantage points, one of which is scientific in nature. Later neuroanatomical studies have revealed that Freud's tightly closed system was greatly oversimplified and overrationalized. Freud appears to have believed that the same logically simple nineteenth-century explanations science proposed for the rest of nature could easily account for complex phenomena in the new psychology. He further reflected the scientific temper of his time by constructing an elaborate systematic model of the mind. Since the time of Freud's early work, science has become skeptical of the existence of concepts which can not be operationally defined and empirically validated. One can no longer be scientific merely by using technological analogies. The Vienna Circle of logical positivists does not seem to have influenced Freud directly, but the more yeasty scientific *zeitgeist* of the twentieth century inevitably shaped his maturer years. As Freud lived through the significant political and ideological events of the twentieth century, he tentatively began to desystematize his earlier rationally satisfying structure.

Freud's theory of needs has also caused moral controversy because his moral beliefs exemplify a naturalistic system of ethics. He judges whatever meets the needs of man's physiological nature as good. This good, embodied in the strivings for instinctual gratification, is opposed by the evil which emanates from man's social needs for security. Not everyone is willing to regard physiological demands for instinctual-need gratification as man's most salient attribute.

A claim for Freud's greatness could be based solely on his discovery that thinking and behaving are motivated. We too easily take this daring claim for granted. However creative and courageous he may have been in abruptly breaking with tradition, in other respects Freud was a more conservative cultural product of his time. The theory of personality in which he rigidly enclosed his theory of needs has received damaging and even devastating criticisms.

Although Freud bases the structure of personality on motivation, modern controversy has arisen concerning what is most basic in the theory of needs. Some are so deeply committed to Freudian theory that they have scarcely questioned the reality of primary process or the basic nature of the pleasure principle, but others find increasing numbers of alternatives to motivate human behavior, other than prurient tensions of sex.

The growing confusion fosters controversy; values are at stake. Freud is controversial because he made sex primary in human life, but one can not fairly single him out for criticism. Other theories of need are perhaps equally arbitrary from a scientific or a moral viewpoint.

Even though Freud's view has been controversial, he had keen vision. From his nineteenth-century vantage point, Freud correctly gauged the temper of the changing times. Motives, not demons or illness, now explain human behavior.

Frustrations

Frustration is the blocking of motivated or need-directed behavior. All behavior has a cause which directs it to meet the need. The term frustration is often used as a synonym for the psychopathological and the abnormal, but it is scientifically more meaningful to speak of frustrations than of sickness. Frustrations are firmly anchored in causal sequence and thus they represent the natural unfolding of a causal sequence. The frustration is the natural result of a need meeting an impediment to its realization.

Another of Freud's lasting contributions was to replace oddness concepts with those of frustration. Freud believed that frustration occurs when the satisfaction of instincts is blocked by social demands mediated through the superego. Man therefore finds himself in a state of perpetual conflict between the impulses that demand release and the stern, forbidding superego, the internalized social voice that prevents instinctual gratification. Somehow one must resolve this impasse to provide some outlet for libidinal impulses. A hydraulic analogy is often used to describe this state of affairs. The dam containing the libidinal impulses will rupture and rather abruptly destroy all ego functioning if the organism does not find some way to lessen this tension before the mounting pressure has disruptive consequences.

The frustration that results from a failure to reduce physiological disequilibrium has unfortunate consequences: The organism becomes upset, and tension is experienced as anxiety. When the organism is blocked in its attempts to gratify instinctual impulses directly, it must resort to subterfuge and indirection. The result is behavior which seems strange and peculiar to an objective observer and often to the individual himself, who feels impelled to this behavior. Freud labeled such behavior psychoneurotic, a regressive move. He did take a notable step forward, however, when he placed the supposed neurosis in a dynamic or causal sequence.

The concept of frustration is clearly preferable to the idea of abnormality. Judgments of the abnormal require an arbitrary, absolute definition of the good as a moral reference point. If the one making the evaluation does not use his personal standards of right and wrong, he must use the collective moral judgment of his society, which may be even more culture bound. Ruth Benedict points out (1934) that the concept of what is normal is properly regarded as only a variant of what is good, and different cultures have a wide range of views of both the good and the normal. The concept of frustration is also preferable to categories of diagnostic illness because illness can be as morally arbitrary as moral judgments of normality and abnormality. Diagnostic labels have a noticeable tendency, discussed in Chapter Two, to betray the values or prejudices of the diagnostician.

Using the concept of frustration does not allow one to escape making moral judgments totally. Although most people today accept the Freudian notion that even the most grotesque acts have natural causes, Freud's conceptualization of the neurotic remains as controversial as his theory of motivation. Freud appears to have been morally somewhat arbitrary in regarding the artist as an aberrant type. In a sense it is immaterial whether the artist does indeed sublimate physiological impulses as Freud charged. What is relevant is that Freud made a value judgment by regarding him as abnormal. Medical license, rather than scientific objectivity, allowed him to diagnose the artist, and from a moral standpoint it is unimportant whether Freud was objectively correct in his causal reconstruction of the artist's early life.

Freud was correct in believing that the so-called psychopathological can be traced to an earlier frustration of basic need. The scientific breakthrough came in 1882 when Freud traced female hysteria to what appeared to be its first cause—seduction by the father. But as Freud himself admitted later, he was wrong about the nature of the need which had been frustrated in his first female patients.

Although Freud changed his mind about the seduction of young girls by their fathers, others believe that he continued to be wrong. If he were wrong about needs, he would have had to have been hoist by his own deterministic petard, and he would have been wrong about the nature and even the identity of the abnormal behavior which resulted from such frustration. The controversy continues. Even within the causal framework of objective scientific method, the judgment of the abnormal remains morally arbitrary and the search must continue for different alternatives to mental illness.

Freudian theory has been unable to resolve the nature of the psychopathological because doubt remains as to the nature of the needs whose frustration produces abnormal behavior. Judgments of the desirability or undesirability of behavior are difficult to make because it is difficult to assess the worth of the underlying needs impelling that behavior. The causal sequence of events locks one into the determined choice of judging behavior dictated by a theory of primary needs.

Counseling and Psychotherapy

If, according to the scientific reality of our time, bad behavior is produced by blocking or frustrating the satisfaction of essential needs, then psychotherapy is conceived to remove this impediment in such a way that the patient ceases to feel tense and anxious and can satisfy his basic needs.

Before 1890, what we describe as counseling and psychotherapy did not exist and nothing indicates that an equivalent process was carried on under other names by other professional groups. The investigator almost immediately encounters a dead end when he searches historical literature for therapeutic prototypes among the professions with which counselors and therapists associate themselves today. Zilboorg's (1941) classic history of psychiatry offers no suggestion that psychiatrists or other physicians made concerted efforts to reverse the course of the so-called mental illness either through the intensity of a single interpersonal relationship or through a carefully focused therapeutic conversation. The results are similarly negative when one investigates the history of the ministry in John T. McNeill's (1951) *History of the Cure of Souls* to find a predecessor to the pastoral counselor. (Although Seward Hiltner [1958] presents the case notes of a pastor who had long conversations with a parishioner who could have been counseled by contemporary standards, the seeming obtuseness of an apparently sensitive pastor appears to support the theory that pastoral counseling appeared later.) One also fails to find any meaningful examples of pretwentieth-century counseling in the history of educational guidance (Brewer, 1942).

Apparently counseling and psychotherapy did not exist before 1890 because they were not needed. May (1953) suggests that before this century modern therapeutic activities were rather intimately a part of other forms of culture. He notes that "in classic Greece one discovers immediately a kind of 'normal' psychotherapy operating spontaneously through certain commonly accepted symbols and practices in the Greek religion, philosophy, art, and drama" (1953, p. 10). May regards psychotherapy as directed toward self-discovery, and therefore he claims the purposes of psychotherapy were previously fulfilled by more personalized types of education.

Several additional cultural forms made counseling and psychotherapy unnecessary until our century. One thinks of the dialogue Socrates held with his students, and the learning experience in which Mark Hopkins sat at one end of the log and his student at the other. Frank (1961) suggests that such religious forms as revivalism and faith healing have inspired a faith analogous to the patient's faith in therapy.

Psychotherapy had not been considered necessary because the educated and religious individual was considered to be rationally capable of solving his own problems. No one supposed that the individual might need external social help. It had not occurred to anyone that improvements might be made in human behavior by interrupting the vicious circle of causally chained events in which the potential patient was trapped.

Again it was part of Freud's genius that he changed this situation by inventing psychoanalysis to remove the impediments which deprived the person of any opportunity to gratify his libidinal instincts. The basic psychoanalytic techniques of free association, dream analysis, and transference are well known. In different ways, these analytic techniques seek to relax the tensions created when the id impulses are blocked by increasing the libidinal flow through the psychological dam.

Freud's therapeutic technique is as controversial as the other parts of psychoanalytic theory. Psychoanalytic technique, which is enmeshed in the same causal network as his theory of needs and theory of psychopathology, is controversial for similar reasons. Not everyone agrees that it is better to heed instinctual demands than to conform and thus gain approval from the significant others in one's life.

If Freud had the first word on psychotherapy, the last word has not been spoken. Many different psychotherapies and many views of which frustrations are significant continue to prosper.

Goals

The causal chain which begins with needs ends with a state of ideal behavior that represents the human embodiment of the highest good. The behavioral sciences require a concept of the good life as a foil to that frustrated human behavior which represents the undesirable and the pathological. This concept provides the general purpose or goal for psychotherapeutic attempts to rid the individual of his frustrations.

Confusion over the nature of psychotherapy is largely due to controversy over its purposes. To say that psychotherapy cures mental illness is little help when the concept of mental illness is itself vague and confused. Even if some forms of disordered conduct, such as schizophrenic and manic-depressive psychoses, do have physiological causes, talk of a cure is still semantically confusing. It is little better to state that the purpose of psychotherapy is the promotion of better mental health. If mental illness is a moral concept, judgments of its nature are even more arbitrarily moralistic.

Greater conceptual clarity can be achieved if one conceives psychotherapy as bringing about attainment of those needs whose frustration produces abnormal behavior. Having begun the causal sequence with motivation, one returns full circle. The usual definition of motivation is anchored in needs and goals, providing a push-pull sequence between them to account for all behavior. The behavioral scientist finds he can deal operationally with needs more easily than with goals—the latter are suspect because they imply purpose. Even the most stringent learning theorist can not indefinitely ignore goals because lawfully determined ultimate consequences exist for even the most behavioristically formulated actions.

During his early scientific career, Freud was deterministically shortsighted in looking backward in a causal sequence, consistent with the scientific myopia of his times. While Freud describes his theory of needs at some length, he ignores the companion problem of the purposes or goals which the need serves. In the twentieth century, Freud found he could no longer ignore questions of teleology. World War I seems to have been especially decisive in causing him to place his theory of motivation in a larger philosophical perspective.

Although Freud had already despaired of the future of civilization, World War I had a noticeable effect on psychoanalysis. Shortly after the war, Freud wrote *Beyond the Pleasure Principle* (1922), in which he adds to (if he does not actually revise) his earlier theory of motivation. The sexual instinct remains, but it now has a rival in the motivational hierarchy—*eros* is joined by *thanatos*, the death instinct. The life instinct impels the organism forward to prolong life; the death instinct seeks a return to that tensionless state of inorganic matter before life began. In the final decade of his life Freud concluded only that "the cooperation and opposition of these two forces produce the phenomena of life to which death puts an end" (1933, p. 147). The purpose of life is the indefinite continuation of the dramatic interplay between two cosmic forces.

Even though this theory represents the later and more mature Freud, it has probably been the least accepted because it contradicts earlier Freudian theory. Furthermore, the sardonic and indecisive nature of the struggle between *thanatos* and *eros* has not inspired psychoanalysts to treat the psychoneurosis successfully.

CONTEMPORARY VIEWS OF GOOD AND EVIL

Freud must be evaluated as a fearless social prophet who sought to release the individual from oppressive Victorian morality. Like Moses glimpsing the promised land from afar, Freud could but dimly envision the world that would exist a generation after his death. Although he was perceptive of his own generation's psychological temper, he failed to grasp the social meaning of life for later generations, as history increasingly reveals.

If Freud had found a comprehensive new reality with universal meaning for modern man, this book would be short, but much more remains to be said. The reality that William James and Sigmund Freud projected into the world of nature remains diffuse and imprecise; it is a fog-bound channel for which man requires a psychic gyroscope as a new world takes on different shapes and forms in the mind's eye.

Although the belief in cause and effect, a basic postulate of psychology, seems firmly established in contemporary thinking, the identity of basic causes remains in doubt. The belief that behavior is motivated has provided the basis for a cause-and-effect sequence by which human behavior can be predicted and controlled. Ironically, the weakest link in that chain is a theory of human needs, however. While the behavioral sciences have generally accepted that thinking and acting are both motivated, most of the confusion is based on a failure to agree on the nature of a basic human motivating force. Freud was led into a metaphysical thicket when he sought to make motives seem physiologically real by grounding them in prurient tensions in the body. Those who have followed him have similarly become lost. For a while psychology was badly entangled in McDougall's long list of the instincts. Although the behaviorists freed themselves from the dilemma of naming basic needs, the delineation of learned and unlearned needs remains a problem. Even scientists who intend to follow a narrow scientific path as B. F. Skinner has done (see his Utopian novel *Walden Two*, 1948), make arbitrary assumptions about the nature of ultimate human need.

Just as no agreement can be found about the nature of basic human needs, so abnormal behavior which results from frustrating these needs also remains in doubt. The behavioral sciences have substantially encouraged the general belief that only a few of the so-called psychopathological conditions can be causally traced either to microbes or to lesions. Although nonphysiological distress is now regarded as functional, no agreement has been reached about the functions that symptoms serve. The nature of the psychopathological remains difficult to describe; Schofield (1964) lists some nine different definitions of the neurosis. If little agreement exists about how to recognize certain abnormal states, even less is known about the cause of such undesirable states. More severely disabling conditions, such as the schizophrenic reaction, although easier to identify, have even more controversial causes.

The confusion about the nature of psychopathology extends to methods of treatment. Just what psychotherapy is or what it does to make people better remains unclear. Because the causes are still unknown, it would seem premature to be categorical about the way psychotherapy reverses the effects of frustration.

Freud's place in history would be secure if he were only known for performing the first talking cure. However, his therapeutic technique is as controversial as the other parts of psychoanalytic theory because it is enmeshed in the same causal network as the theory of needs and theory of psychopathology. Not everyone can agree that it is better to heed repressed instinctual demands than to obey society's demands and maintain the inhibiting blockage which frustrates the release of id impulse.

Other systems of psychotherapy are equally as controversial. Harper (1959) found some thirty-six different systems in a general survey of psychotherapy made before the recent proliferation of existential and learning-theory types. In the course of discussing these theories he concluded that "there is scarcely a psychotherapeutic theory or technique endorsed today by some reputable therapists which has not been skeptically viewed or seriously questioned by others" (1959, p. 4).

If psychotherapy is placed within the moral and social ambiguity of contemporary postrational culture, the confusion becomes more understandable. The only common ground among different therapies is an other-directed situation in which a person who is seeking direction is helped by another. But even the expert practitioner can not perceive clearly what help should be provided because the universal social values required for common agreement are lacking.

Fixed ideas of the nature of good and evil are gone, and with them the consensual validation of society's values. As well-motivated as the therapist may be, the purpose of his assistance needs to be specified more clearly. Therapists must share the relativities of an age which has lost faith in absolutes. Just as general social values become increasingly diffuse, so do the values that practitioners bring to therapy. The result is a multiplicity of value orientations (Lowe, 1959) in which practitioners use varied means because they are attempting to reach different goals.

Thus disagreement about goals becomes the ultimate source of confusion. The present disordered state characterizing therapy, frustrations, and needs can be resolved only when agreement is reached about directing the goals of behavior. The ultimate goal of the therapeutic practitioner is to provide for the complete fulfillment of human needs. The term motivation, commonly defined to include a need and a goal, is a push-pull motivating sequence within which all behavior is causally bracketed. Statements about goals have been distrusted because they imply statements of teleology or purpose which are regarded as alien to scientific objectivity.

While the scientist may prefer not to discuss ends or goals, he can not long avoid doing so in an applied profession. In recent years counselors and psychotherapists have sought to maintain their objectivity by using the term *positive mental health*.

Unfortunately, the use of this seemingly objective term does little to resolve the controversy over causes. Indeed, the concept of positive mental health appears to reap the full measure of the psychologist's confusion concerning the nature of man. Although agreement is general that positive mental health is not simply the absence of mental illness, or normality, or a mere feeling of happiness, it goes no further. Marie Jahoda in *Current Concepts of Positive Mental Health* (1958) surveyed the literature and found nine broad concepts of ideal behavior, many with important but divergent subthemes. She found that none of the many definitions could be unequivocally regarded as more valuable than the rest, and she was forced to conclude that any single definition of positive mental health must be quite tentative.

The myth of positive mental health is far newer than the myth of mental illness. Although it is still counterfeit, it is less tarnished by time, and therefore shines much brighter. The myth of positive mental health, a product of postrational culture, rejects the myth of mental illness by implication because it regards mental health as more than the absence of disease or ill health. In fact it requires a "positively healthy" individual to meet more than the minimal cultural specifications for good adjustment or normalcy.

Although positive mental health avoids the fallacies of the mental-illness model, it is still a myth that effectively provides standards for judging the rightness and wrongness of behavior that would otherwise be hard to evaluate. The criticisms that Szasz directs against the myth of mental illness are even more valid when they are directed against the myth of positive mental health. Mental illness, as Szasz defines it, is a deviation from some moral and sociolegal ideal. The therapist's judgment then becomes even more arbitrary when it is tied to a concept of mental health that is not an existing social norm but a visionary personal ideal. Szasz (1961) notes that the concept of mental illness is so infinitely elastic that any moral, social, or political problem can be cast into a psychiatric mold. Positive mental health will carry counselors and psychotherapists into areas of social life where no problems exist and thus where the behavioral scientist may be allowed to become an ideological despot. Men of science may force improvements upon others in a spirit of scientific do-goodism at the expense of personal liberty.

No easy way can be found to decide which concept of positive mental health is best. Of the two approaches Jahoda contrasts, each seems equally unsuccessful. Jahoda opposes the first approach, which involves the arbitrary selection of a single viewpoint, terming it the Utopian way and rejecting it because it leads to moralization. She prefers the second approach, which is based on research, but it seems almost equally perilous. Research can not determine the nature of positive mental health because choosing a criterion requires a Utopian moralizing that seems universally unacceptable. Without a standard for comparing both behaviors, research is limited to collecting data which have little moral significance. Until positive mental health can be defined, the term itself lacks scientific objectivity and valid research is impossible. In the absence of an objective standard for so-called positive adjustment, research can provide little more than the sheep's clothing for a dangerous moralism which becomes all the more predatory by its false pretensions to be scientific.

Positive mental health is an expression of the ideals which provide the standards for the good life, values which have traditionally been considered religious and not scientific. Its definition transcends scientific method.

ALTERNATIVES TO MENTAL HEALTH

Because agreement about the nature of good and evil is lacking, no simple substitute exists for older beliefs in concepts of mental health and mental illness. Instead of a consensus of values, we find a multiplicity of orientations, each making competitive and contradictory claims to the truth.

Contemporary society therefore finds it rather difficult to replace the concepts of mental health and illness. Faith in reason is gone and no general ideal of the good is rationally acceptable to a preponderance of mankind. Those who cling to older values find their justification from reason is more difficult. Existentialism may currently be popular because the existentialist has been the first to realize that his *angst* before the moral ambiguities of life is an unavoidable human experience. Even if one cherishes older values, he seems to deceive himself by believing that faith in reason can be maintained as a dominant social value in a time when the conflict among supposedly self-evident truths can not be ignored. Modern life requires man to learn to live with certain ambiguities. An easy rationalization for a new moral dogma would not be too helpful even if it were possible to find.

The question to be asked is essentially the one which Freud answered incorrectly: Man is motivated, and behavior meets needs directed towards certain goals. When something blocks need satisfaction, the resulting frustration prevents the realization of that good which became the goal of behavior. Psychotherapy intends to circumvent the frustration and bring about the attainment of goal-directed behavior.

Alternatives to mental health seem to be considered better as alternatives to psychoanalysis. While the values that orthodox psychoanalysis has embraced were too much a part of the late nineteenth century to be universally relevant now, Freud has given us a way of conceptualizing human behavior which outlasted his generation. The author has chosen to place contemporary views of good and evil in such a conceptual model.

SUMMARY

The Age of Reason believed in a rather absolute free will and liked to assume that individual behavior was a pure act directed by a homunculus of reason. Our age has attempted to apply the "scientific" categories of cause and effect to the mind and prefers to consider man as other directed. Although the conformist tendencies of the so-called other-directed man may be grossly exaggerated, the popularity of this description provides its own confirmation: The older myths of mental illness must be replaced by new ideas based on the reality of such concepts as antecedent conditions, intervening variables, and psychological control.

Psychologists have helped modern man gain a more meaningful self-understanding. The first person to apply the principles of the new reality to what is now called psychotherapy was Sigmund Freud. Today many of his assumptions about psychological reality are the basic tenets of all schools of counseling and psychotherapy. The therapist believes that thinking and acting are motivated, and that behavior is pushed from behind by needs and pulled from ahead by goals. When these goals are blocked, frustration occurs. The purpose of psychotherapy is to remove frustrations or psychological blockages so that the client can attain what is commonly called positive mental health.

Psychoanalysis has been controversial both as a system of social morality and as a system of therapeutic psychology. Freud helped perpetuate an obsolescent mental-illness myth, and his model of the mind used mechanistic cause-and-effect relationships that are now discredited. Psychoanalysis implicitly accepts four concepts as fundamental to an understanding of all counseling and psychotherapy: needs, frustrations, purposes and methods of therapy, and goals. The next four chapters will use these concepts to compare four major therapeutic systems.

Psychoanalysis has been controversial for many reasons. Disagreement with its aims and methods is often expressed by therapists who refuse to accept Freud's view that the basic human need is the sexual gratification of libidinal energies. They also refuse to accept the psychoanalytic view of sexual frustration or its implied goal of genital satisfaction. These therapists find their therapeutic systems are also morally controversial.

PART TWO

The Meanings of Mental Health

 *Chapter 5*

HUMANISTIC MEANINGS

It matters not how strait the gate,
   How charged with punishments the scroll,
I am the master of my fate;
   I am the captain of my soul. . . . INVICTUS, *William Ernest Henley*

❖❖❖

There are many different value orientations to which the therapist may choose to be beholden in his practice of counseling or psychotherapy. Accordingly, there are many alternatives to the psychoanalytic model of man examined in the last chapter. Each of these alternative systems of value provides contrasting ways for interpreting the needs, frustrations, therapeutic process, and goals of clients. Personal values are idiosyncratic and unique, and therapists may rightly object to a summarizing and pigeonholing process which systematizes and hardens their unique experiential concerns. Therapeutic value orientations do, however, group themselves into recognizable families. In this chapter and in the following three chapters we will discuss four of these systems: the humanistic, the naturalistic, the social, and the existential.

HISTORICAL FOUNDATIONS

Humanism as a philosophical system is rooted in the renewed concern for the dignity of man which began with the breakup of the Middle Ages and continued through the Enlightenment and the Age of Reason. During the Dark Ages man was so gripped by a stagnant and stultifying social system that he found it almost impossible to achieve personal dignity and could do little more than seek fulfillment in visions of the hereafter. During the High Middle Ages and more especially during the Renaissance there was a revival of man's sense of his own inner life, which had lain dormant for over a thousand years. Indeed, the term Renaissance indicates a rebirth. The rather dramatic reflowering of the Italian Renaissance can be viewed as providing the fertile pollenization for humanistic values which have been significant to individualism for over five hundred years.

The new humanism so captured the spirit of the age that individualism attracted very different types of men. At the one extreme is Giovanni Boccaccio, whose lusty tales have made the *Decameron* a classic in ribald humor. A product of the Trecento, he represents the unrestrained exuberance of the newly secularized city. At the other extreme is Erasmus, who was separated from Boccaccio by a century and a half and nearly a thousand miles. A representative of the Reformation, Erasmus is considered the epitome of Christian humanism. Although he was a committed Christian, Erasmus was born too late to reject the world for the monastery. The pleasures of this life were now too meaningful to be easily renounced even by a faithful Christian. Although Erasmus's humanism was the product of a more thoughtful age than Boccaccio's exuberant Renaissance, Erasmus was also able to laugh at the world. The *Praise of Folly,* however, is a far more scholarly joke. By Erasmus's day humanism had taken a more serious bent: It has become intent on the discovery of wisdom. Erasmus thus illustrates the humanist's interest in reason.

A similar diversity in forms appears in the recent history of humanism in America. During the early nineteenth century, humanism appears to have been best represented by New England transcendentalists such as Henry Thoreau and Ralph Waldo Emerson, although the two men were quite different. But while they disagreed about the emphasis to be placed on the solitary contemplation of nature and the importance of the philosophical search for the oversoul, they shared the same basic humanistic values. Each sought to find within himself the meaning of a distinctive individuality and each found an intensely emotional experience in experiencing oneness with a transcendental world.

During the latter half of the nineteenth century, the mystic contemplations of the transcendental philosopher were replaced by the striving of men of action. The new humanist was an achiever; the new human destiny was to subdue a new world of economic opportunity. The individualists of post-Civil War America were bankers, industrialists, and railroad magnates; men such as J. P.

Morgan, Andrew Carnegie, and Commodore Vanderbilt, who embodied the individual achievement that became a virtual religion. The poet also became caught up in the challenge to the new individualism, as expressed by Henry Wadsworth Longfellow:

> The heights by great men reached and kept
> Were not attained by sudden flight,
> But they, while their companions slept,
> Were toiling upwards in the night.

Humanism Today

Modern humanists seek to draw man's salient experiences of his own worth from the last five hundred years of human history. The Renaissance man, so exuberant in his individuality, has long departed leaving a distinctive humanistic tradition which has been shaped and reshaped in each age. In our day three distinctive values represent the fulfillment of this tradition: belief in man's rationality, perfectibility, and self-awareness.

The first humanistic value is that man is a rational being. If man is valued as a creature who above all else is good, then the rationality which sets him apart from the animal is his crowning glory. Reason is the key to new knowledge of the natural world. In the past man has endured the distress of warfare, poverty, and social disintegration. The fault is not in his essential nature, however, but in his failure to reason and to apply the full measure of his potential knowledge to his problems.

The value the humanist places upon reason is the basis for the objectivist theory of ethics developed by Ayn Rand and Nathaniel Brandon. Ayn Rand views man as having to choose whether to be a rational being or a suicidal animal. Brandon believes that "thinking is man's basic virtue, the source of all his other virtues" (1965, p. 3). According to self-styled *objectivist ethics,* consciousness is man's basic means for survival. If man is to prevail, he must not only initiate the use of reason but also sustain it and be responsible for its results. Objectivist ethics therefore judge good and evil solely by whether or not a given value increases man's reason. To quote Ayn Rand: "Since reason is man's basic means of survival, that which is proper to the life of a rational being is the good; that which negates, opposes or destroys it is the evil" (1964, p. 23).

The second humanist value is the actualization of man's inner potential. Humanists continue to emphasize individual initiative and to believe in progress and in man's ability to perfect his world. Julian Huxley supposes "it is as if man had been suddenly appointed managing director of the biggest business of all, the business of evolution" (1957, p. 13). Huxley believes that this destiny of world mastery has been so thrust upon man that he can not avoid the responsibility for controlling history. Accordingly, he believes that the human being is called upon for "the fullest realization of man's possibilities, whether it is by the individual, by the community, or by the species in its professional adventures along the corridors of time" (1957, p. 14).

The most dramatic examples of the humanistic man of action are provided by characters in Ayn Rand's novels. In the *Fountainhead* (1943) she presents Howard Roark, an architect whose individualism is so unyielding that he caustically defies the conventions and the standards of his profession and of society. In *Atlas Shrugged* (1957) she approvingly recounts the adventures of Dagny Taggart, a woman railroad executive who tries desperately to maintain personal control over a transcontinental railroad empire; and John Galt, an inventive genius who destroys his creative work rather than let his inventions be used for any other purpose than his own self-interest.

A final distinctive characteristic of contemporary humanism is its emphasis upon the individual's experiencing himself. Just as man is called upon to mobilize his energies to thrust into the external world, so he must also develop a greater intensity of inward experience. Although transcendental values no longer have an important influence on American culture as a whole, they are reflected in Unitarianism and in much of liberal Christianity. The contemporary Western humanist has largely forsaken traditional religious thought, but his heritage of Christian humanism has made him more sensitive to the humanistic religions of the East, such as Zen Buddhism and Hinduism, which have had a significant impact upon humanistic intellectuals.

Contemporary humanism can be regarded as philosophically and socially conservative. Many aspects of individualism are being eroded by social change. David Riesman regards the breakup of feudal society as providing a transition from a tradition-directed social orientation to an inner-directed one. The inner-directed man who emerged during the Renaissance displayed the individualism prized by the humanist. Riesman claims that we are witnessing a transition from the inner-directed individual to an other-directed personality. Thus the humanist attempts to maintain inner-directed values despite social changes which he sees as an attempt to grind the individual into an imperceptible part of a social mass.

Humanism in the Behavioral Sciences

Because humanism has always emphasized reason, its influence on psychology can broadly be seen wherever the psychologist studies thought processes and the workings of consciousness. William Wundt's attempts at introspection in his laboratory at Leipzig in 1879 were the beginning of psychology as an academic discipline. As E. G. Boring points out, "it is clear that Wundt came by a rational philosopher's method to his convictions about experimental psychology" (1950, p. 327). Because structural psychology shared the dominant philosophical prejudices of the nineteenth century, contemporary humanism can hardly be blamed for the eventual debacle of the attempts to analyze reason as an entity. After structuralism's failure around the turn of the century, a new generation of cognitive theorists has begun to map out the workings of the mind through more sophisticated experimental methods.

The influence of humanism can also be seen in the widespread interest in the self concept. Like other ideas, the concept of self doubtless originated in antiquity and apparently entered psychology in 1890 when William James devoted a chapter to the self in *Principles of Psychology*. Unfortunately the origins of James's views on the self are unknown, although he was influenced by Ralph Waldo Emerson. Thus James in 1890 defined the self as the total of all that man can call his own; Emerson a half century before had described "this thought which is called I" as the mold into which an inner world is poured like melted wax, a world he defined as "the shadow of that substance which you are" (1843, p. 90). As Lowe (1961) has pointed out, the self concept has many meanings in current psychological usage, some of which continue the transcendental and the Jamesian concerns for a self which is the center of human experience. Other meanings, which are much more intensely humanistic, make an emotional experience of the self the center of religious experience.

The influence of humanism can finally be seen in the current interest in psychology in creativity and in similar descriptions of highly individual behavior. Humanistic values seem basic to assumptions made by Abraham Maslow and by others interested in such characteristics as self-realization, spontaneity, and inner freedom. While Maslow has pursued humanistic values from a philosophical point of view, David C. McClelland has attempted to place human motivation in a sociohistorical context. In *The Achieving Society* (1961), he seeks to relate man's need for achievement to changing social conditions in the post-Renaissance Western world. McClelland assumes that a high need for achievement has been an essential prerequisite to economic progress since the Middle Ages. While McClelland seems to be only minimally concerned with the moral implications of achievement motivation, his composite portrait of the high-need achiever has many humanistic values. McClelland summarizes a far-reaching research program by describing "a composite portrait of a person with high *n* achievement as someone who wants to do well at what he undertakes, who is energetic, nonconforming, and tends to be predisposed towards innovations, toward working at tasks which are not safe and traditional but involve some element of risk . . . " (1958, p. 521).

NEEDS

Humanistic psychology yokes the humanistic concern with man's rationality and the potential which it provides into the construct termed the self. Needs and goals are most appropriately discussed as they relate to that self. Motivation is seen in terms of man's inherent need to enhance the self by expanding his consciousness and by increasing his self-esteem through his powers and abilities.

A Sense of Self

If man is a conscious organism, he must knowingly seek to create structured order from the sensory confusion that exists at birth. At all cost the self needs to maintain psychological control over the myriad stimuli which impinge upon it. This need is met by what are termed cognitive processes, which give man a feeling that he has at least minimal control over events in his psychological environment.

Prescott Lecky (1951) terms the organism's need to unify consciousness as the need for self-consistency. Lecky believes that the act of self-unification offers a pleasure which enables the personality to maintain itself in a world of flux that would otherwise be incomprehensible. The need for self-consistency can also be seen in its obverse, the need to avoid cognitive dissonance. Leon Festinger (1957) theorizes that because people prefer consistency in their perceptions, they will modify conflicting beliefs to reduce the dissonance in their cognitive system.

Because a humanistic self is actively conscious, man must have attitudes toward the self as part of his conscious experience. Humanism stresses the inherent worth of man; therefore the humanist believes that it is morally desirable for man to have self-respect and self-acceptance as a human being for two basic reasons. First, self-respect represents an elemental reality undistorted by so-called neurotic needs which allow the negative attitude of other people to interfere with one's liking one's self. Second, a positive experiencing of self tends to be seen as an appreciation for that humanness which the humanist believes represents man's most sublime experience.

Carl Rogers stresses the need for positive attitudes towards one's self. Rogers's attitude toward the self has become increasingly complex in recent years because his humanistic viewpoint has combined with a more existential concern. In his earlier writing he emphasized the need for self-acceptance, a need so basic to human adjustment that he made it his research criterion for therapeutic changes. Rogers believes that a positive attitude toward self is necessary if the self is to be aware of all experience.

Accomplishment

The humanist does not believe that it is enough for man to have positive feelings towards himself; he must also be able to behave effectively to master the basic parts of his environment. Note that the humanist does not believe that a striving for accomplishment should be motivated by any external gain — virtue is in a sense, its own reward. What matters is that the individual achieves a sense of mastery from reaching a goal that has personal significance.

Robert White claims man has an inborn and primary effectance need based on the desire for competence. White regards the need to become competent as what is omitted from physiological theories of motivation, which he regards as incomplete accounts of human motivation. He defines effectance as "what the neuromuscular system wants to do when it is otherwise unoccupied or is gently stimulated by the environment" (1951, p. 321).

The result of an effectance drive is competence, which White describes both as a neurologically achieved state of skill and as a subjective feeling of confidence in one's ability to master basic life situations. White defines competence as the fitness or ability of the organism "to carry out those transactions with the environment which result in its maintaining itself, growing, and flourishing" (1960, p. 100). White does not limit this need to humans; he finds examples of it in exploratory drives and manipulative behavior in animals. White does imply, however, that the need for competence occupies a relatively more important place in man's motivational makeup.

Man's need to achieve fulfillment in a personally significant manner is also called self-actualization, a term that appears to have originated with Kurt Goldstein (1939). He used the term to describe the organism's need to preserve certain essential humanistic capacities even when it is neurologically damaged. Self-actualization is currently most often associated with the work of Abraham Maslow, who gives it additional meaning.

In Maslow's theory of motivation (1954), self-actualization is the pinnacle of man's need structure. Maslow notes that man has certain lower-order needs—such as hunger, safety, belongingness, and esteem—but that "even if all these needs are satisfied, we may still often (if not always) expect that a new discontent and restlessness will soon develop, unless the individual is doing what he is fitted for" (1954, p. 91). Maslow terms a desire to become everything that one is capable of becoming self-actualization, and he illustrates this need with the observation that "a musician must make music, an artist must paint, a poet must write, if he is to be ultimately at peace with himself" (1954, p. 91). Although Maslow recognizes the specific form of the need varies from person to person, once lower needs are satisfied, each man seeks to achieve his potential.

FRUSTRATIONS

Humanists today continue to judge what is bad in human behavior much as did the humanistic philosophers of the eighteenth and nineteenth centuries. Because they perceive man to be the only species with freedom of choice, his failure to use this choice effectively becomes a basic evil violating his essential nature. Because man's conscious awareness and his free independence are related to this freedom of choice, his failure to be self-assertive and his inability to use his mind rationally are also basic evils that deprive him of his full humanity. Man's failure to exercise his rational freedom effectively and creatively culminates in his failure to master his environment, which the humanist regards as man's most essential good.

In the Age of Reason humanists regarded man's failure to be rational as an unnatural and pathological perversion of nature, an attitude that still exists today. Nathaniel Brandon describes man's rationality as seemingly his only absolute characteristic. Led by what he terms objectivist ethics, Brandon compares mental illness to physical illness: "The standard of mental health—of biologically appropriate mental functioning—is the same as that of physical health: man's survival and well-being" (1964, p. 36). He also notes that "the health of man's consciousness must be judged, like the health of any other organ, by how well it performs its proper function" (1965, p. 5).

Albert Ellis (1967) also defends the practice of labeling people as mentally ill, although he realizes the abuses made by psychiatric terminology. He argues that it is not the labeling process itself which is harmful, but using the term in unnecessarily pejorative ways. He believes, therefore, that terms such as mentally ill can be objectively used to describe individuals who, with some consistency, behave in dysfunctional ways in certain aspects of their lives. (T. R. Sarbin's [1967] refutation of this argument is cited in Chapter Three.)

Contemporary humanists differ from their philosophical predecessors in the Age of Reason in their more sophisticated explanations for the failure of reason to function effectively. It is clearly impossible to maintain the dualistic beliefs about mind and body which developed the original myths of mental illness. Humanistic psychologists and psychiatrists now search for functional and dynamic causes of mental aberrancies. Like many mental-health practitioners of other orientations, humanists may still prefer to use mental-health and mental-illness concepts, but they are most often used analogously. Humanists are particularly apt to explain the symptoms of abnormal behavior as ways of preserving the self from an external threat to self-esteem.

Lack of Insight

A discussion of abnormal behavior from a humanistic viewpoint must start with lack of insight. The humanist deems lack of insight to be bad for three reasons. First, it deprives man of reason, his noblest attribute. Furthermore, lack of insight leads to distortions in self-appraisal and results in an unrealistically low appraisal of self-worth. The third reason is that misperceptions impair the individual's ability to act, reducing his competence and his capability for self-actualization. Such an impairment will ultimately produce failure that is likely to damage self-regard more.

Carl Rogers (1941) offers several reasons for the cognitive failure to assimilate new experiences. Threatened by experiences which are inconsistent with its structure, the self seeks to maintain itself against further erosion by refusing to assimilate new experiences with potential for learning. Such a person, in Roger's view, becomes increasingly detached in his defensive withdrawal from the threat of unperceived inner feelings and the dangers of unwelcome communications from others. The insecure self withdraws and becomes frozen in what Rogers (1958b) terms a state of fixity and remoteness of experiencing in which the individual finds he can not open to new experiences.

Combs and Snygg (1959) deal with insight in terms of what they call the phenomenal field. They use tunnel vision metaphorically to describe how constricting the phenomenal field protects the concept of the self by warding off the perceptions that threaten the structure. If the person lacks a secure concept of self, he is blinded by threats and reacts defensively, just as a baseball player who covers his head with his glove when he is blinded by the sun while chasing a fly ball. Combs and Snygg use their theory to explain different types of abnormal behavior. Neurosis, which results from overreaction to the limited perceptions of tunnel vision, places the individual on a "war footing" that manifests itself as phobias and free-floating anxiety. Even neurotic defenses may not work when a desperate situation requires extreme measures. Then the result is a psychosis, with symptoms which represent attempts to ward off a threat by denying or distorting reality.

George A. Kelly (1955) also finds the basis for psychopathology in cognitive difficulties. In Kelly's psychology of personal constructs, which describes the way man learns to anticipate future events, psychopathology represents a failure in prediction which may occur for either of two reasons. A person whose system of personal constructs is so loosely assembled that his cognitive processes are inadequately organized to interpret events successfully is apt to be diagnosed as schizophrenic. At the other extreme, one may construe events so tightly that he becomes inflexible in his thinking, a disorder that most theorists would term a neurosis.

Kelly illustrates the development of a typical disorder in construction by describing the cognitive growth of a person who as a child had relied upon the belief that God could be inveigled into complying with all his requests. (The construct of God expands to all situations, thus providing an example of what Kelly terms "dilating the field.") Kelly further describes this person as having an extremely literal conception of God. (In Kelly's lexicon, the construct is "impermeable" or "tight.") Because this child's construct of God was so inflexible, the more literal aspects of belief in a compliant God are soon abandoned before rather obvious invalidating evidence. The dilation and the inflexibility of the old constructs prevent the construction of an alternate interpretation of his world. Therefore as an adult his actions are guided by ideas that appear rather infantile to others: "He still wheedles to satisfy his day-to-day wants; except that now he wheedles his associates instead of God or his parents" (1955, p. 837). Evidence that might serve to invalidate this dilated construct is cognitively thrust aside with a "you-don't-love-me" interpretation of events. Instead of experimenting with alternate interpretations of others' behavior, he resorts to self-defeating social manipulations. "He snuggles up to people, whimpers, panders to their whims, indulges his own, and generally postpones his psychological maturation" (1955, p. 838).

Lack of Personal Fulfillment

A humanistic orientation greatly values the unfolding of one's powers: Therefore, anything which prevents the expression of man's inherent humanity is evil. What the humanist regards as pathological conditions occur when man's need for prior satisfaction of lower-order needs traps him in a state in which his behavior is determined by the drive to satisfy what Maslow (1962) terms deficiency needs.

The most complete description of conditions inhibiting man's creative powers is found in Erich Fromm. Fromm's ideal is a productive orientation, roughly equivalent to Maslow's concept of self-actualization, from which he judges a series of contrasting orientations he describes as receptive, exploitative, hoarding, and marketing. The marketing orientation is the pathology which he considers dominant in present American culture.

Fromm resembles the self theorists in his view that man's inability to respect himself inhibits the expression of his creative powers. He differs from the self theorists by seeking the causes of undesirable behavior in cultural conditions. In *Escape from Freedom* (1941), Fromm traces various changes in individualism that have taken place since it emerged during the Renaissance. The contemporary individual finds that the freedom he gained then is now threatened by a sense of aloneness and isolation which tempts him to give up his individuality and conform to social forces in a rough equivalent to Riesman's other directedness. The result is the marketing orientation which Fromm describes in *Man for Himself* (1947)—a cultural dehumanization in which the needs to conform and to please dominate. The criterion for personal worth is determined by a personality marketplace which judges a man by his ability to sell himself, by how well he can "package" his personality in marketable form like the latest fashionable handbag. Fromm concludes in *The Sane Society* (1955) that sickness resides not in the individual but in a society where vices are made virtues in the general social view. For Fromm the tragedy of the marketing orientation is that it destroys the real worth man achieves when he is for himself.

COUNSELING AND PSYCHOTHERAPY

From a humanistic point of view, psychotherapy is an extension of other human experiences which enhance man's dignity and sense of individuality. Rollo May (1953) regards psychotherapy as performing the same educative functions formerly performed by art, philosophy, and religion. He therefore describes psychotherapy as but man's latest attempt to fulfill the Socratic commandment: "Know thyself." The humanist has also discovered continuities between psychotherapy and Eastern philosophical thought forms. Alan W. Watts in *Psychotherapy East and West* (1961) sees Western psychotherapy as offering man the same liberation from his endless struggle with himself that Eastern humanistic religions provide.

Humanistic counseling and psychotherapy use a variety of methods to help the individual secure his inner fulfillment; however, different therapeutic means serve common ends. The purpose of humanistic psychotherapy is to help the individual develop that sense of dignity and worth seen as the hallmarks of humanness.

Reformulation of Thought

If distorted and constricted ways of thinking can so cripple man cognitively that he cannot act purposively or effectively, then the psychotherapist's task is to help man think better. The framework this chapter has been developing shows psychotherapy as increasing man's self-awareness by offering him greater confidence in his ability to think and, as a result, to act for himself. Typical of this view is the definition by Combs and Snygg (1959) that psychotherapy is the freeing of the organism's normal drive for adequacy by removing those threats to the self which cause it to restrict its intellectual awareness. Or, as Wendell Johnson (1946) describes it, therapy changes the person's environment by changing his semantic interpretations of it. The cognitive approach to psychotherapy is also illustrated by the personal-construct psychotherapy of George Kelly (1955). Psychotherapy presents a client with the task of revising his systems of personal constructs by trying out different ways of thinking within the therapeutic encounter.

While Combs and Snygg, Johnson, and Kelly all contribute to a broadly humanistic understanding of psychotherapy oriented to conscious thought processes, little if anything in their writings is humanistic in its specific philosophical sense. Indeed, their approach to insight therapies is so broad that their techniques can be effectively used by those whose therapeutic methods serve completely different value orientations.

The work of Albert Ellis is more specifically humanistic, not only in therapeutic methods, but to an even greater extent in the purposes he believes psychotherapy is designed to serve. Ellis terms his therapeutic approach rational therapy. He states that he chose the term rational "for that, more than anything else, was what I seemed to be doing—demonstrating to patients exactly what the irrational or illogical aspects of their thinking was, and inducing them to think or talk to themselves (or reorient their internalized sentences) in a decidedly more rational manner" (1962, p. 120). Ellis predicates his practice on the assumption that what other people regard as emotion is only an irrational idea. "Emotions" are in effect values which are not in accord with self-determined individualism. "Bad" emotions may be eliminated by attacking the "irrational, groundless premises" (or nonhumanistic values) upon which the ideas are based. Ellis terms this approach the cognitive-persuasive-didactic-reasoning method. After convincing the patient that he has started from the wrong logical premises, the therapist becomes a frank counterpropagandist who contradicts and denies the original self-defeating attitudes and then persuades and cajoles the patient to engage in activities which will help establish a more rational philosophy of life.

The task of the therapist is to free the patient from the ideological ties still binding him to the moral views of the rest of society. Indeed, Ellis rather strongly believes that bad emotions "largely consist of attitudes, perceptual biases, beliefs, assumptions, and ideas which are acquired by biosocial learning and which therefore can be reviewed, questioned, challenged, reconstructed, and changed. . . ." (1962, p. 125). Although Ellis admits that man can not live by reason alone, he does regard reason as the key that opens the door to the good life. He states that "to the degree that man develops rational ethics, he will be able to live more peacefully and creatively with himself and his fellows" (1962, p. 124). Rational therapy must free man from the guilt his social past has planted within him so that he can function more individually.

An example of the application of rational-emotive psychotherapy can be seen in the case of John Jones, a thirty-one year old free-lance copywriter described as having been homosexual since the age of fourteen (Ellis, no date; a portion of the therapy typescript published in Patterson, 1966). In earlier interviews the patient has gained insight into the fact that his homosexuality is related to his fear of being rejected by women and he has also been made aware of both subtle and obvious ways in which he resists heterosexual participation. In the fifteenth interview, Ellis describes the purpose of therapy: "The therapist solidly nails down the circumlocuting patient, and gets him to admit that his sleepiness and lack of sex desire are both excuses for his not wanting to go with girls because he is afraid of rejection" (no date, p. 6). The patient still seems evasive; the therapist carefully explaining that his behavior, if not his actual words, shows that he is continually telling himself how awful it would be if he were in fact rejected by a girl. Ellis in this interview is both simple and direct. He forcefully hammers home the "rational" fact that he does not really need to be bothered about rejection by women.

Positive Attitudes toward Self

Experiencing a positive regard for one's self is an important part of a humanistic orientation. Since it represents man's highest value, this experience in effect becomes a religious experience. When one lacks this positive experience, one has missed the humanistic ideal for man. The task of psychotherapy is to correct this deficiency in the concept of self.

This conception of counseling and psychotherapy is best represented by the self-centered or client-centered approach to psychotherapy of Carl Rogers. Rogers' views of the nature of psychotherapy (and to an even greater extent his philosophy of man) have evolved over the years. However, the title of his second book on therapy, *Client-Centered Psychotherapy* (1951), perhaps best summarizes Rogers' view of the therapeutic task during his most classically humanistic years. Rogers states here that psychological maladjustment exists when the individual denies an awareness of significant feelings because they have not been organized into the concept of self. The psychotherapist's task is to strengthen positive attitudes towards the self in order to incorporate within the self feelings previously considered too threatening for one's self-regard. The therapist communicates his acceptance of the client's self by empathizing with the client as he struggles with the confusions, ambivalences, and feelings that he could not accept were the therapist to reject him as he revealed this negative part of the self.

In his later writings, Rogers' orientation to counseling and psychotherapy is even more explicitly humanistic. He sees therapy not merely as a means of expanding self-awareness but also as a process of becoming more open to new experience. Rogers has increased his emphasis on the need for the therapist to communicate his own humanness to the client if therapeutic change is to occur (1957a). As he describes the characteristics of a helping relationship (1958a), he limits psychotherapeutic helpfulness to a therapist who can be perceived as fully human, trustworthy, dependable, and consistent. When the therapist and the client can start to share the same experience of humanness, therapeutic change takes place as part of what Rogers (1958b) describes as a process with a freer flow of expression about the self and a new acceptance of feeling, which gradually "bubbles through" as direct expression of emotion. Finally an acceptant ownership of these changing feelings emerges and a basic trust in one's own self develops. The self, which has ceased to be an object or even a "concept", is now a positive emotional experience of religious intensity.

The labels *client-centered* and *self-centered psychotherapy* may be taken as fairly literal descriptions of a philosophical orientation in which the individuality of the client is the highest value. The therapeutic purpose is the enhancement of that self which is the center of humanistic concern for man. Psychotherapy has been popularly described as a hothouse that protects the self, which is analogously, a tender plant. Although this seedbox self has great promise for future growth, it needs the warmth of therapeutic protection to realize its potential. The empathic warmth of the therapist shields the self from cold, external threat and simultaneously provides that positive experience which the self needs to grow. The purpose of psychotherapy is clearly to aid the growth and development of a self capable of self-respect and of actualization.

Although tapes and typescripts of a number of Rogers' therapy sessions have been published, his therapeutic approach seems best illustrated by the case of Mr. Lin (Rogers, no date), as his problem is strikingly similar to that of John Jones, whose treatment by Ellis was described above. (For further contrast, turn to page 190 for a description of the treatment of the homosexual by an existential therapist.) Mr. Lin, like John Jones, describes himself to the therapist as a homosexual and willingly admits that he uses sleep and similar escape mechanisms to avoid unpleasant experiences.

The therapists' values and their treatment may at first appear very different. In this interview Rogers displays his characteristic gentle, accepting manner. Instead of confronting the client with the untoward aspects of his behavior, Rogers merely reflects the client's own feeling of frustration at "feeling terrible down." When insights occur, they appear to result from the client's own discovery that the homosexuality, the depression, and the other symptoms must be related to his inability to experience a total life pattern. Among the notable similarities in the two interviews is a concern for the client's label for his problems. Both help the client become more aware of the fact that homosexuality is but the surface manifestation of problems involving other aspects of self. Although the rational and the client-centered therapies are radically different in their means, a similarity of goals is apparent. The purpose of psychotherapy is to free the individual from the tyranny of a compulsive observance of social norms which have no personal meaning for him. Ellis seeks this goal through direct suggestion, while Rogers prefers the decision to be the spontaneous choice of an autonomous client. For both methods, the therapeutic aim is to establish a sovereign self free of external social control.

GOALS

Because humanism is basically optimistic about man, it inevitably stresses that man's potential is not achieved when he is merely free of so-called mental illness; he must also perceive the realization of his potential as his highest good. When the humanist urges man to be himself, his injunction is to be that self which most fully embodies the humanistic values of having feelings of self-worth and of striving to realize more fully that basic potential.

Positive Mental Health

Because the essential premise of humanism is that man has not yet achieved his potential, he must be motivated to continue his efforts to achieve further, unrealized worth. Therefore human goals can not be represented merely as a state of attainment but as a process of continued growth and development.

The same intellectual climate that produced the philosophy of humanism also resorted to the concept of mental illness to explain the obvious foibles of human reason that even an age which gloried in man's rationality could not overlook. The link between philosophical humanism and the mental-illness model is at best an indirect one, however, and today one can hardly blame the humanist for the inefficiency of the illness model as an explanation of the worst of man's idiosyncracies. Obviously, the behavioral scientists who consciously or unconsciously continue humanistic traditions today are men of science far too sophisticated to regard so-called mental illness as something that "happens" to man's mind because of an unnatural process in the body.

Those who operate within a humanistic orientation today focus on the good in man, rather than on explanations for apparent evil in human nature. Contemporary humanists show their interest in man's inherent goodness by their concern for the nature of mental health, a positive term expressing the affirmative qualities they see as most characteristic of human ideals.

The best general summary of uses of the term positive mental health is Marie Jahoda's *Current Concepts of Positive Mental Health* (1958). Her survey indicates that uses of the term are so varied that it would be ridiculous to try to preempt its use exclusively to a humanistic orientation. Jahoda rejects such views of the good life as normality or states of well-being which clearly fail to meet the humanistic criterion. The criteria she presents as suitable have a generally humanistic flavor to them: such as correct attitudes towards self, growth, development, and self-actualization; autonomy; correct perceptions of reality; and mastery of the environment.

Abraham Maslow provides the best-developed theoretical rationale that mental health is more than the absence of mental illness. He notes that "deficit-need gratification and growth-need gratification have differential subjective and objective effects upon the personality" (1962, p. 29). Although satisfying need deficiencies avoids illness, satisfying growth satisfactions is required for positive health. Maslow used the term being to prefix a motivational term which is a growth need. Being needs can occur only when lower-order deficiency needs have been satisfied and the individual is free from a dependence upon his environment to be motivated by goals unique to his own personality.

Self-actualization holds the highest rank in Maslow's need hierarchy. In his view, development is not complete until the individual is motivated by self-actualizing needs that create a restlessness which is in principle impossible to satisfy. For Maslow, self-actualization is a reaching out for man's humanness, achieved only when the demands of need deficiencies have been met.

The portrait of the self-actualizing individual that emerges is so complex that it defies summary. This person is similar in many ways to the individual who fully developed with the Italian Renaissance, who reaches out, unashamably, for all that life has to offer him. In Maslow's words, "self-actualizing people tend to be good and lusty animals, hearty in their appetites and enjoying themselves mightily without regret or shame or apology" (1954, p. 207).

The concept of positive mental health implies that the goal of human behavior is not a fixed state of contentment without "illness," but a process of continual growth and development. Maslow stresses that the satisfaction of deficiency needs frees the individual from dependence upon his environment to satisfy more immediate needs so that he can strike out on his own to realize much longer-term needs. Maslow considers "the process of healthy growth to be a never-ending series of free-choice situations confronting each individual at every point throughout his life, in which he must choose between the delights of safety and growth, dependence and independence, regression and progression, immaturity and maturity" (1962, p. 45).

Individuality

The basic humanistic goal can also be described as creating for every man a sense of freedom to become more truly himself. This goal is seen most clearly in the writing of Carl Rogers, who chose the philosophical journal the *Humanist* (1957b) for an expression of his credo. The good life lies not in a fixed state of virtue, contentment, nirvana, or happiness; nor in a condition in which the individual is adjusted, fulfilled, or actualized. The good life is in process, not in a state of being; and it is a direction, not a destination. Rogers writes: "The good life from the point of view of my experience is the process of movement in a direction which the human organism selects when it is inwardly free to move in any direction, and the good qualities of this selected direction appear to have a certain universality" (1957b, p. 293). The universals that man inevitably seems to select when he has complete freedom of choice include an increasing openness to experience, which permits him to become more aware of his feelings; an increased tendency to live more fully in each moment; and an increasing trust in one's organism that "doing what 'feels right' proves to be a competent and trustworthy guide to behavior which is truly satisfying" (1957b, p. 296).

The humanist typically places the individual's freedom to detach himself from others' expectations under the rubric of creativity. By being creative man expresses himself in a new and unique way and through creativity he forges the unique imprint of self upon his environment. When he is creative, man unfolds his inner self in a way which is uniquely his own. What is creative is so distinctive of one's personality that the creative act can not in principle be duplicated. Thus creativity differs from intelligence, which is defined by one's ability to attain a set standard of behavior, because the creative act is uniquely one's own performance.

After extensive observation, Maslow was forced to differentiate "special-talent creativeness" from "self-actualizing creativeness," which he found sprang much more directly from the person. Self-actualizing creativeness, Maslow feels, is an expressive quality that "is 'emitted,' like radioactivity, and hits all of life, regardless of problems, just as a cheerful person 'emits' cheerfulness without purpose or design or even consciousness" (1962, p. 136). Maslow equates self-actualizing creativity with health itself, but health is only a summary of humanistic virtues which Maslow enumerates as "qualities like boldness, courage, freedom, spontaneity, perspicuity, integration, self-acceptance . . ." (1962, p. 136).

CRITICISM OF HUMANISTIC VALUES

The humanistic orientation is only one among a series of alternatives to the mental-health model, all of which make basic claims to moral truth. The choice of values is a subjective one; no objective proof exists for the worth of humanism as a philosophy of life. In discussing humanism as a system of moral values, however, critics inevitably question its conservatism, its arbitrary moral judgment, and its limited view of man's nature.

Social Relativism

Because its philosophical vantage point is largely conservative, humanism has the highly practical advantage today of being a stabilizing force in a society made giddy by rapid social change. Humanism is conservative in the best sense of the word because it represents an attempt to preserve what seem to be the most lasting parts of post-Renaissance Western heritage as values decline, threatening the qualities which the humanist regards as essential to civilization.

Conservatism also burdens humanism with its greatest weaknesses, however, because it assigns too many abiding qualities to human nature, which is notoriously unwilling to remain static. The values of the achievement-oriented entrepreneur and the morality of the Protestant ethic are now questioned. Because social conditions are changing, it is possible, as van den Berg (1961) suggests, that the nature of man is also changing. Those virtues which seemed so immutable to the Age of Reason seem to many to be disappearing now. If the older rational qualities continue to exist only in exceptional individuals, one may wonder if what was so assuredly virtuous in the past will be regarded as helpful in the future.

Arnold Green (1946) suggests that American psychotherapists have been oriented to so-called democratic values, which stress self-help, independence, and achievement. He finds that these are the basic values of early nineteenth-century Jeffersonian democracy. "Therapy should be nonauthoritarian, individualistic, aimed to promote self-help, independence, and self-achievement" (1946, p. 221). Green wonders if a therapeutic orientation which is non-authoritarian and individualistic can adequately prepare clients for future experiences in a society whose socioeconomic trends are veering sharply away from Jeffersonian democracy.

Green's words seem prophetic. The values that he describes as appropriate to Jeffersonian democracy are also part of a humanistic orientation. The individual entrepreneur, highly prized by Jeffersonian democracy, has been replaced by the organization man and the other-directed person. Automation finds it difficult to reward the hard worker, and in an economic world where consumption is the most relevant economic problem, frugality has a different meaning. The new virtue of cooperation, rather than individual initiative, is rewarded by a complex, interdependent social system.

Humanistic counselors and psychotherapists almost invariably report a drive for self-realization or self-actualization among their clients. One can not know, however, how spontaneous a drive toward personal enhancement is until we know what proportion of clients are somehow related to the Western middle class, which narrowly judges personal acceptability by personal achievement. One conclusion is that Americans are typically activists, who have been lured into frantic activity by their heritage of a beckoning, ever-moving Western frontier. What remains of the great potential of our past may not be a cultural superiority but the cultural pathology of transition so rapid that its highest value is the need for change.

Moral Absolutism

A second criticism of humanism is its rather arbitrary judgment of characteristics selected as most basic to man's nature. Man is his own criterion. Because no external moral reference point exists from which to judge man's worth, the humanist must become self-consciously introspective about his most essential characteristics. Typically he regards a sense of selfhood as his highest value, but since he can justify these values only from self-evidence or inner experience, his argument becomes circular.

The fact that humanistic values represent a highly arbitrary personal judgment is underscored by differences among humanists. The brief historical survey at the beginning of this chapter reveals that humanists are a highly divergent group. As Lowe (1961) points out, a wide variety of definitions of self prevail. Accordingly, one should not be surprised to learn that humanists value quite different characteristics of the self. Ayn Rand's objectivist ethics see man's highest good as the selfishness of an enlightened self-interest. The normative humanism of Erich Fromm's self-love seems equated with self-respect. The contemplative self-love which Fromm theorizes in *The Art of Loving* (1956) stands in marked contrast to the frantic strivings of Ayn Rand's characters. Rogerian therapy of self is distinctive in its emphasis on the discovery of self through exploration of feelings. An opposite viewpoint appears in the rational-emotive approach of Albert Ellis, who emphasizes the need to assert the rational over the emotional.

The arbitrary nature of the humanistic absolute is further underscored by critics who hold other values and charge, in effect, that humanists take too much for granted. On one side are the naturalists, who accuse humanists of being excessively tender-minded. In effect, they charge the humanist with wishful thinking when he endows man with unproven qualities inconsistent with the known physiological facts of man as a natural species. The naturalist criticizes the humanist for emphasizing human virtues which are only examples of a hoped-for but yet-unseen substance. The naturalist would value human qualities which are more observable and tangible.

Although they are on the opposite side from the naturalists, neo-orthodox theologians also charge humanism with overoptimism about man. The theologian believes that humanistic dignity too easily becomes a pride which degenerates into deadly sin when it deceives man into thinking that he is more perfect than he really is. The theologian sees this vainglory as having disastrous consequences for man when it motivates him to undertake actions which are grossly inappropriate to his nature.

Reinhold Niebuhr describes the untoward psychological and social effects of self-deception in several books. In the *Nature of Man* (1941), he traces various psychological implications of the sin of pride. Man, he notes, is afraid to face his own ignorance and thus "the pretensions of final truth are always partly an effort to obscure a darkly felt consciousness of the limits of human knowledge" (1941, p. 184). Afraid that the admission of his limited knowledge will cause him to fall into the abyss of meaninglessness, man becomes a fanatic or uses pride to disguise his imperfections. Niebuhr describes the tragedies of boastful self-assertion in *The Self and the Dramas of History* (1955) and the *Irony of American History* (1952). As Niebuhr looks at post-Renaissance history here, he finds that the ignorance of human limitations has caused innumerable social follies. He charges that the humanistic boast of man's mastery of history causes much that is tragic in modern life. (Rogers [1956] offers a humanistic rebuttal to Niebuhr.)

Moral Incompleteness

These two criticisms are directed at humanism's tendency to endow man with socially relative qualities and to deceive himself into thinking that he is more perfect than he really is. Humanism can also be criticized for ignoring other aspects of man's nature which are morally highly significant.

In "The Uses of Fraternity," Kenneth Benne (1961) charges that the normative orientation of our democratic culture has been based upon the value that the ideal relationship is one between parent and child. Accordingly he sees contemporary culture emphasizing a form of personal maturity described in terms of independence, autonomy, and self-sufficiency. He points out that the result of an overreaction against a dependence upon the parent or upon God has made it "difficult to keep in focus the alternative ideal of maturity—the ability to function autonomously, creatively, and productively in interdependence—an ideal more consonant with the democratic value of fraternity" (1961, p. 234).

Benne argues that it is wrong to believe that man can become independent and self-sustaining at the end of adolescence. He describes the virtues of the experience of fraternity, which encourages people to learn value systems through relationships with peers. Benne believes that fraternity can be integrated with liberty and equality by building "groups with standards that reward and strengthen honest self-expression and self-acceptance, creativity, mutual helpfulness, and the capacity to cope with conflicts (within self or with others)" (1961, pp. 239-240).

In recent years many humanists have themselves become aware of the fact that traditional philosophical humanism has been based upon a truncated view of man. In the last decade such psychologists as Carl Rogers, Rollo May, and Abraham Maslow, who have been the mainstays of a humanistic view in America, have been influenced by European existential thinking to seek a rapprochement between humanistic and existential values. (Existential and humanistic mental-health meanings are compared in Chapter Eight.) Existentialism criticizes humanism for ignoring the inherent contradictions in man's nature.

Succeeding chapters explore other ways of construing man's nature that criticize humanism's self-containment. They seek therefore to lower a drawbridge over the moat of social isolation behind which an alienated individualism has cut itself off from both people and nature. Other value orientations see a need for the inner self to become part of a broader reality.

SUMMARY

Humanism, the first set of mental-health meanings, has grown out of philosophical humanistic values that emphasize the positive qualities in man which differentiate him from the animals. After the Renaissance, part of man's basic credo was that he would become master of his historical destiny through an unfolding of his rational powers. As post-Renaissance individualism has been threatened by social change, humanistic values appear conservative because they are designed to preserve the values of what David Riesman terms an inner-directed orientation despite a social shift toward other directedness.

Views of humanistic mental health center around two primary human virtues—the individual's powers of reason and his capacity for achievement—and regard these values as contained within the self. Counselors and psychotherapists guided by humanistic values typically seek to help the client implement or reconstruct his concept of self in a way that enhances his sense of human dignity.

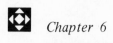

Chapter 6

NATURALISTIC MEANINGS

The end of all our actions is to be free from pain and fear; and when once we have attained this, all the tempest of the soul is laid, . . . Wherefore we call pleasure the alpha and omega of a blessed life. Pleasure is our first and kindred good. From it is the commencement of every choice and every aversion, and to it we come back, and make feeling the rule by which to judge of every good thing. . . . When we say, then, that pleasure is the end and aim, we do not mean the pleasures of the prodigal, or the pleasures of sensuality. . . . By pleasure we mean the absence of pain in the body and trouble in the soul. . . . EPICURUS

Naturalism is the second alternative to mental-health concepts. In the usual philosophical sense, naturalism seeks to limit man's experience to the elements of nature perceived by the senses. Because beliefs can not be perceived in this way, the naturalist usually seeks to avoid becoming concerned with moral values, although he must still make moral judgments. The naturalist is likely to judge something as good to the extent that it serves functions which seem in accord with nature, a propensity that gives him an affinity for hedonistic values. These values are likely to satisfy him intellectually on the grounds that hedonistic pleasure lies in the satisfaction of basic needs which are demonstrably "natural."

As a value orientation, naturalism is both very old and very new. In Classic Greece, Epicurus called upon his fellow man to avoid great tumults which might upset body and soul. As a philosophy of life, naturalism has been somewhat eclipsed until recently, having been overshadowed first by theological values and later by humanistic values. As naturalism finally comes into its own, it seems to be largely a reaction and an opposition to humanism.

HISTORICAL FOUNDATIONS

The beginning of the twentieth century witnessed a general disillusionment with many of those core values which had been central to Western civilization since the Renaissance. In particular, a new skepticism appeared about the rationality of man; basic truths were no longer accepted merely because they appeared to be self-evident. Although man did, of course, continue to reason, he began to lose confidence in the adequacy of his mental powers. As he lost faith in humanistic qualities, he turned to the world of nature to discover those aspects of man which might be understood scientifically. Accordingly he hoped to achieve through science an understanding of self which he could no longer achieve through philosophy.

Psychoanalysis was the first manifestation of naturalistic thinking in psychology. As we have seen, Freud sought to explain the apparent irrationality of man by constructing a model of the mind from the physics and physiology of his day. So also Freud conceived of psychoanalytic practice as a scientific medical technique which would provide a cure for a faltering consciousness.

Behaviorism was a second and much more radical form of naturalism. It relied on the increasingly empirical temper of the time. Behaviorism is a blatant rejection of all man's attempts to reach knowledge through reason. Man's difficulty with logic is seen not as a neurotic distortion which psychoanalysis can cure but as a failure ascribed to his ignorance of scientific method. Behavioristic thought perceives much greater success from man's inductive attempts to secure knowledge by observation and experimentation. Since he regards pure reason as having failed, the behaviorist feels that he can understand human behavior only by scrutinizing man with the scientific instruments that have successfully dissected and analyzed the natural world.

Naturalism Today

Logical positivism is the most extreme attempt to substitute the language of operational definitions for the terms of speculative philosophy. It assigns to science the discovery of a unity of knowledge which philosophy had been unable to find. Science must use objective and exact language; emotive and pictorial language is to be eliminated. Truth is to be limited to scientific fact, or at the most, to statements of what science can potentially verify as fact. What can not be at least potentially measured is considered as unreal.

As logical positivism has purged naturalistic thought, it has had scant use for moral and ethical concerns because good and evil can have no operational definitions. The failure of the new scientific language to deal very systematically with the problem of judgment has not particularly bothered the new naturalists, who regard such words simply as a part of the emotive language lacking in logical properties that had impeded civilized man.

As much as the new naturalism of behaviorism would like to do so, it has not been able to ignore moral issues. While logical positivism could in theory avoid making value judgments, it has been unable to do so in practice. A naturalistic ethics has therefore emerged. Humanism stresses man's uniqueness and bases its decision of good and evil on the qualities of human behavior which distinguish man from other animals; naturalistic orientations assume by contrast that a common good and evil persist throughout all nature. From this philosophical starting point the naturalist deduces an ethics postulated on physiological continuities existing between man and the rest of nature. Since the most obvious continuities are physiological, the naturalist's criterion for good and evil also tends to be physiological. The good is whatever furthers man's physical well-being and contributes to the effective natural functioning of his physiological processes. Evil becomes anything that interferes with the orderly physiological functioning of the organism.

Naturalism in the Behavioral Sciences

Psychology began as an academic discipline with Wundt's establishment of a laboratory at Leipzig in 1879 to analyze the states of consciousness. While the study of the working of intellect satisfied the dominant humanistic interest of that day, the results of introspectionism proved frustrating to the newly emerging naturalists. Introspection was found wanting as a scientific method because it lacked independent verification of individual reports of the self. As a result, two essential scientific canons seemed to be violated: Predictability was difficult because of the highly personal nature of introspective reports and replication was virtually impossible.

The naturalists' disillusionment with introspectionism led to behaviorism, which abruptly sought to change the method and the subject matter of the psychologist's concern. Psychology was to be not the study of mind but the study of behavior. Watson wrote that "psychology as the behaviorist views it is a purely objective experimental branch of natural science" (1914, p. 1). The behaviorist denied the existence of consciousness as an independent entity and substituted the behavioral concomitants of what the humanist had considered consciousness.

In an attempt to find basic elements to explain complex forms of human behavior, the behaviorist has turned to the animal laboratory, seeking what Watson (1914) terms a unitary scheme of animal response. Here the behaviorist has met his greatest success. Because animals do not display consciousness (at least in the sense that the humanist treasures), confining behaviorism to the animal laboratory has only widened the gulf between the behaviorist, who emphasizes those parts of human nature which man shares with lower forms of life, and the humanist, who treasures most that qualitative difference which separates man from the animal.

In recent years learning theory has increasingly left the laboratory and started to apply the principles of behaviorism to a variety of human problems. Watson points out that the behaviorist "recognizes no dividing line between man and brute" (1914, p. 1). As it develops into a program for social action, behaviorism has not hesitated to apply the results of animal experiments to complex social issues. Since behaviorism has developed comprehensive theories of personality and of the nature of society, it is the most appropriate naturalistic model to compare with other views of man which also offer meanings of mental health.

NEEDS

Because naturalism assumes that basic continuities exist between man and the rest of nature, it stresses the basic motives that man shares with typical laboratory animals. The behaviorist justifies generalizing from the rat to man by citing Lloyd Morgan's canon, which assumes that complex human behavior satisfies primitive physiological needs.

By conventional definition, motivation includes both a physiological push (the need) and a teleological pull (the goal). The naturalist obviously prefers to lay aside all questions of goals and purposes because they deal with anticipations which can not be investigated by scientific method. Instead of the molar approach to motivation adopted by the humanist, the naturalist chooses a molecular emphasis. He attempts to avoid postulating any overriding purpose in life and seeks to confine his efforts to describing needs elemental enough to be controlled by laboratory experiments. As a need becomes empirically demonstrated, it becomes a building block. Using other blocks similarly hardened by scientific scrutiny, the behaviorist gradually constructs a wall stout enough to support man's concern for defining higher-order needs and goals.

The naturalist's attempt to avoid taking sides in moral issues has been quite unsuccessful, however. While he may be clear in his own mind that an experiment is in itself morally neutral he can not experiment in a social vacuum. The results of laboratory work are soon integrated into a theory of personality. Needs considered in the laboratory as primary because they are irreducible to other needs are also primary because their satisfaction is most basic and valuable to the organism. Thus primary physiological needs become the keystone of naturalistic values; so-called secondary needs are regarded as having subsidiary value for the organism. What the laboratory regards as secondary needs, the naturalistic counselors and psychotherapists relegate to a lesser good, important only after primary needs are satisfied.

Drive Reduction

Needs may first be described as drives which result from physiological imbalance in the body. This imbalance occurs when certain basic physiological needs are not satisfied. The organism first experiences the imbalance as arousal, and then, if the imbalance becomes extreme, as pain. The tension resulting from the bodily disequilibrium acts much like a watchspring to provide the direct physical impetus to behavior which will satisfy the need and reduce the tension. If pain is in tension-producing disequilibrium, pleasure as its opposite lies in a return to equilibrium. Some learning theorists believe that the *state* of relaxation following the removal of tension is pleasurable; others believe that the *process* of having drives reduced produces happiness.

The most comprehensive learning theorist in drive reduction is Clark Hull. For Hull the basis for motivation is the concept of drive, which consists of aversive stimuli based on deprivation, such as hunger and thirst, or based on noxious stimuli, such as pain and fear. As Hilgard and Bower (1966) point out, Hull's experimental work is based almost entirely upon three drives—hunger, thirst, and pain. Of these, the hunger drive, easily quantified as to the weight of food used as reward, is used most frequently in experimental work. The need to reduce drive aversiveness is for Hull the necessary reinforcement for learning experiences, which are essentially attempts to escape either from internal physiological disequilibrium or from some noxious external agent.

Neural Excitation

Even among naturalists drive reduction is not universally accepted as a suitable explanation for human behavior. Some naturalists point out that the organism does not always appear to seek lassitude. If it did so, as Freud pointed out, the result would be the ultimate state of inactivity—death.

At the other extreme some naturalists assume that pleasure lies in excitement and in activity; thus not drive reduction but stimulation is the basis of pleasure. The need to maintain an excitatory and aroused state in the nervous system provides the rationale for Andrew Salter's theory of personality. Salter (1949) looks to the animal world just as Hull did, but in quite different ways. Salter's model is not the well-trained animal taught to lie supinely in his cage, but the wild animal living in a state of unrestricted nature and maintaining himself according to the law of the jungle. Salter finds the same stimulated need that excites the wild animal to stalk his prey operates in man. He finds man is composed of physical and emotional equipment which most properly belong in the jungle. Excitation, the basis of life in the jungle, is also the basis of human life, the restricting demands of civilization notwithstanding.

Sensory Hunger

Naturalists typically believe that man is driven to behavior that satisfies physiological deficits existing in various parts of his body. Recently, however, laboratory evidence indicates that experimental animals are often motivated by unlearned needs which seem equivalent to human needs for exploration, manipulation, and curiosity. Many learning theorists now believe that certain neurological appetites exist in addition to physiological drives. Because such behavior does not appear to be motivated by the need to satisfy physiological deficits, it becomes necessary to find an additional motivation. Some behaviorists have concluded the nervous system has a sensory hunger roughly analogous to the hunger of physiologically more rudimentary somatic organisms. The nervous system is thus conceived to be hungry for stimulation, which is just as reinforcing as the satisfaction of a physiological need.

For Clifford Morgan (1959), the existence of sensory drives implies that drives build up because of a lack of sensory stimulation and that sensory stimulation can then reduce the drives. Morgan is not certain why such drives should build up, but he discusses two possible causes for them. The first possibility is that the sensory drive is similar to an activity drive. If this is true, a need for physical activity builds up that can not find release until the senses are stimulated so that the organism can respond physiologically. Sensory stimulation thus serves as a trigger to release a pent-up need for activity. As a second possibility, Morgan suggests that sensory drives are due to an interplay of neurological events that are completely unrelated to any physiological need. In support of this possibility Morgan notes that many individuals with rather low activity drives may nevertheless have strong sensory drives. From a philosophic standpoint it is immaterial whether sensory drives are related to an underlying physiological need or whether they have a parallel existence within the nervous system. Both interpretations, as conceived by Morgan and other learning theorists, are similar in operation to visceral drives. Sensory drives can accordingly be reduced in the same general way as physiological drives.

Brain Stimulation

As one might expect, learning theory has been quite responsive to new experimental discoveries. Basic modifications resulting from additional observations of laboratory animals have been discussed above. The behaviorist's views on motivation have also been enriched by new discoveries in the field of neurophysiology. Of particular importance has been the new understanding of the ascending reticular activating formation and the electrical stimulation of the midbrain pleasure centers. At least one Hullian learning theorist (Miller, 1963) has had to revise the Hullian-derived theory of drive reduction to make room for these new "go" or activating mechanisms in the brain which serve to increase arousal, not reduce it.

The newer and more sophisticated approach resulting from recent experimental findings makes the early behaviorists's interpretation of man's internal makeup seem increasingly inappropriate. While behaviorism still believes in continuities between man and animals which are relevant for an understanding of man, the trend in the last few years has been to elevate the entire behavioral realm to a greater complexity than that allowed by traditional interpretations of Lloyd Morgan's canon. The newer viewpoints in learning theory do not change the basic issues, however. Since behaviorism interprets human behavior in the context of its physiological substrata, learning theory must still use a physiological and neurological criterion to judge whether the organism's basic goals and purposes are being appropriately met.

FRUSTRATIONS

The naturalist is apt to consider as undesirable anything that upsets the natural balance of physiological functioning. If man's primary need is to reduce the physiological disequilibrium which results when man's bodily demands are not met, then anything which frustrates meeting these needs is deemed bad. Whatever disrupts physiological equilibrium is considered to be an abnormal condition which is out of harmony with an intended state of nature.

According to one school of thought, the abnormal results from an imbalance in nervous-system functioning, a viewpoint derived from the theories of Ivan Pavlov. Pavlov (1941) regards the neurosis as a chronic disturbance of nervous-system activity, involving an imbalance between the complementary neurological processes of excitation and inhibition. Eysenck and Rachman (1965) use this model to classify different abnormalities according to type and degree of neurological arousal. Although tracing psychopathology to a neurological imbalance has been popular in Europe, it has not become widely accepted in the United States. Salter is one American who operates within a very general Pavlovian tradition, however. He is somewhat distinctive in his viewpoint (1949) that the basic evil is the inhibition of neural functioning which results from the constricting effects of civilization.

Naturalists in the United States customarily use the term anxiety to describe a physiological upset in the natural balance of the nervous system. Thus anxiety tends to be equated with high arousal which disrupts so-called normal physiological functioning. This interpretation of anxiety permits the naturalist to derive evil psychological consequences from such a disordered physiological state. Many difficulties in learning can be traced to the disordered state equated with anxiety. The organism's efficiency is impaired, and it may be so strongly impelled to take action to reduce the anxiety that it neglects meeting primary, organically vital needs. Because the organism's physiological survival is reduced, the core value of organic preservation is threatened. The second reason why anxiety is a fundamental evil is that it is experienced subjectively as painful and the avoidance of pain is a prime naturalistic value.

Since learning theorists in this country have been predominantly concerned with anxiety as the basic manifestation of evil in human nature, the next section examines its origins and its effects on the human organism.

Anxiety Due to Conditioning

One can assume first that man becomes neurotic and even psychotic as a direct result of high-level arousal in the autonomic nervous system. This is the view of Joseph Wolpe (1958) who emphasizes that such typical symptoms of neurosis as tachycardia, high blood pressure, and dryness of the mouth are manifestations of autonomic nervous-system activity, as well as of anxiety. Wolpe believes that these and the other symptoms of neurosis most typically develop in learning situations in which man has been exposed to noxious stimuli in circumstances offering no easy escape. In the opinion of the learning theorist, a phobia results from stimulus generalization. Anxiety is also a response to any stimulus situation which man associates with the original threatening situations.

Although Wolpe believes that neurotic symptoms are produced by autonomic nervous-system activity, he does not believe that the process is limited to the resulting physiological disequilibrium. Because symptoms interfere with the person's behavior, the neurotic becomes ineffective in such important areas as work and sex. Increased muscle tension may impair coordination, cause a socially embarrassing tremor, or result in wasted time and motion as the neurotic makes awkward efforts to avoid the feared situations.

Other undesired consequences can also occur as a result of a phobic situation. One effect is behavior that appears stupid. The neurotic may become fearful in so many situations that he avoids situations in which less anxious individuals learn social and other skills important to social adjustment. Because of unfortunate experiences with other people, a neurotic often has a phobic experience and develops a "burnt-child" reaction causing him to avoid contact with other people even in situations where important social learning takes place. The result is what O. H. Mowrer (1953) terms the neurotic paradox. Potentially intelligent individuals act stupidly because they have used their "intelligence" only to avoid social situations where others learn socially more appropriate behavior.

Learning theorists have used the same principle of stimulus generalization to explain psychotic behavior. Sarnoff A. Mednick (1958) regards schizophrenic symptoms as the result of an even-greater anxiety than the neurotic's. In Hullian terminology, an extremely high drive produces a corresponding increase in the gradient of generalization. The original fear becomes so overgeneralized that anxiety interferes with the ability to concentrate. This overgeneralization explains why the schizophrenic has difficulty in attending to the situation at hand and is distracted by past experiences. Because he responds to the past, others regard his behavior as irrelevant, bizarre, and unconnected. Such tangential associations would not seem likely to produce learning. Mednick believes that seemingly bizarre thoughts do reduce the schizophrenic's anxiety level, however, by filling his mind with associations which are unrelated to the source of his fear. Since inappropriate responses result in drive reduction, they are self-reinforcing. Gradually the schizophrenic learns to experience no emotion at all and presents the familiar flattened or "burnt-out" effect of the chronic schizophrenic.

Anxiety Due to Conflict

Hullian learning theory generally regards anxiety as a learned drive. The organism learns to act to reduce anxiety in much the same way that it seeks to reduce the other drives which Hull postulated. Learning abnormal behavior is somewhat more complicated. As the organism seeks to satisfy different needs, at times the satisfaction of one need may oppose the demands of another, thus causing conflict. Dollard and Miller (1950) trace the origin of neurosis to conflicts between antagonistic drives occurring so early in life that the individual is unable to find a rational solution to this incompatibility of basic drives. They regard the child's conflict between meeting an unlearned need for physiological gratification and a learned need for parental approval as a particularly crucial conflict situation. At this point Dollard and Miller show psychoanalytic influence in their thinking by selecting as critical the learning situations surrounding feeding, cleanliness, sex training, and the treatment of anger responses. They believe that these situations place different combinations of primary physiological and learned social needs in conflict.

In Dollard and Miller's view, the normal individual is one who can be cognitively aware of the nature of conflicting needs. He is also able to use higher mental processes to reason, to plan, and to discriminate among different cues in ways that enable him rather thoughtfully to make the best of a bad situation. For Dollard and Miller, the neurotic is one who is unable to reason effectively to resolve conflict for two reasons. First, his conflicts go back to early childhood when he lacked the verbal tools and higher mental processes to enable him to discriminate between punishing and non-punishing situations. Second, the neurotic is a person who finds it is more pleasant to avoid thinking even when cue-producing cognitions are available to him. This avoidance of thinking about one's difficulties is termed repression by Dollard and Miller. Although Dollard and Miller choose a distinctively psychoanalytic term to describe a lack of cognitive awareness, their interpretation of repression is distinctively behavioristic. The individual who represses awareness of the nature of his conflicts reinforces himself for not thinking about his problems. Not thinking leads to an avoidance of the problem and causes a reduction in the drives produced by thoughts about the problem.

The adult neurotic is easily identified. Dollard and Miller (1950) believe he is one who shows misery, stupidity, and neurotic symptoms. He is miserable because the incompatible nature of conflicting drives makes it impossible for him to take action that can effectively satisfy all his needs. He appears to be stupid because he has learned not to use his mind to solve his most vital problems, instead continuing the primitive problem solving that he acquired in early childhood. He displays neurotic symptoms because however much such symptoms may cripple his ability to meet basic social demands, the symptoms are reinforced because they enable him to avoid situations in which unresolved conflicts become too intense.

COUNSELING AND PSYCHOTHERAPY

If neurosis is regarded as the failure to learn to reduce basic tensions, psychotherapy is defined as a new type of learning experience: Through counterconditioning the psychotherapist provides the patient with a different set of stimuli. If the original experience of learning had been traumatic and negative reinforcement caused avoidance behavior, the therapeutic situation provides the patient with strikingly different experiences. Negative reinforcement with its aversive consequences is replaced by positive reinforcement which elicits less disruptive somatic reactions.

An intense plea for interpreting psychotherapy in naturalistic and learning-theory terms has been made by Leonard Krasner (1962a), who describes the therapist as a social-reinforcement machine programmed by previous training and experience to produce stimulus-response learning. Krasner believes that the therapist should turn to science for a behavioristic interpretation of therapy, rather than to continue placing his faith in such concepts as hope, expectancy, or other unknown factors. Since he sees the therapist as an inevitable source of reinforcement, he should be so programmed that he can produce efficient types of learning.

A somewhat similar appeal for a naturalistically oriented counselor has been made by Sidney Bijou (1966). Describing the relevance of experimental psychology for the counseling process, he concludes: "Instead of conceiving of the counselor as a reflector of feelings, or an explorer of resources, or a habit changer, or a remediator of self-concepts and values, or a releaser of repression, we might come to think of him as a behavioral engineer—one whose function it is to arrange and rearrange the environment in order to bring about desired changes in behavior" (1966, p. 44).

Naturalistic therapies have two common denominators. The first common belief is that alleviating the anxiety should be a primary goal; the second is that learning theory is the best means to this goal. Beyond this point, however, divergencies exist in theory and in practice. While learning theorists have a common allegiance to basic tenets of behaviorism, learning theory is sufficiently general so that the theorist may choose from among different learning-theory principles as the basis of his practice. Naturalistic psychotherapy makes some use of one or both of two basic principles: First, old habits of responding, no longer reinforced, are extinguished; and second, new habits are built up when they are reinforced sufficiently to enter the response repertoire.

The Extinction of Anxiety

According to learning theory, the organism becomes anxious when it is exposed to stimuli which in some way resemble an earlier situation which contained a palpable threat of physical danger. The anxiety would of course be extinguished if the organism would reexpose itself to the original learning situation and find the threat was no longer present. Since anxiety is unpleasant, the organism avoids any situations resembling the original fear-provoking situation, and thus shuts off all possibility of extinguishing the anxiety through nonreinforcement. The therapist is able to expose the client to learning experiences which he has previously succeeded in avoiding. Because psychotherapy is characterized by a basic lack of threat, fear-producing responses are not reinforced and thus anxiety will soon become extinguished through nonreinforcement.

The most distinctive use of extinction as psychotherapeutic technique appears to be made by Thomas G. Stampfl. The purpose of psychotherapy is to teach the victim of anxiety that he no longer needs to be frightened. The therapist does this by deliberately frightening patients as much as he can in psychotherapy without physically harming them. He accomplishes this end by having the patient imagine in as vivid terms as he can what London describes (after having observed it) as "the most thorough-going catalogue of horrors imaginable, perhaps as rich a collection of lore as was ever composed and narrated for the singular purpose of evoking nauseous terror from even the bravest men" (London, 1964, p. 103). The dramatic quality of this threat is quite deliberate and does in fact provide the basis for the name *implosion therapy* which Stampfl gives his therapeutic technique. Although the explosion is caused inwardly, none of the dire ramifications that the patient has dreaded appear outwardly. The patient thus learns to be unafraid of severe threat and thus scarcely needs instruction in overcoming more mundane fears.

Although they use extinction much less dramatically, Dollard and Miller (1950) consider it a necessary first stage for relearning, which can best occur after the original fears are extinguished. In their attempt to reconcile Freudian psychoanalysis with learning theory, they interpret free association in learning-theory terms as a process of extinguishing anxiety-provoking situations by not reinforcing them. The patient is thus encouraged to freely associate in such a way that he alludes as frequently as possible to threatening areas of his life. While the patient previously had been punished for these ideas, he now finds the therapist is permissive and nonpunitive. The benign consequence of expressing previously forbidden thoughts is a continuation of the relaxed atmosphere which the permissive nature of psychotherapy had created. Thus removal of the feared consequence terminates the fear response.

Learning New Behaviors to Inhibit Anxiety

A second principle of learning theory is that new behaviors can be elicited by positively reinforcing them whenever they occur. If certain behaviors are anxiety laden and fear provoking for the patient, a process of counterconditioning can cause him to replace negative anticipations with positive expectations for certain basic events. Hence psychotherapy is seen as providing the impetus to learn new behaviors whose reinforcement inhibits anxiety responses.

The most dramatic use of learning new behaviors is provided by the reconditioning and disinhibiting techniques of Salter (1949). The purpose of psychotherapy is to get the patient to liberate unpleasant emotions, which Salter describes as sticking to the patient like flypaper. Emotions are liberated through increasing the amount of excitation. He lists a series of techniques designed to provide the relearning of what he considers to be excitatory experiences. Salter suggests "feeling talk" for his patients, a term used for the deliberate utterance of spontaneously felt emotions. He advises an emotional truth and frankness which allows one to contradict and attack when he differs with others. Salter also suggests the use of self-assertion: Self-praise should be volunteered with "straightforward naïveté." Finally, Salter advises the patient to learn an emotional improvisation which allows him to live spontaneously on a minute-to-minute basis. Through such techniques, therapy enables the individual "to reeducate himself back to the healthy spontaneity of which his life experiences have deprived him" (1949, p. 103).

Joseph Wolpe (1958) states that he agrees with many of the basic principles on which Salter bases the learning of disinhibition, although he criticizes his flamboyant style of writing. Wolpe emphasizes neurological inhibition, terming his practice of psychotherapy as that of *reciprocal inhibition.* Wolpe grounds his therapy on the neurological fact that a period of reactive inhibition results in a decrease of response strength as fatigue mounts within the nervous system. Spontaneous recovery generally occurs with time, however. Wolpe sees the interim when reactive inhibition is still present as a time when the patient can learn new, antithetical (and hence inhibitory) responses to the fear responses he wishes to eliminate.

The purpose of psychotherapy is to produce a wide variety of responses to inhibit anxiety. Muscle relaxation is another response, since relaxing the muscles is clearly antithetical to the general physical tension of anxiety. Since tensing the body has been associated with certain traumatic events, Wolpe has the patient remain relaxed while he achieves increasing psychological closeness to dreaded events. Wolpe also finds that a similar relaxing effect occurs physiologically by having the patient breathe a heavy concentration of carbon dioxide. While relaxing the muscles can effectively inhibit fear, in Wolpe's view it can also inhibit it through more active behavior. Therefore Wolpe encourages the patient to learn to assert himself in situations in which fear is clearly unadaptive by nature. The result is an action tendency which replaces the former inclination to avoid the source of the threat.

While Wolpe seeks to inhibit anxiety through physiological changes, Dollard and Miller (1950) are more cognitively oriented to the new learning in psychotherapy. Since psychotherapy produces an extinction of fear through free association, the relaxed state of this first step in psychotherapy allows the patient to be less panicky and more thoughtful. The therapist takes advantage of the patient's relaxation by encouraging him to think and talk about those situations whose high degree of threat had previously inhibited consideration. As an increase in discrimination learning occurs, the patient differentiates the original traumatic situation from later phobic experiences only superficially like the original trauma. Learning theory emphasizes that if such new discriminations are to become part of the patient's permanent behavior, they must be reinforced. Accordingly Dollard and Miller emphasize that conflicts and misery can be relieved only in real life and they see the therapist's task to be that of setting up a series of graded tasks to give the patient an opportunity to validate the discriminations learned in psychotherapy.

GOALS

The behaviorist's failure to state his values or to describe his conception of ideal behavior causes serious contention between the behaviorist and the humanist. As B. F. Skinner and Carl Rogers have debated one another (Rogers and Skinner, 1956), one of the chief issues to emerge is a clarification of the scientist's goal in psychotherapy and other types of behavior modification. This issue, so basic to Rogers, is clearly one Skinner would like to avoid. The learning theorist is, however, forced to discover a purpose for behavior modification. Under Rogers' questioning, Skinner acknowledges that the ultimate goal is to preserve the physiological intactness of the organism, or (as Skinner expresses it), to keep breathing. (Later in this book we will find that the existentialist is concerned with why man should keep breathing.)

The behaviorist must have values, even if he prefers to use other terms to describe them. Although behavioristic descriptions of the goal or purpose of human behavior are hard to find, behavioristic mental-health practitioners must select a criterion by which to judge the neurotic or pathological, and to establish a goal or standard for psychotherapy and other forms of behavior modification.

The two behaviorists who have been most vocal in describing the end product of behavior modification differ considerably from each other in their descriptions of the good life. The difference between B. F. Skinner's carefully collectivized society and Andrew Salter's excited and uninhibited individuals is to some extent due to different emphases within the naturalistic tradition. To an even greater extent, however, the differences seem due to the fact that Skinner's basic orientation is social, while Salter's is the individual. Choosing between the values of the individual and those of the society is so basic to an understanding of behaviorism that the discussion here is organized around this distinction.

The Uninhibited Individual

From a naturalistic viewpoint the neurotic is one who has been exposed to negative reinforcement or to punishment too many times. If the behaviorist views overconditioned behavior as undesirable, then he sees behavior so externally unimpeded that the organism can reduce drive without fear and without restraint as the ideal.

A vivid description of such an uninhibited ideal is found in Salter's writings. For Salter, "the objective of mental health is to 'be me, not them'," and he therefore concludes that "society is the sworn enemy of mental health" (1949, p. 103). Since Salter regards society as opposed to the individual, he sees the ideal individual as one who adjusts not to society but to himself. He calls a person who has freed himself from social constraint an excitatory personality.

> The excitatory person is direct. He responds outwardly to his environment. When he is confronted with a problem, he takes immediate constructive action. He is energetic, but here is nothing hyperthyroid about it. He sincerely likes people, yet he does not care what they may think. He talks of himself in an unaffected fashion, and is invariably underestimated by the inhibitory. He makes rapid decisions and likes responsibility. Above all, the excitatory person is free from anxiety. He is truly happy (1949, pp. 45-46).

Because Salter also writes "we are composed of jungle stuff, and ours is a monkey culture" (1949, p. 35), one wonders if the excitatory individual might not ignore the social amenities and become a constant aversive stimulus to others. Salter does not appear to be seriously concerned with this problem, however. He discusses the psychopath, but he regards him as merely another example of an individual so inhibited by early social conditioning that he is unable to express the proper degree of excitement about social feeling. The psychopath's bland exterior is but a disguise for inner inhibition and retreat.

One might also wonder how the need for constant stimulation which Salter postulates can be reconciled with the tension-reducing model that virtually all other behaviorists follow. Salter is not clear on this point. What is clear, however, is that excitation is a basic part of the law of the jungle: "The creatures that survive in the jungle are those that slink and jump and kill" while "the polite and inhibited ones crouch behind a tree and are soon dead" (1949, p. 34). Man is to be governed by "the law of the gut." Emotional expression, grounded in autonomic experience, becomes the highest good for man, whom Salter finds still possesses a human body.

Positive Reinforcement

One way for the behaviorist to view ideal behavior is from the vantage point of the individual, and accordingly to see the good life in terms of the organism's freedom to be left alone by a social system which only inhibits his meeting his basic needs. However, the behaviorist can also examine the social system with the intention of replacing inhibitory or aversive control with a more positive reinforcement that elicits behavior which the learning theorist advises.

B. F. Skinner (1953) sees the learning theorist becoming a behavioral engineer who helps create a new social control that not only ceases to impede the individual from meeting his basic needs but also functions positively to provide basic reinforcements or reward. The result of such control by the behavioral scientist is a smoothly functioning social system where punishment or negative reinforcement is used as an exception, and not the rule.

As discussed above, Skinner consistently refuses to discuss ideal forms of human behavior in moral or ethical terms; instead, he uses terms which originate in science. Skinner is particularly fond of the terms positive and negative reinforcement; the former elicits behavior Skinner considers good, while the latter results in behavior he deems bad. In the Skinnerian lexicon, positive reinforcement is synonymous with such terms as love, admiration, approval, and affection; all considered to be desirable: negative reinforcement is equated with such undesirables as punishment, escape, revolt, passive resistance, fear, rage, depression, excessively vigorous behavior, and defective self-knowledge.

At first glance Skinner's distinction between positive and negative reinforcement appears to be operationally meaningless, subject only to personal taste. Skinner claims, however, an objective distinction exists between the results of the two types of reinforcements; negative reinforcement has a chaining effect which prevents the subject organism from leaving the learning situation. Although he regards negative reinforcement as a tyrannical form of social control because it inhibits effective choice, positive reinforcement is free of enslaving consequences. The positively reinforced individual is still able to exercise one basic freedom—he can leave the learning situation.

The ideal society would be one in which positive reinforcement comprises the sole social control. Skinner describes such a society in his Utopian novel *Walden Two* (1948), set on a farm that is economically and socially isolated from the larger society. Control over all aspects of behavior is vested in the proprietor and founder, a behavioral engineer who has designed this social microcosm to achieve the highest possible institutional efficiency. Cultural anachronisms have been eliminated. By eliminating wasted efforts and instituting a highly efficient centralized economic planning, members minimize expenditures of vocational time and effort. Because centralized dining halls and nurseries eliminate time-consuming domestic tasks, the benefits of increased leisure are not limited to wage earners. In other societies vast amounts of leisure time might be a problem, but recreation is as carefully planned as are all other aspects of the colony's life. Recreation is provided in common, with carefully arranged lists of a multitude of leisure-time activities, rather like a schedule of student activities at a large university.

Skinner realizes the issue of values involved in advocating a highly controlled society such as Walden Two, which appears to be a complete autocracy. Not only is all political power vested in the scientist's hands, but so is every other conceivable form of control that one man could exercise over another. Skinner is nevertheless quite emphatic about the meaningful nature of the new freedoms which the scientist's control provides the individual. Man is now free from the tyranny of the majority, democracy being completely absent. More important, he is free from the tyranny of chance, which Skinner regards as omnipresent in a democracy without effective control. Since only positive reinforcement is used, freedom from the anxiety generated by punishment is complete. Children are raised in air-conditioned nurseries, free from frustration, pain, and fear. Because children develop self-control by standing for five minutes before a kettle of hot soup when they are hungry, everyone is liberated from even the tyrannical control of his own body. The result of complete control is freedom from even "the despotism of neglect, of irresponsibility, the despotism of accident" (1948, p. 223).

For Skinner, the final proof that Walden Two represents the ultimate good lies in the fact that the members have one final freedom. Because control is limited to positive reinforcement, everyone is free to leave. No one does.

CRITICISM OF NATURALISTIC VALUES

A naturalist can describe the ways to achieve basic satisfactions in concise terms that require precise methods. Certainly many people feel that it is time to free man from a morass of metaphysical speculation about ultimate philosophical issues so that he can move forward with a clearly specified program of action. As man feels increasingly frustrated in his efforts to attain the good life, he is drawn to a behavioristic learning theory that offers new tools for forming a radically improved society.

While behaviorism has the potential to be technologically very useful in helping man create a good life, it has companion disadvantages. The two chief criticisms of naturalistic values are that they ignore moral complexities and are insensitive to more broadly humanistic concerns.

Moral Oversimplification

The concise thought which allows the behaviorist to be so technologically efficient is a disadvantage when he must confront the moral implications of behavior modification. Man's social life has become so complex that even the most tentative attempt to unravel the functional from the dysfunctional is controversial. The naturalist, however, refuses to recognize the complex moral quandry which modern man must resolve. The naturalist's solution to the choice between good and evil is to cut the Gordian knot of moral entanglement by excising all the words and terms which can not be given a naturalistic meaning. The problem of morality is indeed "solved"; however, the solution is costly. Banishing the words for subjective experiences limits man to the external world which can be quantified, and banishes science from a concern with the choice of values from which emotional satisfactions grow. The result is a markedly truncated reality which seriously narrows the range of human experience.

The naturalist can not eliminate the reality of man's subjective tastes by pretending that they do not exist, however. He seeks to avoid metaphysical concern, but he is not successful and in fact makes the same mistake as the metaphysicians whom he criticizes so vocally: He confuses his perception of reality with reality as a whole. Basic reality for the behaviorist is the world of the controlled laboratory experiment. As firmly anchored as he may appear to be in a situation that seems scientifically basic, the behaviorist must make a metaphysical venture into faith when he seeks to fashion a larger cosmological realm based on the theoretical blueprint of the laboratory experiment. When the laboratory scientist sketches out grand ideals for future Utopias, he has clearly entangled himself in highly complex moral and metaphysical matters.

B. F. Skinner seeks to construct a bright new tomorrow by using that moral building block which he terms positive reinforcement. The difference between positive and negative reinforcement can be demonstrated in the laboratory on an operational basis of frequency of goal choice. When Skinner seeks to establish social control, positive reinforcement is equated with what people like, such as being pleased, loved, and admired; negative reinforcement is that which people dislike and seek to avoid. Skinner would have man believe that a simple translation of all value-loaded works into the terminology of positive and negative reinforcement solves complex moral problems.

That naturalism has not been entirely successful in resolving moral issues is underscored by Carl Rogers' rejoinders to B. F. Skinner in a well-known series of debates between the two psychologists (see Rogers and Skinner, 1956). Rogers is critical of Skinner's failure to be explicit about the nature of good and evil, accusing him of mixing fact with fancy and of confusing what is with what should be. Rogers asserts that any scientific endeavor must have a prior choice of what values science is to serve. In Rogers' view, the scientist can be impartial only serving a criterion whose choice is beyond science because objectivity implies a comparison of two things by a standard fixed by something other than the variables controlled in the experiment. Scientific objectivity thus requires a statement of the scientist's own values. When the scientist fails to make a conscious choice of the values he has established as a criterion or normative standard, he finds that science (and ultimately the larger society) becomes controlled by the criterion. Science is no longer man's servant in achieving the good life; it now becomes his moral master. Man can therefore become permanently locked in by the rigidity of the scientist's original choice. One can never get free of one's self-determined fate because, as Rogers describes it, "such a scientific endeavor can never transcend itself to seek new goals" (Rogers and Skinner, 1956, p. 1062).

As an example of his concern, Rogers cites Skinner's description of behavioral paradise in *Walden Two* (1948). Rogers concludes that *Walden Two* and Orwell's *Nineteen Eighty-Four* are at a deep philosophical level quite similar to each other because neither offers a clear statement of the purpose of absolute psychological control. Frazier the cultural engineer completely controls every aspect of the farm colony's life. As he looks down on the colony, perhaps he is not God (as he conceives himself to be), but he might, in Rogers' view, be Big Brother.

Dehumanizing Tendencies

In addition to criticism of their being speciously scientific about moral values, naturalists have also been criticized for their insensitivity to more broadly humanistic moral concerns. The humanist seems to be particularly revolted by the heavy-handed scientific destruction of that individualistic freedom he feels is the most basic part of human nature. B. F. Skinner's novel has been the focal point of this issue also. The humanist philosopher, Joseph Wood Krutch was so cut to the quick by *Walden Two* that he wrote *Measure of Man* (1954) to rebut what he feels are the dehumanizing implications of Skinner's view.

Krutch fears that a society which tells its members they are automata risks becoming a society where human capacities atrophy because they are not rewarded. Krutch is unhappy with Skinner's suggestion that humans are not really responsible. He believes that psychological determinism is "something which man cannot afford to know because he can neither know nor even believe it without ceasing to be Man and making way for that something, either better or worse, which the apocalyptically inclined occasionally predict" (1954, p. 54). Krutch is also concerned because if in fact man is not free, there can be no way out of a vicious circle of destructive control should the behavioral engineer choose selfish ends. He wonders what would happen if the son of the commandant of a Nazi labor camp should decide to establish a Walden Three for his own ghoulish purpose of inflicting suffering upon people.

> By what standards could the dictator of Walden Two presume to judge that his utopia was any more desirable than its new rival? He could not appeal to God's revealed word; to the inner light of conscience; or to that eighteenth-century stand-by, the voice of Nature. He could say only that the accidents of his previous existence in a world where accident still played its part in determining how an individual should be conditioned had conditioned him to prefer what he would (1954, p. 65).

As Krutch looks into the future, he is frightened by the prospect that behavioral scientists will increasingly become efficient technicians who are supremely ignorant of the significance of their actions. Distorted values result when all value judgments are rejected except those which a particular mind declares to be self-evident: "First it is 'self-evident' that men ought to be healthy; then self-evident that 'healthy' means 'adjusted' " (1954, pp. 90-91).

Krutch criticizes naturalism because he believes that scientists who are highly trained technicians have not been taught to develop an awareness of the more enduring qualities in man's nature.

> As influence, power, and authority in our society pass, as they are passing, from philosophers and theologians into the hands of those who call themselves 'human engineers,' whether they happen to be functioning as lawmakers, publicists, teachers, psychologists, or even advertising managers, it is passing from those who were at least aware of what value judgments they were making to those who are not (1954, p. 91).

Rogers and Krutch on one hand and Skinner and other naturalists on the other stand for different values. Skinner's ultimate criterion is survival, but Krutch notes that cockroaches have survived in the same form for two hundred and fifty million years. He feels assured that a significant difference exists between surviving as a cockroach and living as a human being. This failure to make a distinction, more than any other, damns Skinner in the eyes of his critics. Older values in our culture proclaim that it is better to be a discontented man than a satisfied animal. Skinner seems to be saying the very opposite: The supreme end of life is to know no frustration. Man in the naturalist's paradise would become like the proverbial cow, raised on farms operated with mechanical efficiency lest disturbing influences occur to prevent getting "contented milk from contented cows."

SUMMARY

Naturalistic mental-health meanings assume that man is basically a creature of nature and therefore that certain continuities exist between man and other animals. While naturalistic values are very old, the philosophy of naturalism has been notably reemphasized within the last century. The rediscovery of naturalistic values can be interpreted as being largely due to a reaction against an over-zealous humanistic rationalism. This mood is particularly true in psychology, where behaviorism has manifestly developed as a reaction to the introspective study of consciousness by structural psychology.

Therapists who are oriented to a naturalistic cosmology are not always guided in their personal lives by principles of physiological need gratification. As personality theorists, however, they are forced by the initial premise of man's naturalistic nature to conclude that human needs and goals must be construed in physiological terms. The same initial premise causes them to conclude that physiological disequilibrium is the basic source of evil in man. The naturalistic therapist regards the purpose of therapy to be freeing the client from tension and anxiety. As a result, the goal of therapy is an uninhibited and unconstricted existence in which the individual ceases to be physiologically pent-up by restrictive social institutions.

Chapter 7

SOCIAL MEANINGS

No man is an island, entire of itself; every man is a piece of the continent, a part of the main; if a clod be washed away by the sea, Europe is the less, as well as if a promontory were, as well as if a manor of thy friends or of thine own were; any man's death diminishes me, because I am involved in mankind; and therefore never send to know for whom the bell tolls; it tolls for thee. . . . DEVOTIONS XVII, *John Donne*

While both humanistic and naturalistic orientations regard man as self-contained, social alternatives regard him as inextricably involved with events occurring around him in social space. A social value orientation does not deny all the assumptions about man made by the two previous value systems, but it does claim that even the most biological needs in man are satisfied in a social context. Social meanings would not deny the value which humanistic alternatives place upon growth and development, but they do emphasize that this growth occurs only in an appropriate social context. They would state further that such actualization should seek to realize shared social goals rather than idiosyncratic and possibly selfish individual interests.

HISTORICAL FOUNDATIONS

Today we are so aware of the dynamics of man's social nature that we tend to assume it has always been a self-evident truth. However, scant appreciation of the influence of the social matrix on man's existence was given until the late nineteenth century. In the wake of the intellectual and ideological ferment which followed Charles Darwin, Herbert Spencer proposed that social evolution was also occurring; however, he proposed a somewhat rigid, mechanical model of social adaptation. Not until the work of George Herbert Mead at the beginning of this century did man become aware of the explicit interrelationships among the mind, the self, and the society, which is the title and the theme of Mead's basic and seminal work (1934).

The discovery of the diverse implications of man's social nature had to wait for appropriate social changes before it could assert itself in man's consciousness. In the terms used in this book, man developed new social insights in the process of a transition from a rational to a postrational moral system. Before the twentieth century man saw little intrinsic reward in considering himself a social animal, preferring the view that he was nurtured in a theological matrix. Although man was aware of the communal nature of society, he believed that the social system was derived from the commonwealth of God and therefore was sacrosanct and beyond question. Man was so intent upon his individuality that he saw his social nature as a fault which he was morally obligated to overcome. Social space was rather open during this period in Western history so that man could ignore the social reality of significant others. When society had to impose its will upon the individual, it found it meaningful to idealize the "noble savage" and to announce as a social goal the return to a much earlier state in which social institutions were notably absent.

Twentieth-century man has suddenly found it rewarding to consider his relationships with other people within a social matrix. The new reality is other people. As man faces more complex social problems peculiar to an other-directed society, he finds that people are both the problem and the answer to the problem. Riesman notes that other direction is characterized by a tendency "to be sensitized to the expectations and preferences of others" (1961, p. 8). According to him, other people, not the material environment, are the obstacles to fulfillment. The inner-directed environment had what Riesman terms "a scarcity psychology" in which the number of men was limited by the growth potential of the material environment. In an other-directed orientation the scarcity of people is replaced by "an abundance psychology" where people are so plentiful that they get in the way. Achievement is less often found in the exploitation of material resources. Self-actualization must now be at the expense of other people. To the extent that man is still governed by the old values of success, he must now learn to manipulate other people. William Whyte's *Organization Man* (1956) gives a good description of the new social context in which older values are to be realized.

A Social Viewpoint Today

Concern with the social aspects of man's nature provides social meanings with a distinctive view of what is good and bad for man. Social values find good in those social ties which link the individual to his fellow human beings; evil, in whatever isolates and alienates man, whatever cuts him off from the social nurturance which provides his basic inner resource. Society ceases to be deprecated as the natural enemy of man which it so often is in the naturalistic and humanistic views. Culture now becomes a source of potential good and man's social needs are given a new dignity because they are no longer regarded as "neurotic" distortions. Social needs have primary importance as the culture provides the basic physiological security.

A social orientation draws support from a wide variety of sources, one of whom is paleontologist George Gaylord Simpson. As Simpson (1949) seeks meaning in evolution, he finds that man's social situation now requires evolution to have a social meaning. He replaces (1966) natural selection with social selection, and he states that naturalistic ethics must be supplemented by moral principles that recognize the effects of social selection. Because evolution is now sociobiological, man must set new goals for his future.

Social values are also supported by the pragmatic emphases of contemporary philosophers, whose best-known leaders are probably William James and John Dewey. Pragmatism assumes that things are good to the extent that they work; in practice, the criterion for success is how efficient is the questioned good in meeting dominant social goals. This philosophy of values is perhaps best known because of its influence upon education, where the goal is typically to prepare the child for the social world of democracy.

From a contrasting vantage point, social values receive support from liberal Protestantism's emphasis upon the social gospel (Rauschenbusch, 1912). Religion is largely equated with social interest; the kingdom of God is drawn from the eschatological future to become a goal of the present. The social gospel concentrates on the great ethical social problems; sin is manifested in a variety of basic social evils, salvation is secured by perfecting the basic social forms of the culture.

A Social Viewpoint in the Behavioral Sciences

A concern with man's social nature seems to be clearest in the behavioral sciences. Indeed, the behavioral sciences can be viewed as emerging in response to man's interest in his social nature. A psychological viewpoint assumes that human behavior is most meaningfully interpreted in the context of past learning situations which are usually social. A sociological viewpoint, which is even more deeply committed to many of the assumptions a social value system must make, interprets social determinants as the basic causes of human behavior. Sociology tends to assume that basic changes in the whole social system make possible basic improvements in individual behavior.

Although social values now have a rather pervasive influence in the behavioral sciences, nevertheless, they can be traced to their historical roots in academic psychology and psychoanalysis. An earlier chapter discusses the introspective method, which characterized the first psychological laboratory, and later seemed artificial and meaningless in content. While behaviorism developed as one form of rebellion against the study of an isolated state of consciousness, a second reaction also developed in what is termed functionalism. The founders and leaders of functionalism were William James and John Dewey. Unlike the structural and the behavioral schools, which studied man within his mind or his body, they were concerned with the way in which various human attributes helped man function in a social environment. Functional psychology did not suddenly become fully aware of the ways in which man relates socially to his environment; social psychology developed later. Because James and Dewey were pragmatists, their new school of psychology demanded to know how man's various attributes could be used to help him adapt to his environment. Although the functionalists themselves do not seem to have been particularly concerned with how one adjusts to a social environment, their ideological descendents have become increasingly interested.

Just as functionalism developed as a reaction to what its founders took to be the dated academic concern of structuralism, so a parallel revisionism was going on in psychoanalysis. Here the rebellion was against naturalistic values, and a social viewpoint was substituted for a physiological one immediately and directly. Alfred Adler broke with Freud because he disagreed with Freud's view of man. Adler saw the fulfillment of social needs, not of instinctual or physiological needs, as crucial to normal development. Harry Stack Sullivan, Karen Horney, and Erich Fromm are also identified with Adler as the center of a movement called social psychoanalysis.

Functionalism and neoanalytic revisionism belong to a period in behavioral science's dim beginnings when ideological currents were so distinct that it was proper to refer to schools of psychology. Since World War I a virtual maelstrom of new ideas has produced so many crosscurrents that the old issues are blended until the ideological flow can not always be traced. Few behavioral scientists fail to recognize the formative effect of early social learning experiences. Today the vital importance of man's social relationships is almost universally accepted.

NEEDS

Social alternatives begin with the same biological rootedness which naturalistic alternatives emphasize. But while the satisfaction of physical tensions is the end of the naturalistic theory of motivation, it is only a preamble to a theory of needs for a social orientation. Because man is biologically helpless at birth, he is completely dependent upon other human beings for survival until he can meet his own basic biological needs.

Love

If an infant is to survive, he must be cared for by other people. Social values assume a basic importance to the way the significant others meet these physical demands. A social orientation maintains that love and affection are an integral part of being fed and clothed. Harry Stack Sullivan (1953) describes how an upset in interpersonal relations between mother and infant can disturb the giving and the receiving of nourishment because the mother's tensions are communicated to the infant.

The very young child has what Sullivan describes as a need for tenderness. The child feels utterly helpless in meeting his own wants, and he becomes aware of his extreme dependence on significant others. Karen Horney describes the child's need to feel loved and wanted, much as Sullivan has. She believes that a child can develop feelings of security only in an atmosphere of warmth and acceptance.

Sullivan and other personality theorists support their belief that the child needs love with clinical studies of infants deprived of psychological mothering. Clinical observations of these infants seem to confirm that lack of affection interferes with even basic physiological functioning. Margaret Ribble (1965) describes how social relatedness is necessary for such basic functions as priming vital reflexes and arousing sensory awareness. Ribble describes love as meeting the need for a life-giving sense of security which will promote an awareness of a mature self. Ribble makes the value judgment that consistent parental love and care is vital in man's ascendancy to a supreme position.

Relatedness

A social value system does not regard man as so self-contained that he can dispense with social relationships even when he becomes mature. The need for love and tenderness in infancy and early childhood is replaced, however, by a more mutual social interchange in adulthood.

The need for social interaction with one's peers is perhaps most often described as a need for affiliation. The desirability of social interchange is so commonly accepted that it is the least controversial of all values. But while other orientations would regard affiliative tendencies as desirable, a social value system sees them as essential for the maintenance of personality organization. Sullivan's attitude seems to represent this viewpoint: "It is a rare person who can cut himself off from mediate and immediate relations with others for long spaces of time without undergoing a deterioration in personality" (1953, p. 32).

Adaptation to One's Society

Man's greatest dread in an other-directed society is of social conformity. He currently has a generalized fear that a mass humanity will panic at the loss of old values and will stampede at the irrational urging of the herd instinct. Man is frightened at his insight into this need for social adaptation or adjustment. An affirmative case can easily be made, however, for believing that it is good for an individual to accommodate himself somewhat to the expectations and needs of others. Without some adjustment to the requirements of a social system, society could easily become chaotic and normless.

The need to conform to basic social demands has traditionally been termed the need to adjust. This need has become the theme and often the title of basic textbooks in the area of mental hygiene. Shaffer and Shoben (1956) compare social adjustment in humans with biological adjustment in animals, noting how one gains favor from others in his group to meet such various social needs as the need for approval and recognition.

In recent years the term adjustment has acquired increasingly evil connotations, implying an undesirable passivity and dependence. Shoben, whose co-authored work was cited above, has come (personal communication) to doubt that the term can be used nonpejoratively. Personality theorists are currently searching for a term which states in a noninvidious fashion the need for active involvement and participation in the social processes of the culture.

A newer way to define a social need is to describe it in terms of a sense of community. Many see a need for mutual participation to maintain one's social matrix is as necessary to man as his need for more personal social relations. According to this view, man can benefit from a sense of group solidarity in ways that are not possible in one-to-one relationships.

Social Concern

A social value orientation assumes that man largely outgrows his infant dependence upon others and assumes an ever-greater responsibility for meeting the needs of others which can be fulfilled only through social relationships.

Alfred Adler calls this social concern *social interest.* In his earlier professional life, Adler emphasizes a different social need; striving for superiority, which enables man to overcome an inferiority complex. Later, Adler increasingly emphasizes man's need to replace his striving for superiority with social interest, or Gemeinschaftsgefühl.

Because it is difficult to find terms that are undistorted by popular stereotype, the translation of Gemeinschaftsgefühl as social interest does not adequately describe Adler's social concern. Walter O'Connell (1965) has suggested that Adler's concept of social interest should be broadly understood as including "fellow feeling," "sense of solidarity," "communal intuition," "community interest," and "social sense." In short, social interest describes a need to enter the fullest possible participation with others as a social being.

FRUSTRATIONS

Social alternatives to mental health often see the individual and his culture as an organic whole. In this perspective the individual is like the branch of a tree, which can be sustained only by remaining integrally related to the nurturant trunk and roots of the tree. Frustration is a blocking off of that social osmosis which allows warmth and tenderness to flow to the individual from other human beings. Clinical evidence has led many to believe that the infant will literally wither physically when he is not given social sustenance. Social deprivation in the adult is not generally regarded as fatal but it does produce a state of frustration which in turn causes the abnormal conduct others term mental illness.

Lack of Social Conformity

A social value system at times replaces illness concepts with oddness concepts. Ruth Benedict, cited above, stresses that judgments of mental illness depend heavily upon cultural values. She regards a "normal" action as one which falls within the limits of expected behavior. Interrelated judgments of the "normal" and the "good" vary widely from culture to culture. Benedict suggests that those whom our culture considers bizarrely psychotic might receive marked veneration in a culture where greater value is placed upon the mystical and the occult. Benedict also stresses that the aggressive businessman whose behavior is so esteemed in Western society would be treated with scornful contempt in any other social system.

The moral judgment that a person's behavior is so deviant that psychiatric treatment and institutional confinement is required may be anthropologically viewed as depending not upon impairment in psychological functioning but upon an inability to act in socially acceptable ways. A corollary of this postulate is that quite disturbed individuals can remain in the community, euphemistically diagnosed as ambulatory schizophrenics, if they are observed by a psychiatrist. A further corollary is that ambulatory schizophrenics become clinical when their behavior deviates far enough from the norm to annoy or embarrass others. Then their confinement is justified on the basis that they are dangerous. The unstructured behavior of the bizarrely psychotic does occasionally pose the danger of physical harm, but most often the dangerous nature of his behavior lies in its threat to the social structure.

Irwin Berg has investigated the relationship between behavioral deviancy and various diagnosed forms of psychopathology. His work is empirical, and he does not attempt to relate his findings to any particular theory of psychopathology. He does claim (1957), however, that when deviant behavior occurs in a seemingly innocuous test situation, it is part of a general pattern of response to any atypical stimulus. He hypothesizes that a deviant response in a noncritical area, such as selecting an abstract design, can indicate deviancies in more critical areas of social behavior. He believes that these deviancies are associated with symptoms of neurosis and psychosis. Berg and Adams (1965) report support for this deviation hypothesis among neurotics and psychotics, as well as among those diagnosed as suffering from character disorder, immaturity, and mental retardation.

Lack of Adequate Socialization

If socially deviant responses are often symptoms of a general inability to conform to basic social demands, the causes should be discovered. A social point of view sees such social deviancy as the result of a failure to be adequately socialized. In other words, the deviating individual remains an undersocialized human being who has not had an adequate opportunity to assimilate cultural norms and expectations.

Social alternatives may view abnormal behavior as the result of inadequacies in the culture or subculture. A society may be so disorganized that it is unable to socialize its younger members adequately or, alternatively, a society may be unable to keep up with social change so that its norms and values may be inappropriate for a new set of social conditions. Sociological field studies have been made of both social situations, and although experimental control is obviously lacking, these studies provide data which are easily interpreted as confirming cultural differences in the type and extent of psychiatric impairment.

The social variable which has received the greatest amount of attention is that of socioeconomic status. The vast amount of data accumulated over the years indicates a sharp increase in the incidence of institutional commitment for mental illness as one goes down the socioeconomic ladder. While earlier studies made no effort to control for obviously contaminating variables, more recent studies such as the Midtown Manhattan Study (Srole, 1962) have made serious attempts to keep constant the variables which are more obviously related to social class. The results of the Midtown Manhattan Study show (Langner and Michael, 1963) a relationship between low socioeconomic class and high psychiatric impairment even when allowance is made for the greater environmental stress to which lower classes are subjected.

Zigler and Phillips also attempt to demonstrate empirically that an impoverished social background is likely to produce later psychopathology. Finding that hospitalized individuals are predominantly drawn from lower socioeconomic groups, they attribute psychiatric impairment to lack of social competency (1960). In their opinion, this deficiency in turn is due to a lower level of development among socially deprived subcultures. In later studies, they relate their measure of social competency to different dimensions of psychopathology, and they conclude that the social-competency dimension applies to all types of psychopathology: "In such a schema the various disorders are viewed as inappropriate solutions to the problems of living at various levels of development" (1962, p. 220).

Lack of Social Acceptance

Instead of blaming a lack of adequate socialization upon the entire culture, one may blame an unhealthy family milieu. As a result of social rejection by the parents who are themselves neurotic, the individual may develop a burnt-child reaction, behaving in a fearful and therefore an abnormal fashion in later social situations. Justification for this interpretation can easily be found in learning theory. The last chapter discussed how avoidance behavior and other deviant responses can be explained by the neurotic paradox. Avoidance behavior is self-reinforcing because it reduces anxiety by "tuning out" the stressful social situation. Avoiding closeness with others reduces the social threat, but it also deprives the person of needed social warmth and affection.

Karen Horney (1937) believes that the neurotic is a person responding to a basic anxiety which results from an early childhood fear of abandonment by ambivalent parents. The adult neurotic remains motivated by the attempt to resolve the same conflict between love and aggression which he first experienced in his relationship with his mother. The relationships he forms as an adult are attempts to compromise between dependence and aggression by selecting to move against, towards, or away from others. None of these three modes of social interaction can be successful; they result in a vicious circle. Because his behavior succeeds only in eliciting rejection from other people, the neurotic becomes even more frustrated in his social relationships.

Horney (1942) illustrates her conception of the neurotic by describing a thirty-year-old magazine editor named Clare. Clare suffers from constant fatigue and lacks self-confidence; these two symptoms prevent her from being maximally productive in her work. Horney describes Clare as an unwanted child who was born after the mother had unsuccessfully tried to have abortions. Clare was rejected both by her mother, who preferred her older brother, and by her father, who was generally absent from home. Clare gained attention only one way. Because her mother thrived on others' admiration, Clare learned that she could win her mother's approval by feeding her this need. Clare was forced to pay a heavy price for her mother's affection, however, because she had to forgo making critical judgments about others. Gradually she lost the capacity for independent thought as she constantly forced herself to respect the feelings of others. The results were not satisfying; inevitably Clare felt she was stupid and the compulsive nature of her dependence made her uncomfortable.

Harry Stack Sullivan (1953) has somewhat similarly traced the origin of psychotic reactions to infant mothering. When an infant's need for tenderness is frustrated by a physiological tension produced by the mother's anxiety, he develops the self system as a defense. In milder forms of psychopathology the self system successfully fends off anxiety by a variety of defense dynamisms, such as dissociation and selective inattention. When the social threat posed by significant others becomes too great, these dynamisms will no longer work and the self system disintegrates, losing control of consciousness. As the schizophrenic seeks to regain control, he may seek to externalize the conflict. He typically uses the paranoid dynamism, which Sullivan defines as "the travail of the self in attempting to patch up some kind of security with the persons of the environment" (1956, p. 350).

Sullivan (1956) illustrates the development of the paranoid dynamism by a preadolescent boy who had received only minute acceptance as a human being in his early years. When the boy entered school, he tried to win the approval of his peers by misbehaving. After he discovered that his schoolmates were interested in him as a problem character and not as a person, he attempted to gain approval by entertaining them with grandiose accounts of his past. Although he was a liar, the boy was not yet psychotic. He did become paranoid, however, when he needed to be intimate with a fellow human being. As he tried to seek out others of his age as potential friends, intimates, or chums, he kept telling himself that others would have no use for him because he was too inferior to get what he must have. Because conscious awareness of this dilemma was intolerable for the boy, he warded off the threat by blaming others for his predicament and developed a persecutory system to make this threat believable.

Lack of Social Responsibility

In the preceding sections, the individual's failure to adjust is blamed on others and failure is ascribed either to the culture or to the family. A reaction in some quarters against blaming others for one's failure to adjust currently focuses on the individual's counterbalancing responsibility to society. The last chapter discussed man's interrelated needs for adapting to basic sanctions and for identifying with a social community, needs which presuppose that man learns to curb his own desires enough to meet certain basic social demands. Psychopathology can also be regarded as a frustration of a need for experiencing a sense of moral solidarity or a "we" feeling with other members of one's culture.

The failure to respond to the basic social demands of significant others in one's culture has been called guilt. Freud believes that guilt develops in the superego as an internalized parental voice, but he does not take the experience seriously because he regards the superego as only a secondary part of personality. He regards the primary task of psychoanalysis as that of weakening the superego to release instinctual gratification of the libido. Freud believes that obtaining release of physical tensions is more important than pleasing others.

A social value orientation reverses Freud's moral judgment. It claims that while frustration of prurient impulses is likely to be of only temporary discomfort to the sexually frustrated individual, shame and guilt are apt to last much longer. Furthermore, debilitating symptoms result from the combination of anxiety, guilt, and shame that one experiences when he violates social values and outrages the moral expectancies of significant others. Subjective discomfort is attributed, not to physiological frustration, but to the pangs of an outraged conscience. Good adjustment consists in responding appropriately to the urgings of the superego rather than obeying the id when expressions of libidinal impulse violate sanctioned social expectations.

This inversion of Freudian logic is basic to the guilt theory of psychopathology of O. Hobart Mowrer. Mowrer believes that psychopathological states are caused by quite tangible wrongdoing on the part of the individual, who thereafter suffers guilt and anxiety from fear that others will discover his violation and will punish him. Mowrer is quite adamant about this expectation of being caught: "My own personal and professional experience and that of a small but growing number of other psychologists, psychiatrists, and social workers shows that the so-called psychoneuroses and functional psychoses can be understood only (*sola!*) in terms of palpable misconduct which has been neither confessed nor expiated" (1964, p. 20).

Mowrer regards the neurotic as an individual whose symptoms provide needed punishment for misdeeds. He notes that the neurotic eventually cures himself by expiating his sins through the punishment of the self-blame by anxiety and depression. The schizophrenic may be no more guilty than the neurotic, but typically he is unwilling to atone for his sins. Instead he organizes his whole life around attempts to conceal his guilt by resorting to a bizarre and noncommunicative use of language lest in an unguarded moment he reveal his past social transgressions. Of all mental-health problems, only the psychopath is free from guilt. The psychopath has also committed tangible wrongs, but he is an "underdone" human being whose failure to be adequately socialized spares him the more "normal" experience of an outraged conscience.

Mowrer seems deliberately to choose terms which will have the greatest shock value; therefore his theories become needlessly controversial. What Mowrer regards as good or evil differs little if any from the views of other theorists cited in this chapter. For Mowrer, the basic virtue is truthfulness because he values man's ability to be open with significant others. The unforgivable sin is the lie, which he regards as pathological because it results in an eventual inability to reveal one's inner feelings to others. The lie is also bad because it perpetuates a hypocrisy which closes the social channels of meaningful social relationship. Sin in the Mowrer lexicon is not the transgression of an absolute and inflexible divine law; it is an out-rage of the basic expectations of those with whom one attempts to maintain a sense of community.

COUNSELING AND PSYCHOTHERAPY

The task of socially oriented psychotherapy is to reknit sundered social ties and to reawaken the client's sense of identity with a surrounding social community. Within a social orientation, therapists use dissimilar means to reach basically the same ends. Counselors and psychotherapists who are guided by social values often define the therapeutic task in terms of the same one-to-one relation as do the other alternatives to mental health. Therapists may often feel that group approaches are more effective and they may consider treatment in the larger context of improving the whole of one's social environment.

Social Attitudes

The purpose of therapy within such a social context may first of all be seen as helping the client to broaden his understanding of his social behavior. The therapist tries to help the client discover more appropriate ways of responding to social situations. Therapy thus becomes a cognitive learning situation whose task is to get the patient to change various perceptions and attitudes affecting the ways he relates to others. In its simplest form such psychotherapy is merely information giving or rather moralistic urging; however, therapeutic techniques may become as complex as any other form of therapy that seeks to produce insight. The therapist is generally regarded as a person who shows great cognitive perspicacity in assessing the dynamic picture but who is also socially adroit in the relationship so that his presence helps the client to relax his defenses.

Harry Stack Sullivan regards the therapist as an expert in inter-personal relationships. The role of such an expert seems relatively impersonal because he performs service like any other professional "who derives his income and status, one or both, from the use of unusually exact or adequate information about his particular field, in the service of others" (1954, p. 11).

Since the dominant role of a Sullivanian therapist is that of an expert in interpersonal relationships, he avoids at one extreme that marked professional anonymity which might lure the patient into regarding him as a parent substitute. At the other extreme the therapist avoids becoming so involved with the patient's problems that his own intense reactions prevent his rendering an objective professional service.

Sullivan believes that the therapist can be of most benefit to a client in the middle ground between these extremes. (While Sullivan uses the term patient, the term client seems much more appropriate in context.) By presenting himself as a professional to the potential client, the therapist is able to convince him that he is not "trafficking in the ordinary commodities of interpersonal relations" (1954, p. 13) as are others to whom the client feels unable to confide his problems. This confidence must not be misplaced. The therapist must be sufficiently skilled in his understanding of interpersonal dynamics to avoid raising the customarily high level of anxiety among people seeking psychotherapeutic services. The therapist must give perceivable assistance. The client must feel that each therapeutic session helps him to improve his interpersonal relationships. In other words, the client needs an immediate return for what he has given the therapist in terms of money and of the pain of self-revelation. Such a *quid pro quo* provides the client with the necessary motivation to continue the painful business of communicating his personal problems to another.

While therapists such as Sullivan attempt to change social attitudes by making the client more aware of why his human relationships are so traumatic, other therapists seek to change the will and the emotions. For them the therapeutic task is more than broadening the patient's understanding of how his social behaviors may become more effective; it also includes motivating the client to change his socially inappropriate behaviors.

Alfred Adler regards the basic task of therapy as that of eliciting a rudimentary form of the social interest he believed is the essential criterion for maturity. Adler appears to have been quite flexible in the method which he used, adapting whatever variation of "the carrot or the stick approach" was most appropriate for the therapeutic circumstances (Ansbacher and Ansbacher, 1956). Upon occasion Adler would cite the pleasantness of the relationship between patient and therapist as evidence of the value of a good social relationship which the patient might thereafter develop with others. At other times the therapist's task would be to attack rather actively a style of life which remained impervious to gentler forms of suggestion.

Hobart Mowrer similarly believes that the therapist must motivate the client to become socially more responsible. He feels that the development of a sense of responsibility for one's misdeeds will stimulate the patient to restore himself to the good graces of those in his social milieu. While Mowrer remains silent about the details of how psychotherapy is best practiced, he has been quite insistent that the only cure either for the neurotic or psychotic is an active attempt at social restoration which involves confession and expiation. Presumably these acts are best done outside of therapy, although Mowrer (1964) notes that the high financial payments which the patient must make to the therapist may be a form of expiation and an important part of the cure.

Therapeutic Relationships

While little agreement exists about anything else in psychotherapy, the therapeutic encounter is indisputably a social situation in which the behavior of the client and the therapist must be understood according to principles of interpersonal dynamics. Because of this fact, many therapists view the relationship as typical of other types of social relationships in which the client becomes involved. In this way therapy becomes a learning situation in which the patient learns to relate to the therapist in a way that is new and significantly better than his former modes of adjusting. Eventually the patient's relationship with the therapist must come to an end, but by this time the patient will be able to generalize from the therapeutic relationship to other significant social relationships.

The last chapter stated that naturalistic alternatives to mental health regarded psychotherapy as a social learning situation in which the client "improved" by having his fears extinguished through the permissive attitudes of the therapist or through learning new social responses which were antagonistic to the old fear responses. Although therapists such as Stampfl and Wolpe emphasize that the purpose of psychotherapy is to reduce physiological tensions, one can also regard therapy from a learning-theory viewpoint as teaching the client a new social adaptation. A distinction can be made within learning theory between approaches which emphasize the satisfaction of biological needs and those which seek to meet social needs. Edward J. Murray (1963) thus distinguishes between what he terms biotropic and sociotropic learning-theory approaches in psychotherapy. The biotropic approach, which Murray describes as symptom centered and manipulative, is oriented to classical conditioning techniques which reinforce reduction in physiological drives. In contrast, the sociotropic approach emphasizes learning acquired social needs. While the biotropic approach is oriented to physiological reality, the sociotropic approach seems rather closely oriented to social values.

Murray recognizes that the distinction between biotropic and sociotropic approaches is not absolute but represents a continuum. He places Wolpe, Salter, and Eysenck on the biotropic end of the continuum and Dollard and Miller, Mowrer, Shoben, and himself on the sociotropic end. Perhaps the most clearcut example of a sociotropic approach is found in E. J. Shoben, who describes psychotherapy (1953) as a social-learning situation which is a microcosm of more general patterns of relating. Since the patient's anxiety has been increased by past social learning situations where punishment has occurred, he must first be made comfortable. The therapeutic relationship must be warm, permissive, safe, and understanding. The therapist allows anxiety to be extinguished by means of a permissive relationship, and in addition he positively reinforces desirable social responses which the client had previously avoided from fear. If the client is to be helped to relate better to other people permanently, he must learn to relate to others in the same way that he has to the therapist. This change occurs through a process of generalization. The ease with which the client has learned to react in the therapy session is now transferred to a more general social situation. Shoben (1960) also describes the therapeutic experience as one in which the neurotic learns to be more loving. Since the neurotic has had basic difficulties in interpersonal relationships, being both unloved and unloving, therapy provides the more mature experience of love which will enable him to overcome loneliness.

For Ann Magaret (1950), psychotherapy is a slightly different type of social learning situation. Its purpose is to help the client develop a new learning set with which to respond to general social situations. The key to successful social change again is generalization, which Magaret constructs as a principle of successful learning from field theory, learning-set theory, and reinforcement theory. Because patients requiring psychotherapy have a learning set which is wrong as well as persistent, the new attitudes provided by therapy are designed to be much more flexible.

If learning-theory approaches can be applied to social values, humanistic values should also serve to improve socialization. The term client centered, which Carl Rogers uses to describe his therapeutic style, could with equal accuracy describe relationship therapy. As a necessary condition of therapeutic change, Rogers (1957a) stresses the "psychological contact" of the client and therapist. He gives as a second necessary condition the patient's perception that he is understood and accepted. Rogers (1958a) describes a number of characteristics for a helping relationship. In order to be helpful, the therapist must enter fully into the world of the client's feelings, remaining acceptant of each facet of the client's personality. When the client perceives these attitudes, a process of sharing occurs which Rogers compares with the dialogue of Martin Buber (1965). Through a shared encounter the therapist confirms and makes real the client's potentialities.

The experiential psychotherapy of Whitaker and Malone (1953) similarly places great emphasis on the quality of interpersonal relationships. They describe psychotherapy as "an interpersonal operation in which the total organismic adaptation of one individual is catalyzed by another individual in such a way that the patient's level of adaptive capacity is increased" (1953, p. 49). Whitaker and Malone's primary value, like Carl Rogers's, is not the patient's social adjustment but his organismic adaptation. The psychotherapeutic relationship becomes the way in which the patient is enabled to integrate what Whitaker and Malone term the biological effects of past experience with a current social experiencing.

Group Therapy

Psychotherapy is customarily understood as a one-to-one relationship between a patient and a therapist. Since social alternatives see man as an inseparable part of his culture, treatment guided by social values does not limit therapy to one-to-one relationships. Group psychotherapy enables the client to develop in depth the types of relatedness which can not be secured in the comparatively solitary traditional one-to-one relationship.

Group psychotherapy may first be seen as providing a "real-life" social situation which can be made to approximate significant social problem areas of the client's life. Various family therapies (for example, Ackerman, 1958; Satir, 1964) consider essential the presence of all the concerned parties in the family conflict in a group situation in which they are encouraged to communicate more effectively and to respond more appropriately to each other's feelings. Other group therapists have developed techniques which enable the client to practice different social responses in more neutral social interactions. Psychodrama, as developed by J. L. Moreno (1946), provides the client with the opportunity to try out different social roles in "playacting" situations in which other patients become social protagonists.

Group therapy also provides the client with the support, encouragement, or fellowship he needs to mobilize his various emotional resources. Indeed, Moreno ascribes his discovery of psychodrama to the observation that professional actors onstage become much more lifelike when they throw away the script. He believes that anyone can become more spontaneous and animated when he develops the freedom to act upon his inner impulses in a supportive social environment. Individual social facilitation has more recently become the basis for the so-called T-group approach. Bradfield, Gibb, and Benne (1964) describe the T group as a miniature society whose members "work to stimulate and support one another's learning within that society" (1964, p. 1). They ascribe the effectiveness of the T group to the fact that the group can mobilize its forces to support the growth of its members as individuals.

Group therapy may finally be seen as providing the individual with shared social experiences that he lacks in an anonymous and impersonal larger society. The mutuality, fellowship, and community of a small group are regarded as being significant in their own right. Sociodrama, which provides such an organic unity, Moreno (1944) defines as "a deep-action method dealing with intergroup relations and collective ideologies" (1944, p. 3), in contrast to the psychodrama, which is concerned with interpersonal relations and private ideologies. The T-group approach also emphasizes the development of a sense of "we feeling." Bradfield, Gibb, and Benne (1964) stress that mobilized group forces must simultaneously support the growth of its members as individuals and as collaborators. Benne (1961) similarly describes the purpose of the training group as providing fraternity. While some kinds of fraternity can stultify man's sense of individuality, the ideal miniature society of the T group makes fraternity congruent with other value orientations. He concludes that "training groups demonstrate that, at least under special circumstances, the practical difficulties of making fraternity serve the disciplines of liberty and equality can be overcome" (1961, p. 240).

GOALS

Social orientations to mental health tend to be in professional ill repute because they are often carelessly or needlessly associated with values which emphasize conformity and adjustment. Certainly many practitioners in mental health have overemphasized the need for cooperation so that group demands have been allowed to interfere with individual needs. Social alternatives, however, can set before man more positive social goals than blind obedience to the social status quo.

Improved Human Relationships

A popular stereotype has developed that the world contains two types of people, introverts and extroverts; the former are termed neurotic because they avoid people and the latter are considered normal because they are gregarious. This popular interpretation confuses mental health with the frequency and extensiveness of social encounter; obviously one can also evaluate social relations for their intensiveness. The criterion of health then becomes the quality of one's relationships with others, rather than its mere quantity.

Evaluating the quality of relationships has two advantages. First, one need not approve social behavior which is not motivated by a genuine social interest, but is driven by a selfish need to manipulate people for other ends. Certainly much social behavior in our culture is motivated by what Fromm terms a marketing orientation, which requires the personality to become in effect a marketable commodity similar to any other economic product. Clearly "gladhand" behavior which is an artificial attempt to "win friends and influence people" must be differentiated from more spontaneous social interactions.

A second advantage to judging human social behavior by its quality is that it provides a reference point with a positive and a negative pole. Behavior can be judged by the degree to which it surpasses a mode or an average, as well as by the degree to which it fails to reach a norm. The ideal for personal interrelationships remains somewhat vague, but nevertheless it provides a transcendental norm toward which all men may direct their social endeavors.

Ideal qualities in human social relationships are described by Martin Buber (1947), who contrasts a social life of dialogue with one of monologue. Buber describes dialogue in terms of I-Thou relationships. It is crucial for Buber that man faces another human being as an I beholding a Thou, not as an I beholding an It. Facing the other person requires one to realize that the relationship between the I and the Thou is personal and demands man's total involvement. Indeed, the I-Thou relationship becomes all encompassing, the reality of dialogue dissolving whatever barriers the individual consciousness had set up between self and object. Whatever reality the I has is the result of encounter with the Thou; through the Thou a man becomes I. Man's further development occurs through active confrontation of what is personal in his world.

A Better Culture

If man can transcend what is normal and average in interpersonal contacts by relating with others at increasingly deeper levels, he can also transcend the average by building a better culture in which the whole social norm is raised. Man is told to transcend what is narrow and parochial in his culture and to grasp the vision of a broader and more humanistic viewpoint which expresses a far broader range of human experience.

The man who uses his capacity for symbolic and communicative processes can transcend the values of his immediate group, and he is then in a position to raise the quality of the whole culture. By refusing to conform to narrow cultural expectancies with their limited grasp of human potential, man adapts the social milieu to his needs.

The quest for a transcultural ideal has been actively pursued by E. J. Shoben. Shoben is a man of wide-ranging philosophical interests whose viewpoints transcend narrow categorization. Over the years his writings reflect a struggle to resolve the dilemma of how man can adapt to his social environment and yet take full advantage of the capacity for symbolizing which allows him to become "the only creature who can look before and after and pine for what is not" (1957, p. 185). While Shoben notes that man has the ability to stand apart from his culture, he also notes that man seems most enthralled by tasks involving participation with others to achieve a shared goal.

Shoben seeks to resolve the human dilemma created by the individual and the social sides of man's nature by enlisting man's capacity to transcend his environment to build a higher cultural order. As he sees it, culture is distinctively human, being in fact the product of the human ego. Shoben views the history of culture as the history of ego development; the unfolding of historical events is an accurate reflection of the degree to which the human being in the culture is ego governed.

Shoben's transcultural ideal is in one sense the ideal which the humanist creates for the individual written large upon the whole society. Thus, "metaphorically and analogically . . . the development of culture is reminiscent of the development of the individual from a superstitious, ego-limited, demanding infant to a more understanding, reality-oriented adult with a wide range of identifications and an acquired ability to discriminate among alternatives and to delay conscious values" (1961, p. 407). Such an ideal culture is also a place where man can enter wholeheartedly into a common social task where ideals can be shared among all. Shoben can but ask what all the virtues would be in such a society built on cooperation.

What kind of world would be ours if we were less concerned about achievement and more fully occupied with understanding each other, participating more wholeheartedly in the corporate venture of building a society which provides more challenges and more satisfactions for more people, and developed a sense of worthwhileness of intimate relationships marked by a high degree of cherishing and the mutual pursuit of essentially private interests? (1956, pp. 330-331)

CRITICISM OF SOCIAL VALUES

If contemporary society can validly be regarded as being other-oriented, a social orientation has the advantage of being most immediately relevant to it. When social conditions make other people the most tangible reality, a socially oriented ideology can be most immediately helpful to individuals who feel that other people's approval has become their most important need. If mental health no longer meets general social needs, social alternatives would seem to have the broadest and most basic support, and evidence supports this view. In a rather extensive survey of self-reports on happiness in the general population Bradburn and Caplovitz (1965) found that positive feelings about being happy were associated with higher rates of social interaction and active engagement in the environment. In what seems to be a representative study, Merl E. Bonney (1964) asked college students to nominate those of their acquaintances who were "highly normal," and found on the basis of test data that the persons selected were heavily involved in interpersonal rapport and in overt social adjustments.

The Dangers of Social Conformity

Many regard the apparent popularity of social values as its own greatest disadvantage. They fear that mass convergence toward a common social value will lead a mass man to stampede in blind obedience to a herd instinct until all types of individualistic value will be trampled underfoot. The literature contains a considerable body of writings which question the desirability of being too well adjusted to one's surroundings. Hadley Cantril notes that "the biographies of most creative persons in every field reveal an unusual loneliness" (1950, p. 124). In this spirit psychiatrist Louis Bisch has written a book for the popular market titled *Be Glad You're Neurotic* (1936), in which he assails the notion that it is good to be normal and bad to be different. Those who comprise the mediocre average are, as Bisch notes, often quite happy. In his view, however, it is far better to be dissatisfied and unhappy with one's life even if this means one becomes anxious and therefore "neurotic."

Social conformity is attacked by both the humanistic orientation and the naturalistic system. The most systematic and thoughtful discussion of the evils of conformity from a humanistic point of view is made by Erich Fromm. In *Escape from Freedom* (1941) he describes man's panicked flight to an external authority as part of "a compulsive conforming in the process of which the isolated individual becomes an automaton, loses his self, and yet at the same time consciously conceives of himself as free and subject only to himself" (1941, p. 241). Fromm describes the unfortunate consequences of man's escape from individuality in his later books. In *Man for Himself* (1947) he describes the evils of the marketing orientation in which the competitive demands of the social market-place force man to sell himself as a standardized economic commodity. Fromm views the marketplace as bad because it demands that man enslave himself to the expectations of others. In *The Sane Society* (1955) he examines the unfortunate consequences of the social ill health of the entire society, noting that there is a *folie à millions,* just as there is a *folie à deux.* Fromm concludes: "The fact that millions of people share the same vices does not make these vices virtues, the fact that they share so many errors does not make the errors to be truths, and the fact that millions of people share the same forms of mental pathology does not make these people sane" (1955, p. 16).

Conformity is also attacked by psychoanalyst Robert Lindner, who decries the soft message of what he regards as a cult of surrender. When the entire society is sick he fears that psychothera-pists will be sorely tempted, like the Biblical false prophets, to take their ease in Zion and to cry "peace, peace, when there is no peace." Lindner vituperatively denounces the therapists' attempts to adjust the individual to an imperfect society. He denounces the values of what he considers to be a majority of the so-called helping professions.

> We are, therefore, I believe entitled to say that most of the accomplishments proudly claimed by members of these profes-sional groups—most of the magic advertised by psychiatry, some of what passes for psychoanalysis, much of clinical psychology, all of religion, and a good deal of the less pretentious arts of medicine and social service—is based upon a cult of passivity and surrender. The transformations worked by the applications of these disciplines are founded upon renunciation and little more. Such wonder-working claims as they make are, thus, by and large specious; and to speak of their "successes" as "cures," or as pro-found alterations of lasting individual or social benefit is to pile falsehood upon untruth. They operate chiefly by the process of weaning a sufferer from the *form* of protest which expressed his woe, and they ignore the woe itself (1952, p. 17).

Lindner believes that every man has the instinct to rebel. He regards society's demand to conform and suppress as an Eleventh Commandment. Stifling the impulse to individuality is instilled in early childhood "by the insidious connection of morality and ethics with functions of toilet and table" (1952, p. 68). Restraint continues in the proletarianization of the mass man, who "has come to embody within himself all the traits and characteristics which are standard, ubiquitous, and mediocre in the world in which he moves" (1962, p. 157). The result is the suppression of all that Lindner deems to be good in man: "Corralled in body and enervated in spirit by these delegated, elected, or self-appointed herdsmen of humanity, our society has been seized and held captive by the delusion that adjustment is the whole of life, its ultimate good" (1952, p. 67).

The Ambiguity of Social Values

Man's present social situation does not offer any particularly obvious social values for his rebellion. If the present social views contain any consensus, it is that so-called mass man is disillusioned with the older values which the past generations found so comforting. As one listens for the voice of social command, all one is apt to hear is a howling chorus of dissent from an increasingly vocal new generation whose only common social bond is the camaraderie of moral revolution.

One can criticize social alternatives from a moral vantage point quite the opposite to the one Fromm and Lindner use. One can maintain that all social values (including the psychoanalytic value orientation of Lindner and the humanistic value system of Fromm) are social in the sense that they are nurtured and transmitted within a social context. The problem is not that man must choose to conform or to rebel against social values, but that he lacks a meaningful basis for choosing among different and actively competitive social values.

The current controversy over the nature of psychotherapy provides an excellent example of the general bewilderment that can result from trying to orient oneself to general social values. According to Arnold Green (1946), all behavior that results in a need for psychotherapy is social in the sense that it involves conflict between personal and social values. In Green's view, the process of choosing values is further complicated by the intrusion of the therapist's values, so that at times three different sets of values are in conflict. Green states that "the history of psychotherapy can be viewed as an unsuccessful struggle to evaluate the role of social values [which] are simply standards of morality, and conceptions of others' welfare supported by the groups of which the given person is a part" (1946, p. 199). Since Green wrote those words the situation has surely become worse. The recent proliferation of different types of therapy reflects an increasing diffusion in the way society seeks to direct the individual to the good life.

Even if one assumes that it is good for man to adapt to his social surroundings, the contemporary individual finds an adjustment to a social system in as much flux as ours to be a doubtful undertaking. To relate harmoniously with rapidly changing surroundings requires nimble social reflexes because adjusting to social change is like leaping from a stationary platform to a rapidly moving train. However, if man's destiny is seen as entering into a dynamic encounter with social other, this accomplishment is similarly fraught with peril. In the fog of an anonymous impersonality, interpersonal relationships with others who are equivocal in their humanity become more difficult.

The individual who attempts to orient himself by contemporary social values is in a sense building on sand when the rain is already falling. The individual who seeks direction from an other-directed truth finds that he has myriad masters, and none of them is constant or abiding in his moral standards. In a culture where social expectations remain unfocused, pleasing others requires a chameleonlike mode of adjustment.

The social irony is that the hypocrisy of being all things to all men is increasingly condemned by a younger generation who perceive the false mask of traditional values. The new generation is in Lindner's term a rebel without a cause because it has not been able to find social values which it feels are worthy of allegiance. Those who seek guidance from contemporary culture are not likely to conform to a given standard of adjustment for very long. Instead, they must inevitably find themselves rent by conflict among different standards of conduct.

SUMMARY

Social meanings are applied to mental health by personality theorists who stress the importance of social nurturance and social relatedness. In a rational historic period, man but dimly perceived himself as a social animal. In our postrational period, other people impinge upon one's life in a more direct manner in a more crowded social space, and as a result, man is more often reminded of the implications of his social involvement in his culture. To the extent that contemporary culture has ceased being inner directed, man is more aware of other's influence upon his destiny. Proponents of a social view of mental health do not usually suggest that the individual should conform to the demands and expectations of others, but they do value relatedness that produces experiences of mutuality or community with other human beings.

 *Chapter 8*

EXISTENTIAL MEANINGS

"This sickness is not unto death" (John 11:4), and yet Lazarus died; for when the disciples misunderstood the words which Christ adjoined later, "Lazarus our friend is asleep, but I go to wake him out of his sleep" (11:11), He said plainly, "Lazarus is dead." So then Lazarus is dead, and yet this sickness was not unto death. . . . SICKNESS UNTO DEATH, Søren Kierkegaard

The fourth and final set of mental-health meanings is the existential. Although existentialism and humanism both cherish individualistic values and would thus appear to complete the circle in this approach to values, the existentialist esteems an individualism that is quite different from the self-affirmation of humanism. Existential values have largely taken root in a younger generation raised during a depression or a war in a new culture in which the old humanistic values can not have the same meaning. The optimism born of belief in the inevitability of human progress has died. Man must now seek his identity in an emotional context of despair and negation.

Because existentialism is not a unified system of thought, generalizations about it are little more than half-truths. In terms of differentiating between it and other mental-health alternatives, existentialism's most distinguishing characteristic is its inward or phenomenological orientation. This inward scrutiny differs from humanistic alternatives, which anticipate a place and time in which man seems destined to rule; from naturalistic alternatives, which look back to man's animal past for signs of his destiny; and from social alternatives, which look to society for signs of man's fulfillment.

Perhaps most distinctive of existentialism's moral values is its emphasis on inner experience, which must ultimately be subjective. The existentialist seeks his own intensely personal experience of good and evil in his experience of being in the world in a particular instant in space and time.

HISTORICAL FOUNDATIONS

The beginning of existentialism is generally linked with the impending breakup of the Victorian way of life during the last part of the nineteenth century. This style of life came abruptly crashing down with the outbreak of the First World War. Paul Tillich (1952) notes that on July 31, 1914, existentialism ceased to be a revolt and became the mirror of an experienced reality. Old beliefs in the inevitability of human progress and the inherent rationality of human thought were shattered. Many individuals experienced an inner turmoil born of despair at the increasing superficiality of the Protestant ethic and unrestrained individualism as values.

Into a social substratum of disillusionment and social conflict existentialism, as well as psychoanalysis, sank its roots. Rollo May (1958) describes how both arose from the same cultural situation as social responses to an increasing fragmentation and compartment-alization of personality. Both occurred as a result of an industrial revolution which depersonalized human worth even as it increased wealth.

Much of what Chapter Four says about psychoanalysis as a natural result of an impending breakdown in rational values also applies to existentialism. Even more than psychoanalysis, existential-ism results from disillusionment with the ability of inner-oriented values to provide a reliable sense of direction. The nihilism that much of existentialism approaches reflects the despair man experi-ences when he starts to disbelieve the old absolutes. Increasing skepticism about the reliability of gyroscopic self-positioning creates the intolerable feeling of *angst*.

Søren Kierkegaard and Friedrich Nietzsche are the patriarchs of existentialism. Each in his own way experienced only emptiness in existing social values. Kierkegaard was a thoroughly inner-oriented man who remained impervious to social pressures to curb an indi-viduality that became heretical by midnineteenth century. Older humanistic ideals were now gone, menaced on every side. May (1958) points out that the individual of Kierkegaard's day was being swallowed rationally by Hegelian philosophy, economically by the increasing objectification of the person, and morally and spirit-ually by soft and vapid religion. Renaissance individualism, which was personified by a swashbuckling adventurer, had shriveled into the distasteful melancholy personified by Kierkegaard's own life.

Friedrich Nietzsche shared with Kierkegaard an awareness of the thinness of the veneer of nineteenth-century values. Rather than the brooding self-despair of Kierkegaard, however, Nietzsche chose a vainglorious self-affirmation. If man must indeed despair at the death of the gods, he must go on living as if nothing had happened. Although Nietzsche chose the will to power over the self-contemplating dread of Kierkegaard, the result was equally as devastating for rational individualism. If all the gods were dead, only the self was left, a self which in Nietzsche's later years was tinged with madness. If man killed God because he could not stand God looking upon his inner self, then man himself is forced to avoid the reality of his inner-directed individualism. William Barrett writes: "The fantasies, the delusions, the grandiose inflation of the ego are only devices to shield him from the sight of the *other side of himself*—of Nietzsche, the sickly lonely man, emotionally starved, a ghost flitting from place to place, always without a home—the dwarf side, that is, of the giant about whom he boasts" (1958, p. 162).

Kierkegaard and Nietzsche were essentially men who lived before their time. Being extra sensitive to the increasingly heavy pressure of culture upon individuality, they felt what few of their contemporaries dared to experience. Socially alert, both were ostracized by the very individualism which they sought to protect. The inner direction of which Kierkegaard and Nietzsche were in their different ways the finest examples had hardened into an individual so encapsulated by social conventions that he could experience only horror at real individualism.

Today, however, the situation is far different. The First World War dramatically ripped away the Victorian facade, whose artificiality Kierkegaard and Nietzsche had first decried. The few traditionalists in Western Europe who could return from World War I with faith in the infallibility of reason and the inevitability of human progress had their values finally shattered by the Great Depression and Second World War. Once the gyroscope of inner direction started to wobble from the fixed point of reason—as it did for the typical European in August, 1914—man could no longer adhere to that amalgam of social morality which had been hardening since the Renaissance. Existentialism has appealed to those who have groped for new meaning in what they perceive to be a moral blackness. As old truths which had so long seemed self-evident suddenly lost all meaning, twentieth-century man has had to find new moral values. And he is still groping for answers.

Although existentialism is viewed historically as a response to social change, not everyone reacts to change in the same way. This difference explains the varied existential responses to the changed human life.

The first view of the human condition is the bleak, atheistic outlook of Friedrich Nietzsche. God remains dead. The possibilities that man can come into his own through the contemporary social structure seem even more remote for such contemporary existentialists as Albert Camus and Jean-Paul Sartre. With at least partial justification, this form of existentialism is popularly identified with beatnik causes and with nihilism. The existentialist of atheism and pessimism shares with the true beatnik and the hippie a disdain for conventional social endeavors because their moral values are false and hypocritical. In the absence of all other possibilities for human fulfillment, atheistic existentialism rebels against the artificial and the conventional.

Kierkegaard remained pessimistic about man's social destiny; nevertheless, he found a reconciliation with God. For Christian existentialism *being* is grounded in God and not in rebellion against indifferent fate. Kierkegaard and other Christian existentialists have, with varying vehemence, excoriated conventional or nonexistential Christianity for a triviality which made belief in God too easy; nevertheless, they have stressed the necessity for man to find being in an act of faith and courage in which he asserts the Being of God even when faith may seem absurd.

If nineteenth-century Christian existentialism must be discussed in terms of Søren Kierkegaard, in the twentieth century it has so far been centered in the work of Paul Tillich. For him as for Camus and Sartre, man faces the continual threat of the nonbeing of conventional society. And like Camus and Sartre, Tillich is aware of how easily religion can itself be a refuge from the threat of nothingness. Indeed, Tillich finds contemporary depth psychology more acutely aware than most contemporary forms of theology are of the way in which man is grasped from below by unconscious processes which represent nonbeing. But there is one essential difference between theistic and atheistic existentialism. For Sartre, being consists only in the freedom to rebel against things which would otherwise depersonalize him; for Tillich, man is secured against nonbeing by that "ground of all being" he defines as God. There is for Tillich what he terms (1957) the New Being, in which possession from above destroys the possession of nonbeing from below, elevating the creative power of the ground into the unity of the personal life.

A third existential concern differs from the other two in its distinctively New-World outlook. American existentialism, which lacks the tragic quality imparted to European existentialism by direct and prolonged participation in two world wars, reflects the continued optimism of a culture which has continued to grow dynamically. Americans find it difficult to perceive the human task as the mythical burden of Sisyphus and remain extremely hopeful about continued progress.

Because American existentialists remain optimistic about man and his potential, they do not draw the sharp line between humanistic and existential concerns that European existentialists do. American psychologists and psychiatrists who a generation ago were clearly humanists in the strict philosophical sense recently have gradually assimilated European existential thinking. Since Americans tend to be less philosophical, they reject atheistic and Christian existentialism in favor of a distinctively American credo of the inherent goodness of man.

NEEDS

The most distinguishing characteristic of existentialism is its belief that man must find meaning for his existence in the face of a perpetual crisis in which nonbeing continually threatens to extinguish his individuality. Existentialists use the term being to describe the perennial struggle for affirmation of consciousness or of self against the perennial threat of physical and social annihilation, or nonbeing.

An existential theory of motivation stresses man's need to assert himself against everything that seeks to depersonalize him and render him an object with essence rather than existence. The word exist means literally to "stand out" or to "emerge." Existentialists most often use the participle being to describe the active process of asserting one's existence. Existentialists do not fully agree how man is to exist in the literal sense of standing out against the environment. They are in general agreement, however, that man can resolve the contradictions in his nature only by asserting his individuality in such a way that his affirmation causes him to "stand out" against those forces in nature and in society seeking to quench his individual nature.

Being through Freedom

Modern man despairs because he feels that the individual has lost his freedom due to the depersonalization of mass society. As a result, many existentialists believe that man must detach himself from the larger society and must seek to "go it alone" by finding his own highly individual meaning in life. This new existential freedom is most often sought by the socially dispossessed who seek new values to replace the old moral system which they condemn as inauthentic.

This value orientation is most characteristically found among a youthful generation born and raised after many of the older values collapsed in the Great Depression. These young existentialists characteristically attempt to find an identity in their own ingroup which they feel conventional society lacks. They "drop out" from "square" or conventional society and "turn on" through an expansion of their own idiosyncratic consciousness. These youth are best known for their existential reliance upon drugs, although there are many other ways in which they seek to add to their existence. Perhaps the bond among the so-called beatnik or hippie existentialists is their common attempt to find an identity through a radically new morality which seems appropriate for an individual caught in a chaotic and disjointed world.

The philosophical godfather of so-called beatnik existentialism is generally considered to be Jean-Paul Sartre (1956). For an atheistic existentialist such as Sartre, the essential human need is freedom, but a freedom that differs radically from the traditional humanistic freedom of man to master his environment. Sartre does not believe man needs to be free to affirm his mastery of the universe because he can not do so. Instead, freedom is necessary to deny or negate the control that nonbeing would otherwise have over man. The individual's basic need is for negation because it is only by acting against nonbeing (or what is more often termed the conventional) that man can affirm his existence in the face of an otherwise enveloping nothingness. Man's freedom is to say no, thus refusing to become a thing of the world. The freedom only to negate would seem to the humanist to deny man's potential, but for Sartre this freedom gives man his only real dignity, which is his ability to transcend the being of a thing, unable to act even in a negative fashion.

Similar values lead Albert Camus to postulate man's need to be free in a slightly different way. Being for Camus is expressed through rebellion which transcends the conventional through self-assertion of the absurd. He finds (1955) human absurdity symbolized in the myth of Sisyphus. Just as Sisyphus's punishment was perpetually to roll a boulder to the top of a mountain from which it endlessly rolled down, so the human condition is to find rest only in the measured pace of retracing one's steps to reassume the torment which shall have no end. But rebellious and powerless though he was, Sisyphus knew his fate. Therefore man triumphs over his fate by rebellion: "The absurd man, when he contemplates his torment, silences all the idols" (1955, p. 123). We learn from Sisyphus that a higher fidelity negates the gods and raises rocks, and that no fate can not be surmounted by scorn.

Courage

A second group of existentialists who are somewhat more hopeful feel that man is destructive when he seeks freedom through rebellion. They stress that the discovery of existence must be an act of faith, that man must seek to believe something which reason tells him is absurd; but they still distrust reason and the older beliefs deduced through reason. Kierkegaard accordingly regarded it as an existential necessity to make a leap of faith. To leap to what rationally seems absurd requires an existential act of courage.

While Sartre writes of freedom to be, Tillich's ultimate need is for courage to be. Tillich is as much concerned as is Sartre with loss of being through a too-easy identification with the nonbeing of surrounding things, but he would meet the need to secure being not by negating, but by affirming. Courage is defined by Tillich as "self-affirmation of being in spite of the fact of nonbeing" (1952, p. 155). As such, it is an act of the self in taking nonbeing upon itself, thus destroying nonbeing in a way that is not totally unlike the way Sartre destroys nonbeing by acting upon being.

Tillich differs from Sartre in believing that ultimately man is secured against nonbeing by the ground of all being he terms God; however, man is separated from this ultimate source of being by the impending threat of nonbeing. In effect, man is separated from God by his anxiety. The belief that God is ultimate existence does not make Tillich's courage to be an easier need to meet than Sartre's freedom to be. Like the assertion of freedom, the act of courage must have an in-spite-of-nonbeing quality to it. Since it is grounded in God, "the courage to be is rooted in the God who appears when God has disappeared in the anxiety of doubt" (1952, p. 190). Because courage is required, Tillich can no more meet the need for the New Being through conventional or nonexistential Christianity than Sartre or Camus could find being in conventional social institutions.

Being through Selfhood

Because of its more pragmatic and humanistic orientation, American existentialism describes man's aspiration to being in a somewhat different way. The motivational context for being ceases to be metaphysical, with little concern for either the negating aspects of atheistic existentialism or the courage in finding the "God above God" of theological existentialism. Instead, motivation is discussed in more immediately psychological terms. The setting for meeting the motivational need for being is the self, in which the existential crisis involves psychologically dynamic forces which being must resolve.

For American existentialists such as Rogers and Maslow the basic motivational concern is to experience the fullness of that being within one's self. The existential task for Rogers is to be that self which one truly is, and he summarizes motivation as meaning "that the individual moves toward *being,* knowingly and acceptingly, the process which he inwardly and actually is" (1961, p. 175). In a somewhat similar way, Maslow sees being as a motivational concept which describes a self-sustaining individual who is intrinsically motivated to sustain himself through peak experiences.

FRUSTRATIONS

What others would regard as a state of malfunction or abnormality, the existentialist is apt to see as a manifestation of nonbeing. Thus if being is the term which best describes the process of humanness, similar value judgments can define nonbeing in terms of evil which blocks or inhibits being. If man's essential qualities are acts of courage, defiance, being one's self, or having peak experiences, then evil is any behavioral phenomenon which stifles his freedom, cuts him off from the ground of his being, or constricts the full flow of experiencing. In other words, frustration or loss of being occurs through unconcern, through inauthenticity, or through constriction of self.

Unconcern

Nonbeing can first be seen as a denial of that perennial crisis state which is an essential part of the human situation. Because this view regards anxiety as a natural reaction to confronting the necessary contingencies of existence, it regards the absence of anxiety as a pathological state. If human comfort is gained at the expense of that reality called being, then psychoanalytic defense mechanisms are typical ways of avoiding the threat of being. Defenses against anxiety serve to conceal the existential situation from one's self, thus making the existential assertion of *being* impossible. The basic evil is not pain, as it is in naturalistic thought, but a feeling of unconcern which blots unpleasant aspects of reality from consciousness.

Søren Kierkegaard discusses this pathological state of not being anxious in *Sickness unto Death* (1941). This sickness is not that of the body: Lazarus whose sickness was of the body was raised from death. Sickness unto a true death is without pain because the part of the self which feels pain has been lost. While everyone is not in despair, everyone ought to be. The degree of despair for Kierkegaard is proportional to being conscious and to being human. Kierkegaard believed that only the true Christian did not have a natural need to despair. The irony of Kierkegaard's life, as he himself notes, is that the one who tries for religious perfection and fails is the one who suffers the most. If despair is the price of the effort to search for the perfection which man can not find, it is a price which Kierkegaard believed must be paid.

Victor Frankl describes existential anxiety in more contemporary terms. Frankl notes a need for tension to replace the boredom which he terms the existential vacuum. Noting that mental health is based on a "tension between what one is and what one should become" (1963, p. 166), he regards the collective neurosis as residing in a nihilistic attitude which enables man to seek refuge from the tension of challenge in the neurotic fatalism of "nothingbutness." Frankl claims that this type of boredom brings more problems to the psychiatrist than distress does. He describes the existence of a depression or "Sunday neurosis" in which man is pained by that inner void he experiences when he becomes bored as soon as the rush of the busy week is over.

Inauthenticity

When the self is lost through unconcern, a self for which being is too painful retreats into nonbeing. In this situation the person takes refuge in a self which is existentially false. Then the individual is forced to disguise from himself the crisis state into which the various contingencies of being places him and to pretend that his being-in-the-world is something quite different from what it really is. He engages in a form of playacting which enables him to disguise existential reality behind a sham reality of social role playing. This process of disguising from oneself the nature of being-in-the-world is called inauthenticity. As J. F. T. Bugental defines the term, authenticity, it is used "to characterize a way of being-in-the-world in which one's being is in harmony with the being of the world itself" (1965, p. 33). One is inauthentic to the degree that one's actions are out of step with a more complete being outside the self.

Jean-Paul Sartre termed avoiding the truth about one's self acting in *bad faith.* Sartre found it necessary to confront the world by saying no, an act of negation that is man's only freedom. Others, however, say no inwardly by negating the truth, an act of bad faith directed against the self. Behind an act of bad faith is an unpleasant truth which the person chooses not to face. Indeed, an act of self-deception is so unpleasant that Sartre regards the Freudian recourse to the unconscious as an attempt to avoid the ethical implications of self-deception by reifying unrecognized bad faith as the so-called unconscious part of the mind.

Psychoanalysis is an intellectual seeking after a psychological excuse for bad faith, but the results of bad faith also extend into the reality of action. Bad faith can take the form of playacting by which one tries to make natural those endeavors whose intent is self-deception as well as the deception of others. Sartre speaks of "the dance of the grocer, of the tailor, of the auctioneer," whose acts deceive when they try to persuade the observer that "they are nothing but a grocer, an auctioneer, a tailor" (1956, p. 59).

The individual's struggles to maintain his authenticity in an insensitive and uncomprehending world form the recurrent theme of the novels of Albert Camus. Arthur Burton (1960b) observes that certain Camus characters are caught up in an existence which is not unlike a schizophrenic condition. A basic condition of Camus's novels is man's confrontation with the absurd. Tillich observed that those who are hypersensitive to the threat of nonbeing turn either to psychological defenses or to a reduced being, but others who are not able to defend themselves against existential threat elude reality. Burton notes that Camus' characters seem to resemble schizophrenics because their modes of being-in-the-world do not confront the question of the absurd directly but practice the continued evasion which makes the schizophrenic a spectator in the game of life.

The central character in Camus' novel *The Stranger* (1946) is Meursault, whose shallow and apparently purposeless existence seems to be increasingly dominated by the absurd. Meursault's existential detachment is underscored by his lack of grief at his mother's death and his shallow feeling about a girlfriend whom he is willing to marry in spite of his seeming indifference. Meursault's passive and indifferent manner appears to be at variance with his absurd and sudden murder of a man who had threatened Meursault's friend. Meursault, however, has been unable to come to terms with his own existence. Just as his actions make no sense to himself, so they also puzzle the authorities, who are unable to sympathize with a murderer like Meursault who fires five bullets into a prostrate form. Meursault's failure to project his existence onto the external world leads others to regard his indifference as a sign that he is a hardened criminal; therefore, he is condemned to die. Meursault sees little meaning in death: "All that remained to hope was that on the day of my execution there should be a high crowd of spectators and that they should greet me with howls of execration" (1946, p. 154). Meursault could not elude the absurd.

Constriction of Self

Existentialists typically relate failure to be anxious to loss of self-affirmation. When a feeling of despair is gone, a completeness of self is also lost. Kierkegaard first noted the human condition in which man's ability to become concerned is swallowed up by mass culture, causing the reduced self to engage in what is now called social role playing. The robot self lives precisely the way he is expected to live; Kierkegaard describes him living in Christendom as a cultured Christian, just as he would be a pagan among pagans, and notes as "a comical thing" that he can even pretend to despair when it is socially appropriate. As the self became lost in a nineteenth-century preview of Riesman's other-directed world, the sickness that Kierkegaard saw was scarcely one that ever calls attention to itself either by its strangeness or its inner turmoil: "The greatest danger, that of losing one's own self, may pass off as quietly as if it were nothing; every other loss, that of an arm, a leg, five dollars, a wife, etc., is sure to be noticed" (1941, p. 49).

Paul Tillich also notes dangers in the loss of self-affirmation. If for him the courage to be is the basic good in human existence, the loss or frustration of such courage results in loss of the self's ability to prevail over nonbeing. It is desirable for man that "he affirms himself as receiving and transforming reality creatively" (1952, p. 46). But man may become so sensitive to impinging boundary situations that he removes the self to what Tillich terms a castle of psychological defenses, defenses that can spare him the need to assert himself courageously. Such a retreat becomes a neurosis, which Tillich defines as "the way of avoiding nonbeing by avoiding being" (1952, p. 66).

Binswanger (1958) points out the tragic consequences of a loss in self-affirmation in the case of Ellen West. He describes Ellen as a young woman whose existence has been caught up in the conflict between a gluttunous urge to eat and a desire for an ethereal thinness. As an increasing amount of her being is involved in this struggle, her existence is more hemmed in because the struggle escalates to include more of her being-in-the-world. The wish for an ethereal existence gradually extends from the physiological aspects of eating to social and personal aspects of her being. Her being or sense of selfhood is blocked by her body as it extends out into space and is weighed down by the distorted perspective of time as "the past, 'weighing down' the existence, deprives it of every view of the future" (1958, p. 295). Ellen feels that she is caught in a tightening noose: All exits are blocked, and she feels that she is mouldering and buried in a tomb. As she becomes increasingly depressed, her condition deteriorates into what would be diagnosed as schizophrenia. The case ends in suicide, in Binswanger's view an act made inevitable by the loss of an existence which "is robbed of its authentic life meaning, of its existential ripening, which is always and only determined by the future" (1958, p. 295).

Carl Rogers also discusses what it means not to be that self which one truly is. Rogers (1958b) describes the process which he has observed as clients move through different stages "from fixity to flowingness." In a state of fixity the self is characterized by a remoteness of experiencing, an unwillingness and inability to communicate, a detachment of feeling, and a denial of the personal meaning of experience. This existential remoteness makes the individual unaware of problems which the therapist might help because he sees all problems as external to the self. The individual experiences life as set in the past, and he is little affected by present realities. Perceiving such an individual as structure bound in his mode of experiencing, Rogers concludes that he has scant recognition of the ebb and flow of the feeling life within him.

COUNSELING AND PSYCHOTHERAPY

If the so-called pathological results from having one's being lost or inhibited, the basic purpose of psychotherapy must be to help the individual regain his lost being by removing the blocks and impediments which prevent him from fully experiencing his existence.

Literature on existential psychotherapy has been somewhat slow in developing. Perhaps it has been inevitable that the morose attitude of European existentialists towards human perfectibility has caused them to be more concerned with analyzing the human condition as a pathological state than with prescribing a remedy. As this book is written, three key books devoted to existential psychotherapy have become fairly well known to readers of English. Two authors, Frankl (1955) and Boss (1963), are Europeans; the third, Bugental (1965), is an American.

Each of these authors contrasts his distinctive existential therapy with that of orthodox psychoanalysis and cites the basic contribution which he feels psychoanalysis has made to treating the conflicts of the disjointed man. All three agree that psychoanalysis fails to resolve the basic human dilemma that the breakdown in social values has created for man and share a common distaste for the naturalistic values which orthodox psychoanalysis embraces. They display a common dissatisfaction with a philosophical view of man which darkens human experience with that deterministic pall cast on the present by the traumatic events of the past. Furthermore, they all reject Freud's pleasure principle in favor of the new value of existential responsibility.

In attempting to transcend what it regards as the narrowly naturalistic concerns of psychoanalysis, existential psychotherapy is motivated by three principle concerns. These overlapping concerns receive different emphasis by different therapists, but they do however provide a recurring theme in the writings of all three.

Freedom from Nonbeing

Since nonbeing is the perpetual threat to man's existence, the first task of psychotherapy must be to free him from the inhibiting and constricting forces which have blocked and stifled his free expression of himself. These three psychotherapists see nonbeing in a variety of forms. For Frankl, the worst forms of nonbeing are an "existential vacuum," or a feeling of boredom and purposelessness; and a transitoriness, which contributes to the void of meaning by making one despair at taking responsibility. For Bugental, nonbeing is somewhat similarly the refusal to take responsibility, but it can also be resignation in the face of tragedy or alienation from self and withdrawal from others.

Existential psychotherapy seeks to counter nonbeing through two general therapeutic devices. First, the therapist helps the patient to work through his resistances and defense mechanisms and, at this point, the influence of psychoanalysis is seen most directly. The means used to lower the patient's psychic resistance may in fact be quite orthodox psychoanalytically. Boss notes the necessity for what he regards as Freud's first rule of psychotherapy: The patient "is obliged to confess everything, whatever may pass through his mind or through his heart, and this without any exception" (1963, p. 61).

In existential analysis, however, the reality that is resisted and defended against is far different. Resistance is directed against the threat of being-in-the-world, a threat that tempts the individual to bar from consciousness the awareness of his actual condition in the world. For Bugental, "resistance is the name that we give to the general defensive wall the patient puts between himself and the threats that he finds linked to being authentic" (1965, p. 103). For Boss, resistance is always an act of an "I" or a total person who "resists" those relationships with a world with which he feels incapable of coping.

Lowering this resistance in existential therapy permits the individual to discover the nature of his existence. Boss notes that if the rules of free association are followed, "it means that all those possibilities of awareness, all feeling, thinking, imagining, dreaming, and acting relationships with the world which either had been fought against until then, or had not even been discovered up to then are now accepted, realized freely, and appropriated with responsibility as constituting one's own existence..." (1963, pp. 61-62). In a similar fashion, Bugental notes "the resistance is not an additive composite but is the life stance of the person in relation to the existential givens" (1965, p. 131). Resistance is a unity which is a "red thread" through all his modes of being.

The second way in which the existential therapist seeks to free the patient from nonbeing is through direct challenge. This contrast between existential analysis, which seeks to assert responsibility, and psychoanalysis, which is charged with condoning a mechanistic, causal-genetic interpretation of self, is pointed up by Boss's distinction between "the psychoanalytic 'Why?' and the daseinsanalytic 'Why not?' " (1963, Ch. 15). The therapeutic issue at stake is not why his adult actions are tied to the fixated libido through early childhood events but why undesired behavior must continue: "Why does he still, this very day, not dare to free himself of the restricting mentality of his childhood?" (1963, p. 248). The question of Why not? becomes an important healing factor for Boss because it frees patients from frustrations of being which have needlessly been repeated by perpetuating past failures in asserting being.

In Frankl the challenge to detach one's self from old existential frustrations is even more direct. If psychoanalysis is represented by a patient lying on a couch and relating things that are very difficult to tell, Frankl's logotherapy means sitting erect and hearing things that are sometimes very disagreeable to hear. Like the daseinsanalysis of Boss, Frankl's logotherapy rejects both retrospection and introspection as only a perpetuation of the form of nonbeing that plays such a decisive role in the development of the so-called neurotic condition. Thus logotherapy seeks to distract the patient from all the vicious circles and feedback mechanisms that influence the development of existential frustration.

The Existential Crisis

After psychotherapy has liberated man from the existential threat, he is free to become more realistically aware of the presence of boundaries between being and nonbeing of which he had previously been unaware. Therefore it is vital for existential therapy to help man increase his understanding of the perennial state of crisis that surrounds human existence. Loss of being through inauthenticity and bad faith, discussed earlier, can be surmounted only through increased awareness of that being-in-the-world in which one is involved.

Although these existential therapists realize that anxiety and guilt are inherent in a human condition which burdens man with a responsibility he does not always feel capable of fulfilling, they make a distinction between existential and neurotic anxiety and guilt. Boss speaks of an existential *being-in-debt* which is experienced as guilt. Man is in a perennial crisis because he can not fulfill the mandate laid upon him. Although being-in-debt guilt is real, conventional psychoanalysis merely deafens a patient to the pangs of an existential conscience. Psychoanalysis (as well as existential therapy) can "free" man from "neurotic" guilt and anxiety. Since the neurotic falls prey to a ritualized and stylized form of life which prevents the full expression of his existence, conventional psychotherapies can help him break the vicious circle created by maladaptive behavior. However, only an existential therapy can transform the neurotic's guilt and anxiety from a narrow concern with a rigidly defended self to a new existence. In this new existence man freely accepts his being-in-debt as it is communicated to him by a conscience freed from the trivial and compulsive concerns of neuroticism.

Existential psychotherapy deals with a crisis of transition as the patient moves from neurotic modes of limited being to a new openness of experiencing. Frankl compares the therapeutic role of making man aware of a wider range of experience to the work of the eye specialist. Just as an ophthalmologist tries to enable the patient to see the world as it really is, so the existential therapist tries to broaden and widen the patient's field of vision so that he may take in the whole realm of what Frankl terms meaning and values.

But just as the sudden exposure to light pains eyes previously adjusted to darkness, so the new perceptions of existential reality are rather uncomfortable. Bugental terms the transition between old modes of limited being and a confrontation with a new fullness of being the existential crisis. This point of choice means a renunciation and a relinquishment, a decision that becomes "a matter of administering death to some possibilities while giving actuality to others" (1965, p. 171). As with any major decision, the choice of how one exists in the world forces one to confront an anxiety-provoking dilemma. Bugental notes that existential anxiety is a fact of being and can not be avoided. What is required is a leap of faith which "is in essence an act of faith in one's own being" (1965, p. 173)—Tillich's courage to be. The existential therapist must realize that this courage is centered in an act of existential crisis which is peculiarly the patient's own. Even if he is but a witness to the birth of another's self, the therapist is still the midwife who acts neither to stifle existential birth pangs through premature therapeutic intervention (as Bugental sees occurring in orthodox psychoanalysis) nor to allow the patient to remain in perpetual unproductive labor (as occurs in the typical neurotic whose anguish serves only to enmesh him deeper in defensiveness).

Will to Meaning

After psychotherapy has freed the patient from entrapment in neurotic defenses against responsibility, the patient must learn to face the challenges imposed upon him by his new existential awareness. Frankl describes taking up of these new responsibilities as the *will to meaning,* an acceptance that forms the final therapeutic task of existential psychotherapy. This decision requires the patient, now free from neurotic bondage to the past, to live in the present and in the future. In this way all contingencies of being which are linked with the past are broken.

Frankl differentiates the will to meaning from the will to pleasure, which he considers the center of Freudian psychoanalysis, and the will to power, which he imputes to Adlerian psychology. Frankl also seeks to differentiate the will to power from what he terms a moral drive or a religious drive, with moralistic and Pharisaical attitudes that Frankl eschews.

Frankl limits the will to meaning to making the patient fully aware of his responsibilities. He leaves the patient with the choice of what and to what or to whom he is responsible so that he must imagine that the past has been left behind and even the present is now past. Frankl lists the categorical imperative of logotherapy as the following: "So live as if you were living already for the second time and as if you had acted the first time as wrongly as you are about to act now!" (1963, p. 173). Frankl sees this maxim as confronting him not only with the finiteness of life but also with the finality of what he makes of his life and of himself.

The assumption of personal responsibility is also emphasized by other existential therapists. Boss does not consider that it is therapeutically important to recall how neurotic behaviors were acquired in childhood; the important issues are what keeps the patient chained to past neurotic behavior patterns and how he can be freed from perpetuating and stereotyped accusations against the past. As stated earlier, Boss' own categorical imperative is the rhetorical Why not?, which in effect commands the patient to free himself from childish neurotic modes of being.

Bugental views man as becoming responsible as soon as he accepts his own "thrown" condition in the world. He sees man as thrown into the present moment in such a way that he must be responsible even for events over whose beginning he had no control. Man can not blame the present upon the past; he must accept his thrown condition and make the best of what seems subjectively to be a bad situation. Bugental notes that many therapeutic systems seem content "to act like parents 'writing an excuse' to a teacher for the patient so he can (apparently) avoid contingency-responsibility-tragedy: 'Please excuse Mr. Smith from contingency. He had bad parents' " (1965, p. 45). While the patient is not to be blamed for developing undesired behavior patterns, enacting those behaviors now is his responsibility.

Bugental presents the case of Frank to illustrate the dangers involved when the psychotherapist is an unwitting accomplice in the theft of the patient's responsibility. (Although Frank was one of his patients, Bugental labels him a therapeutic failure.) Frank is described as a forty-year-old homosexual who came to therapy seeking, in Bugental's paraphrase of the patient's words, "confirmation as a human being." Bugental describes the therapeutic crisis as occurring in the second year of treatment when Frank suddenly was strongly tempted to seduce a bisexual male friend.

As a result of this temptation, Frank experienced intense conflict. Bugental records the patient's description of one pole of his conflict.

Change is possible. What will change me is not some new drug or different therapeutic technique—both of which I have tried many times—it is not something external to me that I just haven't been lucky enough to find yet. What will change me is —and always has been—within me.

I can be loved by others who are not homosexuals, and I can love other heterosexuals (1965, p. 167).

At the same time, however, Frank is also pulled by the other pole of the conflict to deny responsibility, and thereby succumb to nonbeing.

I am indeed forty years old.

My life is half over, and, if these new awarenesses are true, it has been needlessly wasted on bypaths.

I can't bear the awful pain of thinking I brought this about; yet I no longer can blame my mother or my heredity.

Bugental believes that therapy failed because Frank was unable to accept his responsibility for twenty years of failure, and therefore he was unable to make the necessary "choice of taking responsibility for the past in order to have opportunity in the present and future" (1965, p. 168).

Bugental believes that he failed as a therapist because he also failed to be authentic and to assume responsibility. Being unaware that Frank was weighing his being in the balance, Bugental was content to interpret to Frank the way he had been twenty years before. He was unable as a therapist to accept his own thrown condition. Because of his past training and his current need to defend against his tragic losses, Bugental encouraged Frank to emasculate himself of the responsibility for his own life.

GOALS

The existentialist sees man's final destiny as one of achieving conscious awareness of the ultimate nature of reality. At times he seems mystical in his yearning for an experience of at-oneness with absolute Being. Typically, he seeks to achieve this goal by transcending the structured dichotomies which the nonexistentialist has created in man's mind. Therefore the experience of being which he seeks must transcend the usual sense experiences of space and time within which ordinary man finds himself rigidly bound.

Existentialists describe this ontological fulfillment in varied ways. That ontological reality experienced by the burdened Sisyphus bears little outward resemblance to Tillich's ultimate concern, grounded in God. Nevertheless Camus, Tillich, and other existential thinkers seek a distinctive approach to reality in common: an inward experiencing of feeling which draws man into a heightened awareness of an inner world by means of an expanded consciousness.

Affirmation of Being

Existentialism is at least in part a reaction to the individual's feeling of powerlessness in a mass society that seems to display little tolerance for individual differences. Existentialism seeks to counter this leveled sameness by asserting an inner experience of being to negate socially induced conformity. The first goal of existential concern is to develop an inner vitality to permit the affirmation of being confronted by social depersonalization.

The task of finding the affirmative nature of man's existence has in recent years been a major concern of Carl Rogers. Rogers describes the enhanced individual as experiencing new feelings with immediacy and richness of detail. Such an increase in feeling is accompanied by a growing and continuing sense of acceptant ownership as the individual develops a basic trust in his own process. The primary role of consciousness is replaced by a total organismic process. Thus liberated, experiencing ceases to be structure bound and becomes what Rogers terms a process: "The situation is experienced and interpreted in its newness, not as the past" (1961, p. 152).

Just as Rogers has redefined the basic goals in human experience in the transition from a humanistic to an existential view, so the goals which Maslow sets for human behavior have undergone a similar evolution. Maslow has attempted "to redefine self-actualization in such a way as to purge it of its static and typological shortcomings" (1962, p. 91). He calls this existential self-actualization the *peak experience* and defines it as "an episode, or a spurt in which the powers of the person come together in a particularly efficient and intensely enjoyable way . . ." (1962, p. 91).

Maslow regards a peak experience as the final purpose of man's existence: "The peak experiences of pure delight are for my subjects among the ultimate goals of living and the ultimate validations and justifications for it" (1962, p. 75). This is the one unquestioningly good experience in man's life, as he states, "the peak experience is only good and desirable, and is never experienced as evil or undesirable" (1962, p. 76).

Maslow regards peak experiencing as an unequivocal good because it enables man to transcend the limitations of space and time so that he can stand apart from the rest of the world. He becomes godlike "in the complete, loving, uncondemning, compassionate, and perhaps amused acceptance of the world and of the person" (1962, p. 87).

> One aspect of the peak experience is a complete, though momentary, loss of fear, anxiety, inhibition, defense and control, a giving up of renunciation, delay and restraint. The fear of disintegration and dissolution, the fear of being overwhelmed by the "instincts," the fear of death and of insanity, the fear of giving in to unbridled pleasure and emotion, all tend to disappear or go into abeyance for the time being (1962, p. 89).

> At the higher levels of human maturation, many dichotomies, polarities, and conflicts are fused, transcended, or resolved. Self-actualizing people are simultaneously selfish and unselfish, Dionysian and Appolonian, individual and social, rational and irrational, fused with others and detached from others, and so on (1962, p. 86).

Paul Tillich is also actively concerned with finding positive aspects in man's existence, which is the focal concern of his *Courage to Be* (1952). As discussed above, he sees the courage to be as the affirmation of being in the face of the threat of non-being. Tillich thus contrasts the power of being, which is good, with the power over being, which he says is the conventional ideal for personality. The undesired power over being deprives the individual of his ability to affirm his real self by subjecting his being to a "rationalized and intellectualized consciousness" which in turn seeks vengeance upon the self for repression in the "chaotic and destructive outbreak of repressed forces." By power of being, however, man affirms the good side of his nature. Through power of being, man comes into proper relationship with things, people, and his own unconscious, as "the power of the thing is discovered and affirmed by the personality" (1957, p. 124). Consciousness is transcended as "all sides of human existence are drawn into the spiritual life of the whole" (1957, p. 132).

Authenticity of Being

Affirmation of being refers to completeness of experiencing; authenticity of being describes the genuineness of being. Authenticity of being can hardly be divorced from affirmation of being: The same neurotic defenses which make it impossible for the person to affirm himself also deprive him of his authenticity. But while affirmation of being is an act of assertion or of courage, authenticity of being is an act of integration in which consciousness and experiencing of feeling are congruent with each other and with Being, which many existentialists regard as an absolute reality transcending personal idiosyncratic experiencing.

Authenticity is to be regarded as man's highest value and represents "an ultimate state of at-oneness with the cosmos and the immense continuum leading toward that ultimate ideal" (Bugental, 1965, p. 32). Bugental also describes it as a state of being in harmony with the being of the world itself. The nature of such being is somewhat difficult to spell out because the authenticity equated with being in harmony with reality is little more than a credo of one's faith in the ultimate good. Bugental seems to be aware of this fact himself and thus stipulates that his view of authenticity is not to be reduced to adaptation or adjustment, which have connotations of resignation or conformity that are odious to many people, nor is it to become so detached from practical concerns that it appears mystical and otherworldly.

Bugental represents a philosophical school of thought that sees being as an ultimate goodness which transcends the thrownness of the human condition, but other existentialists reject anything which transcends direct human experience. The good in this second faith is seen in one's being authentic to one's self. Thus authenticity for Sartre is represented by what he terms good faith, which lies in keeping faith with one's self by refusing to deceive one's self.

CRITICISM OF EXISTENTIAL VALUES

Since existentialism is so directly born of despair at the irrelevancy of old social values, it is uniquely sensitive to the current alienation of socially detached individuals who feel disillusioned and even angry with the moral irrelevancy of existing social norms. Existentialism comes to grips courageously and imaginatively with the current human condition. It has developed an empathic understanding for human beings who seriously doubt the relevance of old social values and yet who find themselves unable to forsee the fashioning of a new social order where the older values of individualism can be realized.

Although most observers seem willing to commend existentialists for the challenge which they have accepted, many have become critical of the solutions which existentialism proposes for contemporary individualism. These critics have attacked existentialism for its personal morality, its moral conservativism, and its social radicalism.

Subjective Detachment

Existentialism has become socially relevant as an ideological reaction to values which reflect the impersonality and overrationality of modern industrial society which subordinates individual feelings to the economic demands of the machine. Existentialism has accordingly ridden the swing of the pendulum back to an extreme in which feeling becomes as absolute a value as was thought in the preceding view.

Many now believe that overemphasizing subjective experience is as dangerous as seeking to make an absolute of the mind. Modern man suffers from a loss of rational certainty and feels that general social values have ceased to be meaningful. Thus he suffers from a loss in his own identity. Existentialism encourages man to embrace values that are highly personal and thus may not be particularly relevant to society. Existentialism may therefore indirectly intensify that estrangement which the modern individual experiences in his relationship to his culture.

The result of this new attitude to society is a new morality. One's private feelings are now the only justification for values and there is no longer any recourse to a consensually validated morality. Each individual's inner feelings become his own private highest good and therefore ultimate law. But since nothing outside the individual is recognized as socially authoritative, the danger is that a "new morality" will produce a moral anarchy in which others' behavior can in principle never be seen as bad.

Maslow (1962) examines some issues which a subjective or peak-experience morality raises. If a man finds beauty in a Yosemite, is his responsibility to keep it private and untrammeled by other men or the larger responsibility to share it with the millions, who will lessen its beauty or even destroy it? Maslow does not know, but he cites the dilemma of Buddha's enlightenment: Was it a purely personal, private possession? Must one, through writing and teaching, step back from bliss or ecstasy, "giving up heaven to help others get there?" (1962, p. 113).

Maslow himself is not sure which value orientation is appropriate and concludes that each side has some right. Those governed by a social system of values, however, can have few doubts. When man values his inner feelings more than his social responsibility, he increases his alienation and estrangement by severing human bonds that are already frayed by the social abrasions of a mass, depersonalized society.

An inner experience which lacks a social point of reference can easily degenerate into maudlin emotion and selfish hedonism. Benjamin Wolstein (1962) charges that "existential practice verges on solipsism because, after the experience of therapy is immediatized and empathy overcome, no one can discuss the transaction with confidence or competence" (1962, p. 73). He also suggests that existential therapy must appeal to patients who are excessively bound up within themselves and therefore are alienated from more genuine forms of social experiencing: "A philosophy without meaning or outlook, existentialism uses symbolic structures that are alienated from immediate experience to pursue an anxious search for personal existence" (1962, p. 65).

Wolstein explains that the socially estranged individual is attracted by existentialism because he typically wants to use the immediacy of existential experience as a defense against a more social experience which, if less immediate, is nevertheless more ultimate: "It compels him to screen his compassion for fellow humans in anxiety, and prevents him from carrying out his self-appointed task—to listen, assimilate, and respond to actual experience, both immediate and reflective, as conveyed in any form of communication at their command" (1962, p. 71).

Many sociologists also feel that the plight of the so-called other-directed man is more appropriately described as an anomie resulting from a breakdown in the social structure. If this view is correct, the solution to contemporary *angst* does not rest in morbid intro-spection of experience but in opening the communication channels through which meaning may flow from one person to another.

Placed in a sociohistoric perspective, existentialism may be regarded as part of the travail that has been caused by a general loss of social cohesiveness. When the individual can not find basic satisfaction in society, he turns inward to private consciousness and seeks a subjective substitute for social benefits. If this analysis is correct, existentialism is a symptom, but hardly a cure.

Moral Conservatism

Existential concern for subjective consciousness appears to be quite helpful in understanding the individual psyche, but it has been much less successful in prescribing a cure for ontological estrangement. Existentialism's subjective orientation becomes a hindrance when man wishes to act in society to produce forms of social understanding which are more conducive to highly subjective concerns. Existentialists experience a common moral repugnance for what they perceive as other-directed evils, depersonalization, and loss of autonomy. Distrust of anything that is not individually experienced has made it difficult for existentialism to discover any general social solution for the depersonalization of mass society.

The existentialist must eventually bridge the gap between inward feeling and outward action. Søren Kierkegaard described this transition from subjective experiencing to formal belief as a leap of faith. Philosophizing about the ultimate nature of being can not relieve the existentialist of the responsibility of making a leap across the moral chasm which separates his inwardness from an external social reality. Unless he resigns himself to utter despair, he must link subjective inwardness and the particular culture which seems most conducive to the realization of existential values.

Wolstein believes that it is unlikely that an existential jump can in any sense be a great leap forward. He notes that when the existentialist completes his ontological leap, "he enters a conceptual paradise well furnished with the objective principles he had already accepted prior to both the dichotomy and the leap" (1962, p. 23).

Wolstein believes that existentialism has in fact made a socially backward leap. He doubts the social relevancy of existentialism because it adopts a limited view of human nature that is deeply rooted in the outmoded ideas of the nineteenth century, such as Newtonian science, which other disciplines have discarded.

[Existentialism] actually falls back on the presuppositions of Newtonian science that are no longer workable in their original forms—the metaphysical absolutes of time and space, inter-action at a distance between self-enclosed and discrete entities, the failure of reason in the domain of absolute immediacy, and the 'I-am' experience as a sort of personal *deus ex machina* that makes the ego move—all of which were continued into the nineteenth century conception of man and his universe (1962, p. 97).

If this charge is true, existentialism may represent the refusal of those with individualistic values to accommodate themselves to the new thought forms of an other-directed period. Existentialism may be the rational man's last attempt to preserve an absolute self in the face of modes of thinking that are quite alien to traditional individualistic values. If this analysis is correct, the core of existen-tial despair may be a fear that social change has made old values worthless.

In one sense, existentialism provides new philosophical lyrics for a traditional moral tune. Absolute individualism remains the basic value; the only unequivocal good is still that man is the captain of his fate and the master of his soul. But as he seeks to be his own moral master, man must whistle in the dark to keep his courage up. Now he can choose neither of the conventional alternatives of lighting a candle or cursing the darkness; he must continue to tremble inwardly at the undefined forms in the ontological mist.

In another sense the existentialist is like the well-known Molière character who is greatly delighted to learn that he has been speak-ing prose all his life. At various times and in diverse ways man has his own inner consciousness, and at times he has even experienced mystic ecstasy. Man has had to lead a life of *dasein* all through recorded time, but not until our century has he known how onto-logical he has been. It would now seem incumbent for the existen-tialist to demonstrate his ability to put his newly discovered prose to better use than Molière's naive and suggestible character does.

There is a danger that existential terminology will suffer the same fate that mental-health concepts have: Their meaning may rapidly fade as their social relevancy diminishes. Rollo May has in general been quite sympathetic to existentialism. He notes (1962a), however, that in America existential psychotherapy has produced a confusion of tongues which has become virtually a Tower of Babel.

He perceives a growing trend in existentialism to become so wrapped in semantic devices that human experience is bypassed. He charges existentialism with too often trying to resolve with a single word age-old problems of human existence with which thinkers have struggled since human consciousness began.

May notes that language and symbols are the form and content of all types of thinking. Existentialism, which is no exception, must describe ontological reality with socially meaningful words. The usefulness of symbolic forms are appropriately assumed by the philosopher, but they must also be evaluated by the larger society which is the final judge of their social relevancy. Time makes ancient good uncouth. Existential thought must keep abreast of social truth.

Social Radicalism

Existentialism reveres a number of values considered highly traditional in the great world cultures. As a philosophy and a system of psychotherapy, existentialism is morally conservative, seeking to maintain absolute individual freedom in an age of conformity and mass depersonalization. Despite its conservative and esoteric nature, existentialism increasingly takes on the character of a mass social movement among the young. The conservative values remain, but a younger generation is increasingly trying to gain conservative moral ends through somewhat radical social means.

The aims of the existential avant-garde are in themselves neither new nor controversial. The quest for heightened and expanded consciousness has had a long and honorable history in eastern and western cultures. While society has not always tolerated those with different social values, it has always accepted the need for a seer and a prophet who can attain a broader social vision by delving deeper into personal experience. Even the most encapsulated society has made such elaborate institutional provisions as the monastery and convent for those who would seek intense personal experience by renouncing more typical social forms.

The social tragedy of our time is that the moral anomie resulting from the decay of older values is so great that those who would deviate from modal mass-cultural values no longer feel they can entrust themselves to traditional forms of social detachment. The culturally dispossessed now feel that they must combine their search for the purity of mystic detachment with a rebellion against the whole social and moral structure.

The mystic search for an expanded awareness increasingly involves a rebellious new generation seeking a nirvana of worldless bliss through drugs. Although existentialism has provided an important focus for the new generation's rebellion, it is hardly fair to equate it with psychedelic religion, with the beat generation, or with hippies: These phenomena are certainly far removed from the ontological concern of early philosophic and psychiatric existentialism. It is nevertheless apparent that a new generation of existentialists has given the concept of existential freedom a more active meaning.

Even a person as sympathetic with existentialism as Rollo May takes concerned notice of the "faddist and bandwagon tendencies which lead man to seek instant satori by means of psychedelic drugs." May notes that such an oversimplified attempt to expand awareness tends to bypass and evade anxiety, tragedy, guilt, and the reality of evil.

May (1962a) seems to forecast astutely the trend of events. To a sharply increased extent, existentialism ceases to be controlled by academic philosophers and mental-health practitioners and is seized by avant-garde youth who use its highly individual and subjective values to justify the formation of a social movement which seeks not ontological understanding but overt political aims often approaching nihilism in their fearful antipathy to society.

Surely the danger of anarchism exists in a social system in which anomically detached individuals may become desperate in their search for moral structure. If this happens, they may solipsistically demand every individual's absolute right to complete and utter freedom to pursue his own inward experiencing with no regard for any external value. The existentialist's inner experiencing transcends spatiotemporal boundaries as well as any other limits that people seek to impose to provide "normal" limits upon one's inner world. A new individualism which refuses to be bound by social limits now transcends the boundaries of social space.

A few years ago Wolstein (1962) described the new myth of another Sisyphus in rebellion now against even the compulsion of the former struggle. "He wants the whole answer to the problems of living, and if he cannot have it all, he prefers to have none" (1962, p. 117). The new Sisyphus simply abandons the whole enterprise in despair.

Tired and bored, Sisyphus finally surrenders to an irrational fate and absentmindedly resigns himself to climbing the mountain again. While suffering the resentful anger of disillusionment in silence, he has also recognized the nihilism of this refusal to modify the strain of living without having the final answers. In response to desperate inner strivings for absolutism, he willingly settled into the bleakness of his belated discovery that life was gradually losing its meaning. And he preferred the absolute of a meaningless life to a relatively meaningful life: absolute absurdity was better than no absolute answer at all (1962, p. 118).

Wolstein may yet be right. There are many tired mystics who have turned their backs on the world in cynical disillusion. But, as Wolstein also notes, this new hip existentialism has the atmosphere of a magical cultism. Even those who are most anomically bereft are easily swept up in an ideological fanaticism where the seduction of feeling allows one to become an emotional prostitute before a phantasmogoria of shifting emotions.

The new generation finds its social identity by being in the vanguard of yet another type of inner experiencing in even more active rebellion. It seeks new vistas of mind which older generations have not been bold enough to experience. The new Sisyphus does not repeat himself.

The new individual is impelled forward once more by the delusion that he will at last glimpse a mystic vision if he can only lug Sisyphus's boulder up yet another mountain from whose summit the view will somehow be different. But he toils up one mountain only to rush pell-mell down the other side so that he can toil up the even higher and steeper mountain ahead. And the mountains keep getting steeper and the precipices, deeper. Although the view at the top is always hindered by the stone walls of other mountains looming still higher, the new Sisyphus is not willing to go back.

SUMMARY

Existentialism has been interpreted here as modern man's attempt to regain an individualism lost through the various social, economic, and technological demands of an urbanized and industrialized culture. Existentialism has attempted to combat tendencies towards compartmentalization and fragmentation of personality by encouraging the individual to develop an intense inwardness. Such existence or being enables man to emerge or to stand out (literally to *ex+sistere*) from his social surroundings so that he can transcend the old rational dualities of self-society, subject-object, and mind-body imposed by preexistential rational thought. Certain similarities are inevitable between existential thought and humanistic values discussed in Chapter Five: both value man's individuality or sense of selfhood. But the humanist believes that selfhood is relatively contained within the self, while the existentialist emphasizes that selfhood is realized only through dynamic confrontation of the nonself or nonbeing. Existentialism sees that man's individuality is in crisis, and only active stirrings at the depth of his personality can save him from becoming an unfeeling automaton.

 PART THREE

The Therapist: Scientist or Moralist?

Chapter 9

THE THERAPIST'S CHOICE OF VALUES

And if the bugle gives an indistinct sound, who will get ready for battle? . . .
PAUL'S FIRST LETTER TO THE CORINTHIANS

❖❖❖

Man requires a new conceptual schemata with which to structure his perceptions of good and evil. The preceding chapters have discussed what seem to be the four most important alternatives which contemporary society has constructed to replace the mental-health model, whose social relevance appears to be steadily decreasing.

While all four value orientations seem important, they are significant in quite different ways. There are no clear signs that any of them will provide a moral motif which can be as dominant in our age as was belief in witches and in mental illness in earlier periods. Either an entirely different alternative to the mental-health model may suddenly emerge and sweep to ideological victory, or man's moral ideals may become even more diffuse until conceptions of good and evil become so individual that social morality will largely disappear.

Because ours is a time of social transition in which old values have been lost and new ones are not yet clearly established, the definitions of good and evil are confused. The ideological successors to mental health and mental illness are not apparent. The views of good and evil in man that guided our forefathers no longer satisfy the present generation. Traditional and rational periods of history held core values in common, and because they were socially sanctioned, these values provided clear perceptions of good and bad. But this moral clarity has been succeeded in a postrational age by a moral blur.

There is no current agreement even about the source of an authority to provide a new ideology. The twentieth century is frustrated in its search for truth because it does not know where to look for it.

205

Of the four alternatives to mental health, each is in its way an epitaph to the passing of mental illness and mental health as morally useful concepts. Each alternative judges the concepts of mental health and interprets modern man's moral and ethical situation differently. Each presents itself as an alternative to mental health and illness and makes a claim for man's allegiance to its definition of truth. Thus the problem is not that the demise of mental-health systems has left us with an axiological vacuum, but that there are too many would-be moral and ethical guides.

DIFFERENCES AMONG ALTERNATIVES

The four alternatives to the mental-health model which contemporary society offers as answers contradict one another. The naturalist's assumptions contrast starkly with the existentialist's view of man; and in their most logically consistent forms, social and humanistic values are no easier to reconcile. While one can quite properly claim that all four value orientations have elements of truth, each makes an absolute claim for what it believes is most basic about human nature.

Inevitably, therefore, these four ideologies compete with one another and make contradictory claims for the allegiance of the counselor and psychotherapist. In practice a behavioral scientist often places the different philosophical theories side by side and then fuses them together eclectically. Lest he be torn ideologically asunder by these competing moral standards, he must reconcile them by ranking their competing demands for allegiance. The therapist must choose.

Conflicting values about the ultimate good result in what Lowe (1959) has described as an ethical dilemma in which different value orientations compete with one another for the practitioner's allegiance. And there is no easy way out of this dilemma of competing claims for the truth. Many practitioners seek to remain tentative and open-minded in their approach to truth, but a value orientation demands for itself an absolute which transcends individual efforts to remain detached, to compromise, or to ignore philosophical issues.

To resolve these competing claims for truth, a single individual would have to combine the attributes that every theoretical orientation values. This person would surely have an imposing array of attributes. Free from anxiety-provoking tension, he would relate harmoniously in a wide variety of social situations. Although sensitive enough to meet the basic expectations of others, he would be autonomous and able to detach himself from their expectations. But while he would not need to meet others' demands slavishly, he would successfully adapt himself to perform in social situations involving love, work, and play. He would have basically favorable attitudes toward himself, although he would not become so self-satisfied that his growth and personal development cease. He would also be in good contact with reality and make minimal use of defense mechanisms. Thus he would confront the mystifying ambiguities of life with an existential courage that would enable him to find a unifying outlook on life. Lest such an overload of desirable attributes expose this person to the jealousy of the psychologically less fortunate, we would add the final quality of humility to his composite portrait.

The contradictions of this theoretical portrait are obvious. The greatest disparity is between the physiological stimulus-response model, whose goal is a driveless state of bliss, and an existential view, which sees as man's glory his ability to live creatively with the anxiety-producing ambiguities of life. Both groups wish man to be in good contact with reality, but while one believes that basic reality lies in the careful analysis of minute parts, the other believes that it exists in an organismic wholeness found only as part of a venture in faith. The naturalist chooses for his ideal that sense of certainty which results from being able to tuck all the loose ends of experience into a verifiable theory. The existentialist is in his glory, however, among those ambiguities which provoke an anxiety that he regards as a challenge. An unreconciled difference in values exists between the choice of feeling secure because one feels he has mastered certain basic learning situations and the choice of that creative doubt which results from existential crisis. One view is that man's crowning glory is his depth of feeling, while the opposing view is that man's essential dignity is in his ability to learn more efficiently than other animals.

An equal polarity appears between the other two alternatives, the social and the humanistic. Here the contradiction is one of meeting social demands or of following one's creative inclinations to be individualistic. Loyalty to basic social institutions seems increasingly incompatible with what a growing number of individuals regard as the essential right of self-expression and self-determination. In the past, the needs of the individual and of society have fortunately been the same. Today, however, evidence is increasing that the welfare of the individual and of society may no longer coincide. It has become difficult to be a maverick in a more compact social herd. As the other-directed social space becomes more crowded, the self-actualization of one individual could not go on forever without infringing upon others. The inevitable has occurred. Collisions in social space have become more frequent as more pressures are made to conform. Increasingly the self-actualizing individual must detach himself from the social matrix by rebelling. The term self-actualization, which may seem to be loosely used, is generally considered to be synonomous with creativity, which has been intensively studied. Although these studies are of different types of creativity, they consistently present the creative ideal as an individual whose ability to be different comes at the expense of his ability to conform and to adapt to the behaviors others deem most desirable in basic social situations.

Many have indeed attempted to merge existential and humanistic concerns. There is nevertheless an ultimate antinomy between pride in outward accomplishment and despair at inward nothingness. The humanist's pride in individual accomplishment becomes the existentialist's self-deceptive *hubris* which contains the seeds of its own downfall. The positive self-concept so prized by the humanist is often regarded by the existentialist as but a shield against the threat of a nonbeing that man would rather not face. And the existentialist's perennial crisis of man who is on the verge of succumbing to nonbeing is hardly understandable to humanists nurtured on the supreme goodness of man who is little less than a god in his ability to rise from the animal realm to tame a manageable world.

Existentialism is no more compatible with a social value orientation. The existential aloneness of a Kierkegaard or a Nietzsche is apt to terrify anyone closely wedded to social values. Indeed, the very nature of the security of his social matrix makes man confront existential dread in utter loneliness. And if it seems that many are the Job's comforters for the existential man is despair, the false counsel of social relativities becomes the existentialist's worst enemy, for he is the man whose task is to wrestle with absolutes.

If naturalistic values are incompatible with existential values, they are equally difficult to reconcile with social or humanistic approaches. The enduring mark of Freud's genius is that he was the first to see the inherent conflict between the natural man and the controls that civilization places upon him. Indeed, there must be an antagonism between the creature demands for immediate gratification and the social demands which label as selfish the gratification of impulses impeding the socialization process. While naturalism prizes an individual who has minimal anxiety, a social orientation is apt to label such a person a psychopath who lacks all motivation for social concern.

Although naturalism and humanism both prize the individual organism, the qualities which they cherish are not the same. The briskly efficient comfort of *Walden Two* is scarcely compatible with humanistic achievement and self-actualization. The classic humanistic ideal is embodied in Longfellow's vision of how "great heights by great men reached and kept, were not attained by sudden flight." Probably the humanist's naturalistic contemporaries would meet their creaturely need for sleep while the great achievers were "toiling upwards in the night."

THE THERAPIST'S ETHICAL DILEMMA

In an anomic society where older moral laws have been discredited, the individual is apt to find that moral choice is difficult. He experiences what some term an existential crisis. Individuals who can think for themselves creatively may weather this moral crisis and, according to the individualistic orientation, may even be improved by the experience. Other individuals who feel that they are less able to tolerate moral uncertainty seek the behavioral scientist's help.

While many individuals continue to wrestle with their personal values, the behavioral scientist is in a much more difficult ethical position. He is the new moral authority. When contemporary man is in conflict over moral choices or in despair about the uncertainty of good and evil, he turns to the behavioral scientist in general and to the psychotherapist in particular. Because the scientist's moral views affect others, his values are no longer personal, but social.

All men find it easier to view the conceptual foibles which have receded into historical perspective than to judge a more recent period in whose cultural idiosyncrasies they are themselves involved. The scientist whose training has provided him with an objective attitude may gain special satisfaction from knowing that man has learned to expose the myth and the magic of the past. He may feel that the objective attitude of science can prevent a repetition of past mistakes.

But it is one thing to analyze and dissect the past and quite another to find a new cosmology which will enable our generation to place current experiences into a philosophical framework that allows man to find sufficient meaning in his experience to confidently differentiate between what is considered good or bad. And if it is difficult to view with detachment the efforts of one's contemporaries to write new meanings upon the present, it is still more difficult to prophesy and identify the values of a better world yet to be born.

Ideas die when their social time is past, but people go on living. They need leadership. In politics, man's need for governmental structure insures that the death of one ruler is followed by the inauguration of his successor. To proclaim that the king is dead is also to proclaim long live the king. The same continuity appears with the demise of an ideology. Mental health as a system of values seems short lived. If one set of social attitudes passes away, the culture must discover another credo or it will fall into the same lack of moral regulation and normless despair which afflicts the body politic when basic governmental institutions can no longer elicit the allegiance of its citizens. The result in an ideological situation is moral anomie, in which despair becomes the only consensually validated feeling.

As the public looks to the counselor or psychotherapist for new moral leadership, he finds the exercise of this leadership to be increasingly difficult. No objective certainty can be claimed for the new solutions to problems in living. Should he believe that his values are ultimates, he soon feels the hostile sting of critical colleagues who are equally certain of an opposing truth.

The therapist looks in vain for an escape from the ethical dilemma into which the conflict over morals and values places him. He hopes that perhaps he can refuse to be the social arbiter of morality. He may seek to limit his assessment of human behavior to descriptive, rather than evaluative, terms so that he can eliminate from his lexicon such value-laden terms as creativity, neuroticism, and even intelligence. In psychotherapy he may seek to be morally neutral, rejecting all the client's attempts to direct therapeutic conversation into problem areas with moral implications.

The counselor or psychotherapist may also hope to resolve the discrepancies among conflicting value orientations by taking what seem to be the most valid elements from each value orientation and blending them into a harmonious whole with a more basic truth than that of any constituent element. An attempt would thereby be made to combine the advantages of different orientations and at the same time to eliminate less desirable viewpoints.

The eclectic view which such a practice describes does have its advantages. Far-ranging social thinkers successfully take ideas from many value systems and combine them into personal values which frequently reveal the highest ethical concerns. Eclecticism itself, however, requires a prior value or a schematic core around which subordinate values are gathered. If one has no prior commitment to some theory, combining different ideas becomes a syncretistic attempt to force incompatible ideas into an ideological marriage which can not be justified morally or scientifically.

Finally, the therapist may hope that with time some new system of values will emerge with an increasing coalescence of agreement. He may hope that leadership will emerge in his profession to provide him with the meaningful moral structure which his patients and clients ask him to supply. Thus he may listen intently to addresses at conventions and may seek the opinions of colleagues whom he respects. He may also read more in various professional journals.

Since the opinions of others obviously shape the autokinetic effect of a perceptually unstructured light, it may not be too much to hope that a similar process will gradually occur with moral judgments as behavioral scientists exchange opinions. The tendency to imitate and to identify seems to be deeply rooted in human behavior, and no doubt it has helped increase social cohesion on numerous occasions. As essential as imitation may be to socialization, however, its utter lack of objectivity renders it inadequate as a way to achieve scientific consensus.

The therapist must choose his own values. By his decision to respond to human need, he has made a commitment to some brave new world which he hopes will result from his efforts to improve human behavior. To attempt a moral neutrality is to reject those needs which society is most insistent that he meet. The responsibility is a personal one. He can not relieve himself of the dilemma of conflicting values by selecting from psychiatric folklore the clichés which seem socially most appropriate. Nor can he be saved by the personal judgments of esteemed peers, no matter how worthy they may be as leaders of science.

THE DILEMMA OF SCIENTIFIC VALUES

Because the professional development of counseling and psychotherapy has been an outgrowth of advances in the behavioral sciences, the therapist naturally turns to science for help in choosing values. The therapist typically expects science to help with this choice in two basic ways. First, science provides the therapist with systematic knowledge which enables him to be better informed about the implications and consequences of human behavior than the nonscientist. Second, science provides him with an objective temperament to ponder ethical issues with greater detachment and impartiality.

Science, which is generally regarded as value free, can not therefore embrace any particular personal tastes and preferences. Many scientists believe, however, that much can be done in the name of science to improve human behavior. Physicist Jacob Bronowski was inspired by the apparent immorality of the atomic destruction at Nagasaki to write *Science and Human Values* to "show the place of science in the canons of conduct which it has still to perfect" (1956, p. 13). In support of his plea for the scientist's moral involvement he suggests that "men have asked for freedom, justice, and respect precisely as the scientific spirit has spread among them" (1956, p. 90). While Bronowski is concerned with solving larger social problems, therapists who identify with science can find an analogy between his suggested involvement in social problems and their own scientific involvement in psychological problems. The scientifically oriented therapist is apt therefore to conceive himself as a rock of imperturbable moral objectivity to which the client can safely moor amidst a sea of bewilderment and confusion as to values.

Two therapeutic orientations are particularly insistent that the therapist remain scientific in his attempts to help clients with problems involving morals and values. These orientations are based on Freudian and learning theories.

Freudian or orthodox psychoanalysis regards the analyst as an expert who can objectively analyze the thoughts, the behavior, and the dreams of the patient. The insights which the analyst seeks to have the patient attain are regarded as unquestionably objective in nature, and the patient who refuses to accept the analyst's authority as trustworthy is considered resistant.

Since the psychoanalyst's objective stance is regarded as allowing him to remain morally uninvolved, he sees his task as that of freeing the patient from the oppressive and burdensome moralism which the superego has imposed upon the ego. Because he believes that the father originally imposed the guilt-producing morality upon the patient, the analyst tries to become a surrogate father through therapeutic transference. The original father imposed an irrational morality based upon superstition and myth, and imposed through fears and threats; but the therapist's scientific orientation permits him to be a more reasonable and objective moralist. He can therefore encourage the patient to discover his own values through a liberated reason.

A classic description of how a psychoanalytic viewpoint can objectify moral problems is found in J. C. Flugel's *Man, Morals, and Society* (1945). Flugel believes that psychoanalysis is justified in condemning conventional morality because its restrictions and inhibitions are more than human nature can comfortably bear. Therefore, if the analyst must make a value judgment in condemning repressive social forces which act on behalf of morality, he is scientifically justified in doing so. To those who object to the analyst's attempt to abrogate conventional morality in the name of science, Flugel offers the following rebuttal.

> As against these charges, the psychoanalyst could reply (though in fact he seldom troubled to do so) that his only concern, as a medical psychologist, was to cure his patients, as a pure scientist, to understand the nature and causes of the psychological problems that confronted him; that he had only reported matters as he found them, that he had no subversive designs against existing moral conventions, and above all that his discoveries showed that in nervous and mental disease there was already a failure of satisfactory moral control, resulting in moral unhappiness, inefficiency, and moral maladjustment, and that his endeavors as psychotherapist aimed at bringing about a new attitude to life which would make the patient into a more reasonable, helpful and cooperative being (1945, pp. 30-31).

Flugel recognizes that there is always the danger that a few over-enthusiastic and ill-informed supporters might illogically conclude that all repressions were bad and all conventions should be flouted. He regards this danger as but a typical hasty generalization that follows advances in knowledge, and he concludes therefore that "he, the psychoanalyst, was no more responsible than any other scientist for the misuse of his discoveries" (1945, p. 31).

More recently, Jan Ehrenwald also attempts to convince the public that the analyst is a scientist. In *Psychotherapy: Myth and Method* (1966) he describes psychotherapy as modern man's attempt to replace reliance upon magic, myth, and superstition with a more reasoned approach gained through a scientific temper. If psychotherapy must be the modern analogue to primitive healing, all psychotherapies, psychoanalytic or otherwise, differ from earlier attempts at mental healing in their uncompromising rejection of magic.

Ehrenwald believes that although all the major psychotherapies have been able to avoid magic, they have not all been completely able to forsake myth; therefore he contrasts "mythophobic" psychoanalysis with other, less scientific, "mythophylic" therapies. Ehrenwald believes that psychoanalysis, in common with other scientific discoveries, can be refined and made more precise. Since psychoanalysis was derived from scientific evidence available at the turn of the century, he believes that it must be reconciled with more contemporary scientific views. Ehrenwald believes that psycho-analysis can make impressive claims for itself, these historical limitations notwithstanding. In his words, "psychoanalysis represents the boldest step in arriving at a naturalistic and scientifically verifiable concept of man viewed as *homo natura*" (1966, p. 69).

The second therapy which seeks a scientific solution to the problem of values is based upon learning theory. Psychoanalysts and learning theorists are rather irreconcilably opposed to one another in their views of how to make psychotherapy scientific, however. The learning theorist, who rejects the analytic structure of mind because it can not be observed, substitutes the principles of behavior modification for mental categories. But if the analyst and learning theorist start from different premises, they reach quite similar conclusions: In the name of science the therapist must oppose the oppressive and restrictive moralities that oppressively inhibit the patient or client.

B. F. Skinner in *Science and Human Behavior* (1953) contrasts the social control exercised over the individual by traditional social institutions with a more benevolent control exercised by the therapist. Since Skinner believes that all behavior is controlled by external reinforcement, he in effect denies that the individual has the personal choice which this book defines as a value orientation. Skinner does seem to imply, however, that man can choose the type of control he exercises over others and therefore he can exercise freedom of choice over what we define as a social morality.

Skinner's various writings, such as *Walden Two* (1948) and *Science and Human Behavior,* contrast the social, and therefore the moral, control exercised by the behavioral or cultural engineer and the psychotherapist with the traditional controls exerted by powerful social institutions. Skinner (1953) describes how such older social agencies as government, religion, and education use negative reinforcement, or punishment, to a large extent. He regards punishment as morally evil because it causes such undesirable traits as escape, revolt, passive resistance, fear, phobias, anxiety, anger, rage, depression, excessively vigorous behavior, excessively restrained behavior, defective stimulus control, and defective self-knowledge.

Skinner regards the psychotherapist as exercising a benevolent moral control which contrasts sharply with the Machiavellian tactics of other social agencies. Therefore Skinner describes the therapist as a person who uses rewards to reverse the crude and misguided attempts at social control by agencies using punishment. Skinner denies that even morally benevolent social controls can produce that human freedom which the humanist describes. Nevertheless, he does agree that the client should be freed from the symptoms, inhibitions, and emotional blockages produced by the wrong type of moral control.

Since Skinner believes that in an ultimate sense man is never free to choose his own values, he sees the basic moral issue as the decision of which group in our society is best prepared to exercise control. Skinner believes that because moral control is inevitable, those who exercise it should be those with the most knowledge of the consequences produced by different reinforcements—the scientists. In *Walden Two* (1948), Skinner portrays two types of morality. The first, which is exercised by the "charlatan, the demagogue, the priest," leads to the despotism of ignorance, neglect, irresponsibility, and accident. The ideal culture contained in the Utopian colony of Walden Two contrasts with the immorality of the outside world. All aspects of man's life are carefully controlled by Frazier, the behavioral engineer. Because Frazier uses only positive reinforcement, the members of the colony possess one final freedom: They may leave the colony and be controlled by other methods. No one in the novel makes this choice.

How to Become Scientific

The first dilemma faced by the therapist who identifies with science is the manner in which he is to become scientific. The term science has become a sort of shibboleth among psychotherapists. The therapist likes to describe his efforts in scientific terms, lest he be accused of wallowing in a morass of subjectivity. The terms can have no real meaning, however, until they are related to bona fide experimental data such as that which has provided the empirical building blocks for other sciences.

Learning theorists have been quite contemptuous of psychoanalysts because the latter use scientific theories to deduce various ingredients of mind (such as id, ego, and superego) whose existence can never be proven because they can never be observed or measured. Learning theory itself, however, has been criticized because it fails to demonstrate that its terms derived from laboratory experiments and used to describe psychotherapy are in fact any more justified than the use of physical and neurological theory to justify the conduct of the psychoanalyst.

Breger and McGaugh (1965) suggest that those psychotherapies which seek justification in learning theory may in point of fact be devoid of tangible scientific content.

> Claims of scientific respectability are made with great frequency by the behavior therapists. Terms such as laboratory based, experimental, behavioral, systematic, and control are continually used to support their position. The validity of a theory or method must rest on empirical evidence, however. Thus, their use of scientific sounding terminology does not make their approach scientific, but rather seems to obscure an examination of the evidence on which their claims are based (1965, p. 339).

Breger and McGaugh argue that the scientific respectibility of the behavioral therapist rests heavily upon his attempts to associate his brand of therapy with the prestigious field of experimental learning.

They attempt to demonstrate the logical fallacies of this approach. Thus they argue that a concept such as counterconditioning is no more objective, controlled, or scientific than terms such as classical psychoanalysis, hypnotherapy, or treatment with tranquilizers.

While psychoanalysts and learning theorists have attempted to become scientific in completely different ways, they have at least agreed that a world of experimental fact stands distinct from an inner world of the mind. A skepticism is growing within the scientific community that science can be kept so free of personal values that the private needs and purposes of the scientist never intrude upon his theorizing or even upon his scientific observations. Einsteinian theories of relativity, and to an even greater extent new developments in quantum physics, question the Newtonian assumptions that a rational mind is fully able to understand a universe governed by mechanical, physical forces.

Many physicists now believe that man's perceptions of what has heretofore been considered an objective world of nature are in fact determined by psychological processes closely akin to what I describe here as personal values. The effects of these subjective factors are described by such prominent physicists and biologists as Werner Heisenberg (1959), Percy Bridgman (1958), and J. Z. Young (1951). The philosophical view of these scientists has an interesting parallel in psychology among the students of the perceptual process who conclude that man's perceptions are influenced by his needs and his expectations. Empirical studies of what has become termed the New Look in perception have related values to such common perceptions as coin sizes (Bruner and Goodman, 1947) and tachistoscopically presented words (Postman, Bruner, and McGinnies, 1948).

If these new views about the nature of the physical universe on the one side and individual cognitive processes on the other are correct, one must question whether science can in point of fact ever be value free. Attempts to find "scientific" solutions to controversial issues involving personal values and social morals often merely beg the question. The therapist's problem is not to decide whether or not to be scientific but how to become scientific. It would be foolish to charge that the wish is so fully father of the thought that science is little more than a rationalization for man's inner urges and desires. However, one might reasonably suggest that a professed loyalty to scientific method can hardly guarantee the therapist's moral neutrality. The therapist who dodges moral involvement under the guise of scientific neutrality may merely be begging the age-old question, What is truth?

Deciding the Ends of Science

The second dilemma which the therapist faces when he seeks a scientific solution to moral issues is that of deciding the goals or the purposes which a scientific approach to therapy is to serve. The experimental method requires a criterion. The therapist who seeks scientific guidance in his counseling and psychotherapy must become involved in the decision of which goals and purposes the scientifically oriented therapy is to serve.

The problem of the end or purpose which psychological control is to serve has been debated by Rogers and Skinner in their well-known dialogues (Rogers and Skinner, 1956; 1962). In the first of these debates, Rogers argues that: "In any scientific endeavor—whether 'pure' or applied science—there is a prior subjective choice of the purpose or value which the scientific work is perceived as serving. This subjective value choice which brings the scientific endeavor into being must always be outside of that endeavor and can never become a part of the science involved in that endeavor." Rogers accordingly asks: "Who will be controlled? Who will exercise control? What type of control will be exercised? Most important of all, toward what end or what purpose, or *in the pursuit of what value* will control be exercised?" (1956, p. 1060; italics added).

Empirical research merely compares two variables along the standard or scale preselected as the criterion. In studies of mental health the criterion is determined by values. In such a situation research can be but an attempt to lift one's self by the bootstraps from the horns of the ethical dilemma on which one is impaled. Research can not determine its own criterion. Without a sense of direction, increasing the technological efficiency of science has the same result as increasing the horsepower of an automobile which has no steering wheel. Without an ideologically well-grounded criterion, the search for truth through research is in danger of becoming circular as it meanders from premises to conclusions that logically depend upon one another.

Research within the mental-illness model can relate a neurotic's anxiety to certain early childhood conditions; however, it can not judge the morality of anxiety or the propriety of the preceding socializing experiences. Research on the same behavioral phenomena can also be conducted within a learning-theory framework. In this context anxiety may be related to an increased speed in learning, but science must remain morally neutral about the desirability of easy conditioning. Research in psychotherapy can be conducted within the mental-illness and the learning-theory models. Although the effectiveness of different modalities producing behavior and attitude change can be precisely assessed, one can hardly state the desired outcome either of psychotherapy or of that longer-range goal termed positive mental health. In applied situations with a multiplicity of value orientations, the scientist must look beyond the mere delineation of the variables to that basic standard for excellence which the experiment is designed to serve.

A flaw in an otherwise thoughtful book, *Current Concepts of Positive Mental Health* (1958), is Marie Jahoda's suggestion that research can select which of the many concepts of positive mental health is best. She contrasts two approaches to the definition of positive mental health: "The Utopian way, which leads to moralizing, and the scientific way, which leads to experimentation and deliberate action" (1958, p. 109). She clearly prefers an experimental approach because it is more effective than exhortation.

Jahoda discusses how research can be conducted within the frame of reference of each major view of positive mental health. From the viewpoint of a particular theory of personality much can be gained by research; but all approaches clearly benefit from discovering which of many means will best attain a desired end. Jahoda can not suggest ways in which to compare the various positive mental-health views because obviously no objective standard or criterion exists for empirical comparison.

As vital as research is in determining the effectiveness of various means to a desired end, the scientific method clearly can not produce a rational and objective definition of the ends to be served. The objective method reveals with the greatest precision the degree of difference between two variables, but until an absolute standard is found, it can tell us little about the ultimate nature of either the dependent or the independent variables. Attempts to discover final truth from relative measures result in a pseudo-science which describes the important variables incorrectly.

The therapist finds it more difficult to divorce his scientific concern for what is from his moral concern for what should be. Carl Rogers has described this problem two decades ago.

One cannot take responsibility for evaluating a person's abilities, motives, conflicts, needs; for evaluating the adjustment he is capable of achieving, the degree of reorganization he should undergo, the conflicts which he should resolve, the degree of dependence which he should develop upon the therapist, and the goals of therapy without a significant degree of control over the individual being an inevitable accompaniment. As this process is extended to more and more persons ... it means a subtle control of persons and their values and goals by a group which has selected itself to do the controlling. The fact that it is a subtle and well-intentioned control makes it only less likely that people will realize what they are accepting (1948, p. 212).

Since Rogers wrote these words, the psychological control which he prophesies has been at least partly realized. As psychological control is in fact practiced, learning theorists are also finding it necessary to confront the problem of values. Thus Leonard Krasner admits that the learning-theory therapist is in the paradoxical position of telling the patient "we will change your behavior but we do not really want to change your behavior" (1962b, p. 200). Krasner suggests that one of the reasons for psychotherapists' denials that they do in fact control the behavior of others is their fear that descriptions of this control would raise moral, ethical, and legal problems which the therapist is not professionally equipped to handle. Krasner's attitudes are rather pithely summarized by the title of a recent article (1965): "The Behavioral Scientist and Social Responsibility: No Place to Hide."

As more is written about the ethical problems raised by the intrusion of the therapist's personal values into counseling and psychotherapy, therapists who seek to derive their orientation from science have become much more thoughtful about the ethical implications of their practice. Many learning-theory therapists now suggest that the therapist should force the client to state his goals or purposes in therapy. The therapist would be expected to limit himself to the instrumental role of helping the client to modify his behaviors so that he can better attain values or satisfactions in life which would remain rather uniquely the client's.

Three reasons suggest that this solution to the problem may not be completely adequate. Often the client is so bewildered and confused that he can not clearly focus his values. Andrews (1966) suggests that even those individuals bothered by rather specific phobias are often extremely dependent and have difficulty stating their values. Second, clients are often so suggestible and impression-able that the therapist's values can be communicated and condi-tioned through such subtle cues that neither the therapist nor the client is conscious of them. This conditioning is particularly apt to occur if, as Andrews suggests, the learning-theory therapist's client is dependent. Finally, a scientist can no longer avoid responsibility for the nonscientific uses of his technological contributions. Even when the client chooses the ends to be served, the therapist has difficulty ignoring the moral implications of therapy.

THE DILEMMA OF MORAL VALUES

If many therapists seek a scientific orientation in their thera-peutic methods and goals, other therapists want more subjective guidance. Therapists of this second type hardly consider themselves nonscientific, although they differ from the therapists discussed in the previous section not only because they define the term scientific somewhat differently but also because they see science as having a different relevancy for therapy.

Therapists who refuse to depend on a traditional science in selecting their therapeutic values can be termed moralists because they are aware that therapy must be guided by some particular personal value. Although they are called moralists in their profes-sional identity, they are not to be regarded as moralistic in the sense of seeking to impose some particular social standard of morality upon a reluctant client. These therapists are morally con-cerned in the sense that they see the purpose of therapy to be that of helping the client to develop certain basic values whose ultimate worth both client and therapist can accept.

The first type of moralistic therapist is the pastoral counselor. He is likely to be guided in his counseling by transcendental moral standards or goals, such as the love of God, a personal religious experience, or the I-Thou dialogue. The pastoral counselor typically seeks to establish a relationship with a parishioner in such a way that he may experience these ethical or moral principles on a more personal basis as part of his experience of God.

The therapists who identify themselves with the so-called "third force" in psychology can be considered a second type of moralistic therapist. Since members of the third force are by definition those who express basic disagreement with the first two forces of psychoanalysis and behaviorism, they provide an obvious foil to the scientific orientation discussed previously.

Members of the third force are hardly antiscientific. But while they characteristically believe that science can tell man much about himself, they also believe that science alone can not provide man with significant self-understanding. Thus Shoben seems to express the basic third-force attitude when he writes that "psychology's great opportunity lies not in discarding its sturdily expanding methodological apparatus, but in informing it with humanistic vision" (1965, p. 218). Bugental (1964) somewhat similarly describes the third force as a convergence of science and the humanities, which results in a world of values previously inaccessible to science or to humanism alone. Bugental points out that while the third force does not disavow statistical methods or experimental tests, it must insist that experimental methods are but the means to some other end, and the ultimate criterion is human experience. Shoben (1965) points out that these experiences (or personal values) are derived not only from the experiencing of the self, but also from experiences in interpersonal relations, society, education, art, religion, and even science.

Being a Religionist

Therapists who are moralists must base their therapeutic values on their own highly subjective personal commitment. Using Paul Tillich's definition of religion as "ultimate concern," therapists who are moralists can also be regarded as religionists. From an existential perspective, third-force pastoral counselors and secular therapists alike have made a personal commitment to an inner experience they regard as the highest possible good. The secularized religion of the third force is not apt to be based upon belief in the supernatural, however. The fact that the third-force therapist seeks "the ultimate good" not transcendentally in God but more immanently within man makes neither the nature nor the commitment any less religious.

The first problem the moralist faces as a religionist is a difficulty in being frank and open about the fact that his therapeutic values are based upon the same type of venture in faith which the great world religions have always demanded of their adherents. This reluctance to admit one's religious motivations appears to be partly personal and partly professional. Typically, the therapist finds it personally difficult to identify with traditional institutional religions, as Chapter One shows. His professional reluctance is largely based on his knowledge that if the client is to be helped, he must have faith in the therapist (recall Frank's [1961] evidence concerning persuasion, healing, and faith). Sensing his clients seek guidance and support which they have been unable to find from traditional religion, he finds it difficult to admit that his own therapeutic practice is also based upon faith.

The second problem which the therapist as moralist faces is the inherent difficulty every religionist confronts when he seeks to communicate his own intense concerns to others. Inevitably religious and quasi-religious concepts are highly ambiguous. In discussing these attempts to combine human, humanistic, and humane, J. A. Cardno states that the concepts of third-force psychology "suggest theology to those who have no religious beliefs, and atheism to those who have" (1966, p. 175).

In an age popularly characterized as one of disbelief, supernatural values are inevitably greeted with skepticism. Values based upon man's inner experience are likely to be only slightly less misunderstood, however. As society becomes more heterogeneous, the inner worlds individuals experience may become more dissimilar. Whether therapists or laymen, individuals run an increasing risk of being misunderstood when they attempt to communicate their highly personal inner concerns to other people.

The traditions of religious freedom and tolerance, which are part of the morality of American democracy, impose the final difficulty in being a religionist. American democracy strongly opposes trying to impose one's private religion upon other people, since it strives to treat different religions as equally as the citizens who believe in them. Thus one is undemocratic, even gauche, when he tries to convince another of his own religious values without invitation. Third-force therapists are typically nondirective in the sense that they refrain from moralizing and from urging their clients to accept their personal values. Nevertheless, the therapist still communicates his attitudes and feelings to the client in extremely subtle ways.

Because a man's religion involves highly personal experiences, recent court interpretations of the First Amendment have rejected even the most tangential connection between government functions and expressions of religious belief. In private practice the therapist may use religious freedom openly to proclaim himself a guru, a zen master, a priest, or anything he wishes. When he works in an agency or a hospital receiving financial support from the government, however, his ability to be a religionist is severely limited.

Being a Social Movement

Just as therapists who forsake their scientific identification can be accused of being religionists, so they are also charged with being merely one more type of social philosopher or political theorist. The therapist as religionist is called upon to justify his moral doctrines in the perspective of age-old philosophical concerns, while the therapist as social planner and political activist must justify his professional endeavors by his ability to resolve socially relevant human concerns.

The moralist's dilemma is that he must be part of the culture so that he can provide leadership for moral reform and yet not be so involved with conventional morality that his social messages have only temporal significance. The moralist must therefore be wary lest his theories become only political ideologies, narrowly bound by cultural relativities. Such a morality can only reflect the culture. Just as water is incapable of rising higher than its source, so a behavioral science beholden to the *zeitgeist* is also unable to transcend cultural limits. In short, this behavioral science would lack any more authority for its pronouncements than any other social group.

If the therapist ceases to be a scientist, he must in a sense become a member of a social reform movement with the same strengths and weaknesses as any other social movement. As part of a social movement, he might select for his crusading efforts a goal of great social promise. If such a psychotherapist should find social values with subjective meaning for the general population, the mental-health practitioner would become a highly regarded member of society.

The practice of mental health as a social movement, like any other movement, would soon face cultural and historical obsolescence. As useful as many social movements have been in providing the onward push of social change, they have inevitably lost their relevance after a time. Indeed, as the rate of cultural change increases, the time in which a social movement can make a relevant contribution becomes shorter. Social change is now so rapid that a youthful crusading zealot becomes a middle-aged conservative and a standpatter. As cultural change continues, he ends his productive life as a reactionary who merely fends off rather desperately the new reform movements of a different day.

A social movement must in a sense have a rather tragic fate. If it succeeds in rallying the society to its values, its very success is its undoing. As its distinctive values are assimilated by the culture, it is no longer a reform movement. The social reason for its being has come to an end and its very successes are seen as failures by a new ideological generation of visionaries. They blame the remaining cultural inadequacies on the reformers of yesterday and organize new crusades to rally society around new values.

The fate of unsuccessful social movements is tragic in another way. Since these movements can not prove the worth of their values to the body social, their failure is more spectacular. Indeed, they may become the pariahs of their time because they threaten existing values. The very intensity with which new values are rejected may be an unintentional tribute to their social relevancy, however. In this case rejection means only that at the time other ideologies were socially more dominant. Reform movements which are rejected may find consolation in speculating what might have been. While the vigor of successful social movements is soon spent, the vitality of those which are socially unsuccessful may endure much longer. Since their panaceas have not been tried, their suggestions can not be disproven. Even when they are finally relegated to history books, they may, if they have had an intellectually martyred fate, yet inspire future generations to more fruitful social action.

The specific fate of the counselor and psychotherapist, were they to relinquish their scientific tradition and become an ideological movement for social reform, is hard to predict. Much would depend upon the therapist's specific value orientation. Should he accept those values which seem to be most popular with society as a whole, his message might enjoy rather prompt success and might soon claim a position of prestigeful and useful leadership in a wide range of social situations. The success of such a movement might rapidly lead to its failure, however, should the adopted social values merely represent a passing fancy of the body social. In this case, society would soon reject the temporary leadership of the mental-health practitioner and turn to other leadership.

The fate of the successor to mental health would be quite different were it to adopt less popular value orientations. In this case success in terms of marketable skills would be much less marked and the term of leadership might be minimal. The ideology would probably be somewhat longer lived, however, by having a greater resistance to the whim of general social fancy. Resisting the temptation of too-easy success would not guarantee future success. The future of the movement would still depend upon its ability to assess correctly the current cultural situation and at the same time to envision a future still unseen by contemporaries.

THE THERAPIST: SCIENTIST AND MORALIST?

This discussion implies that the counselor and psychotherapist face an ethical dilemma because they must choose values based either on science or on some arbitrarily selected morality. Our culture firmly believes that essential differences exist between the objective and the subjective, the biased and the impartial, and the scientific and the philosophic. Since these distinctions have become so ingrained in Western thought, the distinction between a scientist and a moralist has been a natural starting point for a discussion of ethics.

A suspicion is growing in Western culture that the scientific and the moral may not in fact be two different phenomena. Attempts to break down this subject-object dichotomy are being made by the existentialist on one side and the quantum physicist on the other. The behavioral sciences also show a trend toward reconciling the scientific observer's subjective involvement with his objective concern for truth. Rogers (1956) suggests that the psychologist can be simultaneously concerned with science and with persons, and describes how he can transcend the traditional dichotomy between subjective and objective involvement. More recently, Maslow (1966) suggests that the time has come to rededicate science.

Counseling and psychotherapy are new professions which emerged during a period which questions not only the older categories and structures of thought but also the social functions and roles of traditional professions and occupations. Therefore it is becoming more difficult to describe the therapist with the categories of a past age whose world view has become alien to ours. It is also less likely that therapists will find an acceptable solution to their ethical dilemma in outworn conceptions of science and morality.

Unfortunately, just how the therapist is to combine being a moralist with being a scientist is not clear. The subject-object dichotomy still runs deep in Western thought, and deeply entrenched mental patterns can not be adequately bridged by words which lack substantive meaning. In addressing an audience of third-force psychologists, Rogers questions the direction of therapy.

We are not fond of a mechanistically oriented, hard-headed empiricism. But what will we put in its place? An existential mysticism will not, in my judgment be good enough. Private subjective opinion will not be good enough (1965, p. 2).

Accordingly, he asks his audience (1965, p. 5): "What kind of discipline are we? Do we resemble physics? Oceanography? Religion? Or?"

If the solution to the problem of professional identity defies someone as creative and as farsighted as Carl Rogers, perhaps it should be regarded as a conundrum for which there is no current solution.

Since he is faced with basic ethical problems, the therapist's most realistic solution to the dilemma over values and morals is to admit somewhat humbly that he does not know all the answers. With such a sense of professional incompleteness, he becomes motivated to reach out to other professionals who are experiencing similar incompleteness in their professional roles and social functions. The world is so complex that it defies solutions by any single professional group. The next chapter considers ways in which therapists may integrate their professional concerns as moralists with other professions concerned with similar issues.

SUMMARY

While the therapist must swear his allegiance to some particular system of values, his choice frequently appears to be arbitrary to others. In this situation he seeks to justify his choice in one of two basic ways. First, he may turn to science in the belief that it will offer an objective truth free of values. However, he may choose to become a moralist, admitting that his choice of values is guided by subjective considerations.

Therapists are confronted by ethical problems regardless of their self-identification as scientists or moralists. Although scientists and moralists face somewhat different ethical dilemmas, neither is easily resolved. Although it is sometimes suggested that the therapist try to transcend the traditional distinction between objective and subjective knowledge, this proposal offers little toward solving the therapist's ethical dilemma.

Chapter 10

RESOLVING THE ANTINOMIES BETWEEN SCIENCE AND MORALITY

Now the whole earth had one language and few words. And as men migrated from the east, they found a plain in the land of Shinar and settled there. And they said to one another, "Come, let us make bricks, and burn them thoroughly." And they had brick for stone, and bitumen for mortar. Then they said, "Come let us build ourselves a city, and a tower with its top in the heavens, and let us make a name for ourselves, lest we be scattered abroad upon the face of the whole earth." And the Lord came down to see the city and the tower, which the sons of men had built. And the Lord said, "Behold, they are one people, and they have all one language; and this is only the beginning of what they will do; and nothing that they propose to do will now be impossible for them. Come, let us go down, and there confuse their language, that they may not understand one another's speech." So the Lord scattered them abroad from there over the face of all the earth, and they left off building the city. Therefore its name was called Babel, because there the Lord confused the language of all the earth....
GENESIS

❖❖❖

Because the therapist has no satisfactory way to combine the moral and scientific aspects of his work, he must look to other professions similarly concerned with social and psychological issues involving morals and values. To an increasing extent, counselors and psychotherapists share the moral authority that the minister or priest and the social philosopher or political theorist exercised in the past. Because these groups also experience difficulties in satisfactorily defining their moral functions, it seems appropriate for the therapist to relate his ethical dilemma to the equivalent concerns of other moralists.

Counselors and psychotherapists face an ethical dilemma because they have too often addressed themselves to the wrong question. They have dealt with mental health as a scientific problem when it would be better dealt with as a moral issue. They have sought an objective truth which past natural scientists sought in the physical realm. When the behavioral scientist's new task is seen to be that of relating man's scientific knowledge to his search for values, the moral enigma of modern man can be stated more clearly.

Part of the new task of the behavioral sciences is to relate the information which man is acquiring in an accelerating fashion to his current social condition. To ask what the future uses of the new discoveries and the new inventions are to be is to seek answers to basic questions concerning meaning and purpose. In short, the question becomes one of values, since judgments of good and evil are involved.

When one admits that science is not value free, but is inevitably an instrument of social and therefore of moral change, much of the fog of contemporary moral ambiguity is dissipated. As the therapist realizes the moral implications of various objective facts, he can use his expanded awareness to anticipate the moral consequences of social events. While the therapist can not state with objective finality that a given consequence is desirable or undesirable, he can provide contemporary society with a deeper insight and a broader understanding for making a more relevant moral judgment.

Man is currently having great difficulty in differentiating between good and evil because in the past he has gone to epistemological extremes in search of moral wisdom. The speculative philosophy of the Classical and Medieval periods was followed by scientific and technological advances in the post-Renaissance. In all these periods man was encapsulated by the *zeitgeist* in his search for truth. In terms of Hegelian historical logic, the Renaissance speculative approach to truth was followed by an equally incomplete antithesis which attempted to tear the universe apart conceptually by analyzing it mathematically. As an antithesis, this approach ignored the larger philosophical and social issues of which earlier history had been acutely aware.

In terms of Hegelian logic, we need to meld these encapsulated extremes into a gestalt to provide knowledge with a meaning and significance it now lacks. This synthesis must integrate man's new knowledge of himself and his world into a schemata which will enable him to relate the objective knowledge of science to the moral concerns traditionally regarded as philosophical.

At present a rather serious gap lies between those who conceive of the world objectively and those oriented subjectively. A concern over this cultural abyss is the focus of the writings of English novelist and essayist C. P. Snow. In a well-known essay (1959), his theme is the increasing polarization between two cultures; one the scientific, the other the humanistic. Snow's short book unloosed an avalanche of comment, leading him to conclude later that it was as if "a nerve had been touched almost simultaneously in different intellectual societies in different parts of the world..." (1963, p. 54). Since Snow is a novelist, it is not surprising that most of the comment is concerned with "two cultures" as the term is used in its more classical sense. Snow's short book has acted as a catalyst for a wide-spread concern over reconciling the humanistic concern of the liberal arts with the quantitatively more exact descriptions of the sciences.

The behavioral sciences have a vital role to play in bridging this cultural abyss. Addressing himself to the science-humanism antinomy, Sigmund Koch (1961) sees the social sciences as a third force which must take the lead in achieving a rapprochement. In Koch's opinion, what is needed are individuals with sensitivities overlapping those of the humanist and with aptitudes for scientific analysis.

The two-cultures problem which C. P. Snow and Sigmund Koch describe is part of a larger concern, however. One aspect of this larger problem is the relationship between one "culture" which subjectively derives moral values and another "culture" which seeks to deal with the problem more objectively in terms of mental-health concepts.

The problem of finding conceptual alternatives to mental health is a part of the larger problem of what man believes to be objective truth in conflict with what he feels to be subjective and affective concerns. The concept of mental health has been useful because it purports to be an objective, and therefore a scientific, term. The concept of illness will continue to be meaningful to the medical profession in situations where it is concretely and immediately useful to compare the action of an organ or the behavior of a whole organism with an objectively specified norm. But using mental-health concepts to objectify rather abstractly particular moral values is not appropriate to the new purpose of a science which no longer seeks to maintain the illusion that it can free itself from value judgments.

As the therapist seeks to bridge this gap between man's subjective and objective concerns, it should be evident that he requires a conceptual strategy which is radically different from previous attempts to find truth. The behavioral sciences can not lend their support to an ideological attempt to seek moral certainty through philosophical methods whose usefulness is now discredited, and yet they can not achieve objective certainty by using methods which have been useful for the natural sciences.

If man's need for moral knowledge is to be met, therapy must find ways to reach from its objective, scientific tradition to those professions which have been more subjective in their approach toward moral values. Of these contrasting theoretical orientations, the two most important are theology and jurisprudence. Those whose professional activities derive from these contrasting approaches to truth have been concerned with the same moral issues which the behavioral sciences have now inherited.

Chapter One presented the behavioral sciences as a new authority whose social mandate has become inextricably entwined with that older authority which the church and the law continue to exercise. Counselors and psychotherapists can not exercise the full measure of their new authority without becoming involved in that moral and ethical dilemma which results from having to choose among the conflicting values presented in Part Two. Thus therapists should not attempt to wield all of this new authority single-handedly but should seek to work with other professions that are also required to judge social good and evil.

The truism that religion is too vital to leave to theologians implies the need for an active laity as well. An equally obvious fact of current social life is that the affairs of state can not be entrusted to politicians to the extent that voters are uninformed of public issues or relieved of the opportunity of voting. While technocratic control of society is conceivable as its own self-contained morality, such a moral standard seems so alien to contemporary values that the scientist can not make this choice. The embodiment of man's highest ideals can hardly be made the exclusive province of the behavioral scientist, no matter how relevant his professional knowledge may be. The same need for public concern that requires religion to be broader than theology and democracy more pervasive than politics also forces science to look beyond itself to other social groups. Science, theology, and politics are all intertwined with the same search for a universal social good. The relationships among these three disciplines must be so ordered that each may make its most appropriate contribution to the discovery of moral truth. Finding acceptable moral standards must become a group effort which benefits from the interaction of diverse social and professional viewpoints. If the behavioral scientist is to make an appropriate professional contribution, he must find a strategy for relating his social concern to similar concerns of others who approach the same basic problem from radically different professional vantage points.

RELATING THERAPY AND RELIGION

Chapter One shows that the therapist, who has taken over many of the clergyman's functions, has thus become a new moral authority. To the extent that science becomes a pseudo-religion in this way, it supplies man with a belief in a new highest good that he previously found in religion.

The Therapist as Secular Priest

Now that the theologian has lost so much of his former authority, many therapists would happily preempt the theologian's traditional role completely. Freud regarded man's religious interest as a sign of regressive tendencies. For him, religion symbolized an attempt to gain security by returning to an early dependence upon the father. Freud had very little hesitancy in letting the psychoanalyst temporarily assume the authoritarian role of father figure to free the patient from his dependence.

Somewhat similarly, Erich Fromm (1947, 1950) criticizes traditional religious systems, which he terms authoritarian, preferring to substitute for them a more contemporary humanistic religion based on an appreciation of man's inherent worth. Humanistic religion expresses Fromm's values so directly that he equates religious concern with his interpretation of neo-Freudian psychoanalysis. Fromm concludes that the "psychoanalytic cure of the soul aims at helping the patient to achieve an attitude which can be called religious in the humanistic, though not in the authoritarian, sense of the word" (1950, p. 93).

More recently, O. H. Mowrer is also extremely critical of contemporary theology (1961). While Fromm and Freud criticize theologians for assuming too active a role in directing human affairs, Mowrer is concerned because the church has abdicated responsibility to the Freudian psychoanalyst, to whom Mowrer is exceedingly unsympathetic. Mowrer wants to strengthen traditional institutions, but he also wants to change theology to accommodate his religio-psychological views. Thus he wishes to see theological doctrines "modernized" to fit his theories of the psychological origin of sin and guilt. The church in effect would cease to be a theological undertaking and become an instrument of psychotherapeutic technique.

Certain obvious dangers appear in the scientist's attempt to assume the theologian's role. The controversial nature of the undertaking is underscored by the noticeable incompatibility of the ways that Freud, Fromm, and Mowrer (probably the three best-known scientific religionists) would assume the theological undertaking. However, it would be somewhat naive to suppose that scientists who try to answer questions heretofore answered by theologians can be less arbitrary and capricious than those theologians whom they accuse of being superstitious, dogmatic, and authoritarian.

The behavioral scientist has an advantage that in theory his terms should be more precise because the empirical nature of science frequently permits operational definitions of increasing precision. But this very objectivity blinds the behavioral scientist to the subjective judgments necessary in selecting the criterion at the very heart of experimental knowledge.

The theologian has certain advantages over the scientist. He finds himself better equipped to deal openly and forthrightly with issues of good and evil which many consider alien to science. The theologian is also better prepared to consider in a more systematic fashion the many philosophical implications of moral choices. At the same time, however, the theologian is at a disadvantage because he is frequently unable to ground his terms in concrete experience so that they are plagued with ambiguity. The language of science may fairly be described as the universal language, but the language of theology is continually blocked because the personal nature of truth is difficult to communicate.

A Willy-Nilly Interchange of Concepts

Perhaps the least satisfactory approach in the search for a way of relating theology to the behavioral sciences is what John Maguire (1962) terms "the willy-nilly interchange of concepts." This approach juxtaposes scientific and theological terminology. The churchman borrows and adapts psychiatric terms and concepts in an attempt to make the church's methods seem more "contemporary." William Douglas (1960) deals rather critically with a process by which sermons become popular psychology and pastoral care is a form of "cut-rate psychiatry." When the behavioral scientist attempts to place theological concepts within a scientific context, the results are apt to be equally unsatisfactory. The recent writings of O. H. Mowrer provide a good example of a communications impasse which can result when familiar terms are placed in an inappropriate context.

A Division of Labor

An equally unsatisfactory arrangement is the proposal to divide labor between the two disciplines. The argument is that the behavioral sciences are appropriately equipped to find the causes of human problems while religion is better prepared to find a cure. Carl Jung is perhaps the best-known advocate of this approach. In a familiar passage, he states that of all his patients over thirty-five, "none of them has been really healed who did not regain his spiritual outlook" (1933, p. 264). Certain existential therapists have adopted a similar approach in their attempt to stimulate the patient to find meaning and purpose. That there may be a difficulty in this approach arises from the suggestions made to divide the responsibility between theology and the behavioral science in an opposite way. This approach is more apt to be suggested by the theologian who views man's estrangement and alienation within a theological context and who seeks the therapist's help in reknitting sundered relationships.

A division of professional labor has customarily been made on the basis of the degree of abnormality. The psychodynamic and religious experiences of neurotics and psychotics are assumed to be radically different from those of so-called normal individuals. Furthermore, these differences are assumed to represent separate realms of truth. These assumptions are the basis for the assignment of responsibility: Theology is concerned with normal religious experience, psychiatry deals with equivalent experiences among those diagnosed psychiatrically. The current attempt to differentiate between so-called neurotic and existential anxiety is an example of this distinction. Existential theorists such as Victor Frankl and Paul Tillich base their attempts to differentiate the role of the clergyman from the psychiatrist on the types of defenses used against being.

The difficulty with this strategy is defining the line between normal and neurotic religious experience. Anton Boisen believes that an acute psychotic break is at times a constructive religious experience. Indeed, Boisen cites as an example his own psychotic break, which he regarded as having been an integral part of his solution to his own religious conflicts. (Boisen [1960] describes how he founded a hospital chaplaincy as a result of his psychotic break.) Lowe and Braaten (1966) cite empirical evidence to refute the view that psychotics are bizarrely religious. Differentiating a "healthy" from an "unhealthy" religious experience is a value judgment. The relationship between religion and neurosis would seem to be a special application of the mental-illness myth: Religious experiences that differ from one's own are judged to be symptoms of neurosis. Where cultural differences exist, unaccustomed forms of religious experience are likely to be diagnosed as a psychosis.

All these strategies fail for the same reason: They assume psychiatry and other forms of behavioral science to be a fully objective body of knowledge and they overlook the aspects of science which give it the important characteristics of an alternative religious system. The terms and concepts of mental health again appear to form a serious stumbling block. Because diagnostic labels are too often falsely perceived as disease entities with their own objective existence, a foreclosure on ideological interchange results between the mental-health practitioner who uses this language and all those who think in different terms.

Alternate Modes of Moral Knowledge

Fortunately a final way exists for dealing conceptually with the overlapping concerns of theology and the behavioral sciences. This resolution involves an application of the thinking which George A. Kelly (1955) terms "constructive alternativism." This approach allows the theologian and the behavioral scientist to "construe" the same behavior according to the distinctive conceptual approach which each possesses with no limits on the varieties of behavior which they are allowed to interpret. The only limits set are self-imposed restrictions of meaningfulness because not all behavior can be equally meaningful to the theologian and the scientist. Insight can occur only when a given perception can be connected conceptually to existing constructs. Each profession is thus left to its own creative ingenuity in erecting cognitive edifices which can provide understanding for a wide range of human behavior. Virtue in this instance is its own reward. The purpose of the construct is to allow one to predict. The effectiveness of theological and scientific "explanations" can be judged according to the utility of each in predicting future events.

For Kelly, the hallmark of effective thinking is a permeability of constructs which allows one to assimilate new perceptual experiences previously not a part of the cognitive framework of reality. If either the behavioral scientist or the theologian is to be maximally effective in his thinking, his construction of human experience must allow the alternative constructions of contrasting professional approaches. The theologian and the behavioral scientist must be prepared to learn from each other. They can do so only when they are open to the possibility that constructive alternatives exist for their own professional biases.

In Kelly's theory of personal constructs, impermeable constructs also tend to be preemptive. A preemptive construct is an Aristotelian or a pigeonhole construct in that what has been put into one category can not simultaneously be put into any other. Both the theologian and the scientist are at times prone to use preemptive constructs to manufacture a rigid and self-contained body of theory or doctrine which then becomes impermeable to relevant insights gained by other professions or viewpoints.

The church has invited outside intervention by science in its affairs because it has itself meddled in scientific affairs in times when churchmen felt scientists were heretics. The same lessons of history which make the theologian repent his past impermeability to new truth should caution the therapist, however. He must not commit the same mistakes as earlier theologians whose shortcoming was an overcommitment to a narrow, parochial truth. Within the last century the positions of the theologian and the scientist have been reversed. Since the Renaissance, power has gradually shifted from the theologian to the scientist. The church which forced Galileo to recant did so at the high tide of its metaphysical influence. The world view supported by theology has since ebbed steadily while a new metaphysical reality based upon science has grown.

If the tragic flaw of the theologian has been his encapsulation within a too-rigid theory of truth, today society allows the scientist to believe that his metaphysical presuppositions are absolute truth. The scientist faces the temptation to make absolute the relativities which are culture bound to space and time. Those theologians who at various times have been too tightly bound to traditional values would largely have escaped their cultural captivity had they heeded the new metaphysical theories of the scientists. That theologians have not always responded to a new call should be a lesson to the modern scientist who finds himself as dominantly and as firmly entrenched in his new cosmology as the theologian once was in his limited supposition of truth.

RELATING THERAPY AND LAW

The last section showed how the common moral concern of the theologian and the therapist requires some conceptual format for understanding similarities between the two professional roles. The therapist and the jurist also meet in a need to judge human behavior. Although the basis for evaluating behavior in terms of mental illness clearly differs from the process of judging a man guilty or not guilty of committing acts which society deems bad, nevertheless the same types of behavior inevitably come under both psychiatric and legal scrutiny. At stake in this overlapping concern is not merely the philosophical issue of deciding between right and wrong but also the more practical concern of finding a stable basis for maintaining social control and law and order.

Illegal Behavior as Mental Illness

Just as many behavioral scientists seek to become authoritative in religious matters, so a number of them also wish to have science seriously concerned with law. They regard deviant individuals who threaten the social stability not as criminals but as potentially treatable psychiatric cases. Crime is not a responsible act of one who acts rationally but an irrational act caused by a deep-seated personality disturbance.

The social offender may be viewed as a psychopath or sociopath who has successfully resisted all attempts at socialization or enculturation. The most familiar description of the psychopath is in Harvey M. Cleckley's *The Mask of Sanity* (1964). He describes a psychopathic type who appears to be normal, but whose sanity is only a mask. Inwardly he lacks the capacity to form meaningful social relationships and remains insensitive to the social needs of others. He seems unable to learn from his mistakes as others do because he has not experienced socially those stimuli which guide the behavior of more successfully adapted individuals.

Social deviates are also frequently considered from a psychoanalytic point of view. Alexander and Staub (1931) classify the criminal according to the degree of ego functioning which he displays. They regard the chronic criminal, for example, either as one who has lost ego functioning from toxic or organic destruction or as one whose behavior is conditioned by a neurosis. David Abrahamsen is even more categorical in his use of unconscious determinants to preempt criminology for psychiatry, arguing that the normal offender is a myth. Abrahamsen claims: "In all my experience I have not been able to find one single offender who did not show some mental pathology, in his emotions or in his character or in his intelligence" (1952, p. 125). Thus he can define crime as "a psychobiological disease" which is caused by a variety of physical and emotional defects or predispositions. His varied list of the guilty includes, in addition to the psychopath and the character disorder, the neurotic, driven by unconscious forces he can neither understand nor control, who perhaps wants to be caught and punished in response to repressed guilt feelings; and the more "normal" momentary offender who overreacts to temporary stresses as a result of emotional-arousal patterns learned as a child.

Abrahamsen's solution to crime is psychoanalytically fairly orthodox, even if it is judicially quite revolutionary. He believes that the person who is prone to commit antisocial acts should undergo psychoanalytic treatment to settle permanently conflicts among the id, ego, and superego long before he resorts to crime, since the psychological processes responsible for crime can be anticipated long in advance. Abrahamsen believes that it is useless to wait until a crime is committed to punish the malefactor because the effect of imprisonment merely increases the patient's resistance.

To implement this strategy of social control would certainly require a major readjustment in the role large social institutions play in our society. The extent of the necessary realignment is reminiscent of Samuel Butler's novel *Erewhon,* where all crime is treated as mental illness and such illness is a crime. One can apply Kelly's constructive alternativism to such a problem: Whether "deviant" behaviors are construed as "illegal" or "unhealthy" would appear to depend largely upon how useful each approach is in preventing the undesirable action.

If the problem were as simple as merely choosing between legal and psychiatric constructs, it could easily be solved. Empirical research could measure the relative effectiveness of penology and psychotherapy as preventive devices. Research is obviously needed, but it can not answer the larger question of the basis for judging whether a given behavior is socially deviant.

To regard crime as a form of mental illness serves merely to compound the severity of the problem of moral values. This strategy creates precisely the situation which Thomas Szasz decries in his *Law, Liberty, and Psychiatry* (1963). The psychiatrist's values are used not only to make moral judgments but also to give legal sanction to depriving a person of his liberty without the customary safeguards of due process of law. Institutional incarceration ceases to be governed by a legal system in which juries decide that guilt results from the breaking of democratic laws and becomes part of the autocratic prerogative of a psychiatrist, justified solely by a "mythological" mental-illness model.

Social Pathology as Mental Illness

Fortunately there are alternatives to regarding crime as mental illness. Although the first of these alternatives also relies upon an illness model, instead of basing antisocial behavior on individual psychopathology, it includes the whole social system in the concept of sickness. Therefore the individual alone is not sick, but the culture as a whole is unbalanced and maladjusted.

This viewpoint is commonly derived from psychoanalysis. In *Totem and Taboo* (1938) and in *Civilization and Its Discontents* (1930), Freud developed the viewpoint that man's psychic difficulties are related to the social group's need to impose libidinal restrictions upon the individual. Civilization is in a sense a necessary evil in Freud's view. It provides man with a needed sense of security, but at the same time it intensifies his conflict over the expression of instinctual needs which Freud apparently regarded as more important than man's sense of belonging to community. The idea that the state is man written large is not new with Freud and is hardly central to his thought, but he did see society as the inherent source of the irrational. In his analysis of the relationship between psychoanalysis and political thought, Thomas Johnston

(1965) describes Freud as believing that society has its own peculiar psychosis, which is much more than the effect on it of having psychotic members. Johnston concludes that the sickness of society that Freud described was its own sickness, not merely the sum of the sicknesses of its members.

While many have seen as society's sickness its too-strict social control, others would blame the wrong type of social control. Typical of such a viewpoint is Erich Fromm, whose views were discussed in Chapter Five. He believes, as we have seen, that there is a *folie à millions* in which an entire society has the same vices, which hardly become virtues because all members have them. Fromm's standard for judging a society is a "normative humanism" which permits a creative productivity unfettered by external social pressures. While he is much less pessimistic than Freud about an inherent antinomy between the individual and social control, he does find serious social defects in the contemporary capitalistic system, which he finds guilty of exploiting the individual for economic gain. The social overhaul advocated by Fromm is a general one, requiring simultaneous changes in the economic, political, and cultural spheres. While Fromm is not concerned with jurisprudence in a strict sense of the term, he includes law in his suggestions for a general reorganization. The political transformation reinstitutes a more democratic social concern in a manner reminiscent of a town meeting as a prelude to general cultural changes for restoring social sanity.

Placed within the context of current social needs, a system which relates social control to the whole culture has definite advantages over one which sees mental health only in terms of individuals. While terms such as health and sanity are still used, their meaning necessarily shifts when they are used to describe the body social. Since the concept of illness is still defined by what Sarbin terms its metaphorical meaning, there is less likelihood of misunderstanding. A broader use of the term in fact denies that narrower medical model which makes the so-called disease the unique possession of the individual. At the same time, this strategy recognizes the need for far-reaching social changes which include everyone involved in any form of social planning. The concerns of psychiatry or of any other behavioral science are not set against the social functions performed by the legal profession; instead a broad new vision transcends parochial professional concerns.

With a view toward keeping objective fact and subjective value separated, judging the psychological health of a whole culture has one serious shortcoming. If diagnostic terms are but thinly veiled judgments of the behavior in question, such judgments are even more apparent when applied to a whole culture. With equal aptness, therefore, Fromm could have titled his book either the *Sane Society* or the *Good Society* because the sane society has Fromm's personal values and ideals writ large upon the body social. While Freud and Fromm both describe a sick society, they hardly paint the same picture because their conceptions of man's nature differ so radically.

Social Control through Learning Theory

A third way of relating politics and the behavioral sciences uses learning-theory terminology. The learning-theory approach views government as a stimulus which is in principle the same as all the other stimuli which impinge upon the individual. Immoral and antisocial behavior is regarded, not in terms of the wanton perversity of individuals who freely and rationally choose to break the law, but as a direct reinforcement of the wrong kinds of behaviors caused by society and its different institutions.

A behavioristic description of the legal system is most fully developed in B. F. Skinner's *Science and Human Behavior* (1953), which devotes a chapter to government and law. Government in a narrow sense is defined as the use of power to punish. The terms legal and illegal are operationally defined by whether or not the behavior has any aversive consequences for the controlling agency. Law is defined as "a statement of a contingency of reinforcement maintained by a governmental agency" (1953, p. 339). Legal power is the ability of a governmental institution to reinforce behavior. Skinner sees governmental agencies as most customarily using negative reinforcement or punishment. Governments which present only aversive stimuli to the citizenry are seen as severely limited in their ability to encourage legal behavior. Even when the power of a government is limited to the ability to punish, it can still reward legal behavior by using the removal of threats of punishment to reinforce the individual responses which it deems desirable.

Skinner is able to find behaviorally defined equivalents for various principles of jurisprudence. He considers justice to mean simply that the "just" government reinforces the behavior of supporting it. Being free is not the ability to operate apart from external controls but merely a state where aversive stimuli are absent. Such freedom is generally associated with governments that govern least, since governmental action and negative reinforcement (or punishment) are likely to be closely related. "Human rights," which exist as restrictions on the power of government to control its citizens, become a countercontrol of government by the individual. Human rights are more likely to be perceived by the individuals exercising them as a countercontrol when governments exercise the original control behavior by positive reinforcements (or rewards): Those who are so reinforced feel that they are free. And finally Skinner describes the welfare state as a government that reinforces its citizens through the removal of aversive stimuli, such as hunger, cold, and general hardship.

If one carries this terminology to its logical conclusion, jurisprudence becomes behavioral engineering; precisely what happens in Skinner's Utopian novel, *Walden Two* (1948), described in Chapter Six. There is no "abnormal" behavior because there is no punishment. Punishment in turn is absent because in the narrow sense in which Skinner defines it, government does not exist.

In a conventional sense, *Walden Two* is Utopian because it describes an ideal which has not yet been realized. But if no efforts have been made to realize the bold vision of the novel, it is because the principles of behavioral engineering on which the colony would be based are still in an experimental stage. Knowledge of behavior modification is increasing rapidly, and there is every indication that for Skinner and like-minded neobehaviorists, the principles of behavior modification represent man's only real hope of social and political progress.

Walden Two must be taken for what it is: a novel. Most behaviorists would probably consider it too premature to use as a blueprint for reforming our present system of jurisprudence. The behavioristic principle that government and law should be studied empirically in terms of their consequences has far-reaching consequences for jurisprudence. If Skinner's claim that present methods of punishing criminals are almost entirely ineffective should prove experimentally true, far-reaching changes in the administration of penal justice would become inevitable. Similar far-reaching consequences of both a practical and philosophical nature would also result from substantiating a similar claim that the punishment of others is no deterent to would-be criminals.

The behavioristic conception of social control overcomes one serious handicap of the mental-health conceptualization of jurisprudence. Because its terms are operationally defined, it provides a model which can be directly translated into social action based on existing learning theory. Politics is a form of behavior, and like all other forms of behavior, it is to be understood in terms of its antecedent conditions in the same way. Thus disease entities or other philosophical concepts too abstract to provide the means to immediate behavior change need not be invoked.

The behavioristic approach to law and order is, however, conceptually even more poorly equipped than the medical model to deal with the nature of social good and evil. Skinner uses skillful ingenuity to make operational equivalents of goodness and badness in the distinction between positive and negative reinforcements. It is one thing to define good and bad in terms of pleasure and pain, but quite another to design a whole social system around the maximization of a happiness which is not further defined. A recurrent theme of this book is that conceptions of the good life differ. I (1959) have pointed out that *Walden Two* is an expression of B. F. Skinner's personal values. *Walden Two* may describe a skillful feat of behavioral engineering, but the book has only intensified the problem of defining social good.

Social Control and Political Encounter

The therapist who seeks to preempt authority in the realm of politics and jurisprudence faces many of the same ethical problems which the scientist confronts when he seeks to exercise religious authority. In the three cases, he is tempted to preempt more traditional roles and propose new social controls which utilize current psychological, sociological, and psychiatric insights. But in prescribing a "cure" for a "sick" individual or society suffering from the wrong social control, the scientist must again make a value judgment of the purpose of the social control.

Religious and political involvement have important differences for the counselor and psychotherapist. Religion is a personal encounter in which one man's experience can never be exactly the same as another's. In contrast, law is based upon the uniformity of a consensually validated morality to which all citizens are asked to subscribe. In our society political ends are democratically chosen. If the therapist is to behave ethically, he can not actively encourage the client to adopt values which are contrary to general social morality; therefore, his social control over the client remains subservient to the public moral will.

Behavioral sciences have at times taken rather gross liberties in religious and theological areas. On occasion they have avoided significant rebuke because past encounters with science have rendered the church a rather toothless, clawless tiger. The counselor and psychotherapist can not expect to enjoy the same immunity from persecution in their involvement with law and jurisprudence. The behavioral sciences in general and therapists in particular have already encountered vocal but irrational opposition from political far rightists. Right-wing political extremists realistically perceive the new human sciences as a threat to traditional values which they have long cherished. The conservative's intense need to isolate the behavioral sciences from important areas of social concern can be perceived as an attempt by a decreasing inner-directed remnant of society to maintain sociologically inappropriate values despite social change which makes new values more appropriate.

Counselors and psychotherapists should not be unduly troubled by highly irrational attacks made upon them by the political far right. If the historical analysis which is the premise of this book is correct, the strength of these groups must continue to wane as their proposed ideological viewpoint recedes further into the historical distance. Therapists should take warning, however, from the degree of vehemence which these groups display. When the therapist arbitrarily advances his personal values as desirable social norms, he can expect rebuttal from groups whose values are threatened.

The individual's freedom in religion is not possible in social control, which must bind all members of society. The same separation which exists between church and science is possible between church and state, but not between science and state. Hiroshima proved that even the most detached theoreticians are involved as citizens. The behavioral scientist whose coin is man's social nature finds his knowledge is directly and immediately involved in social planning.

The therapist can contribute much to man's political search for a more effective system of law and order. The behavioral sciences possess methods of behavioral control which can immeasurably increase the efficiency and the effectiveness of legal and judicial processes. Caution is required, however, if the counselor or psychotherapist is not to impose his subjective values autocratically upon the whole social system. Until democracy is replaced by some other consensually validated system, the therapist must keep his values subservient to the majority will as the majority value is defined by existing political institutions.

SCIENCE, RELIGION, AND SOCIETY

The therapist, the theologian, and the politician share a common social concern with implementing the good life, but each must continue to conceive of the so-called good life in his own unique way. The loss of consensual values has been so great in contemporary society that no member of these three professions can agree even with his coworkers about the nature of the good life. As one might expect, the approach to truth is even more varied when we cross disciplinary lines.

Primitive cultures have communalities in values and in social functions among government, religion, and science. A similar universal agreement seems quite impossible in modern society, nor does a common approach to truth seem in fact to be desirable. For at least the last two thousand years a rather dynamic form of tension has existed between theology and politics. The theological ideal has been that the church should be in, but not of, the world; the political ideal has proposed a separation of church and state. Attempts within Western civilization to force religion and politics into the same mold have not been very inspiring. Early in the Christian era Roman emperors tried to force Christians to worship the emperor as god with no apparent long-term political advantage for the Empire. Attempts by Gregory VII to force political unity upon the Holy Roman Empire and by Calvin to coerce the city of Geneva into theological control have similarly failed. Our society, therefore, has strong sanctions supporting the separation of church and state.

The rather intricate organization of contemporary society makes it unrealistic to suppose that Western culture can return to the simpler social organization of an earlier day when a single social institution could provide man with a comprehensive moral structure. The behavioral scientist can not preempt for himself the whole of moral authority; he must share concern for moral values with theology and jurisprudence. Each discipline has a distinctive social function and each approaches moral knowledge with different purposes. These purposes in turn result in incompatibilities that make it unlikely that science, theology, and law can ever see moral problems in the same way.

Therapy, as an additional and essential social institution, has been a third force complicating the traditional dynamic tension between church and state. Were counselors and psychotherapists to align themselves professionally either with institutional religion or with political activism, the balance between the sacred and the secular which has seemed so necessary to Western civilization would be upset. But the therapist's distinctive approach to truth and to reality makes this supposition unlikely.

The therapist can regard himself as a scientist, a religionist, or a jurist. Certainly he can not combine all three roles, and it is highly doubtful if he can combine even two of them. If he adopts the role of the priest or lawmaker, he becomes a moralist whose social function is to provide man with unambiguous descriptions of the purposes and goals of individual and corporate existence. The present human condition is such that moral meaning must be taken on faith. The moralist often experiences the worth of human experience with great intensity, and he may possess great inward certainty. If he attempts to convert others to his experience, however, he must forego any attempt to be objective in his search for truth.

If the mental-health practitioner chooses to regard himself as a scientist, he remains objective and he can not evangelize values which he believes nor proclaim laws binding the society to observe moral standards which he personally believes to be just and proper. With a broader understanding of science, however, the behavioral scientist can play appropriate roles as an other-directed age seeks moral structure in the seeming social chaos of change.

The therapist may prove his worth by developing a breadth of social knowledge which gives him insight into a wide range of human experience. And it is on the basis of such accumulated knowledge that moral judgments can most effectively be made. While his training as a scientist has not given the counselor or the psychotherapist any magical powers of moral judgment, it has trained him to remain open-minded to the possibility of his own error. If Nevitt Sanford is correct in his judgment that science is the only discipline that "can criticize itself and still go on much as before, improved but not shattered" (1965, p. 62), then the behavioral scientist has a right and even a duty to make his value judgments as a citizen in an open society which encourages the expression of even the most divergent values. M. Brewster Smith (1961) points out that since the psychologist has made an especially careful study of the human situation, he is better equipped than the average person to make value judgments. A society with such divergent values as those espoused by nudists, ethical culturalists, Communists, and members of the W.C.T.U. certainly should offer an open forum for the counselor or psychotherapist.

SUMMARY

Due to divided allegiance and authority, no single group in contemporary society can provide the sanctions for a social morality which is at the same time personally satisfying and universally accepted. The fragmentation of personal values among individuals has a parallel in the splintering of social functions among different occupational groups who play moral roles. Different professions typically fail to speak the same "language," even though they address the same moral concerns and may at times even use the same words. This chapter discusses various conceptual strategies which will allow different fields to "speak" to one another. But while the therapist, the theologian, and the political theorist can learn much from each other, it is still appropriate that members of each profession continue as moralists in their own distinctive ways. A positive benefit results from the dynamic tension among the different professional groups whose social roles must of necessity complement each other.

Chapter 11

THE THERAPIST AND THE
NEW MORALITY

"Behold, the days are coming, says the Lord, when I will make a new covenant with the house of Israel and the house of Judah, not like the covenant which I made with their fathers when I took them by the hand to bring them out of the land of Egypt, my covenant which they broke, though I was their husband, says the Lord. But this is the covenant which I will make with the house of Israel after those days, says the Lord; I will put my law within them, and I will write it upon their hearts; and I will be their God, and they shall be my people. And no longer shall each man teach his neighbor and each his brother, saying 'Know the Lord,' for they shall all know me, from the least of them to the greatest, says the Lord...."

JEREMIAH

❖❖❖

Even though man can no longer be certain about the nature of good and evil, he must still direct his behavior toward goals whose selection requires a choice of values. Moral standards are, by definition, involved in all social behavior. Man once believed that he could base morality on reason, that the nature of good was a logical part of what he perceived as a contrapuntal unity in the universe. Although man has lost faith in his rational powers, he must continue to face a world which provides at least minimal moral structure if his society is to avoid social disintegration.

Our discussion of the confusion resulting from the loss of old values in sociological and historical perspective has largely followed the social typology of David Riesman's *The Lonely Crowd* (1961). Because current use of the terms tradition, inner directedness, and other directedness have grown out of the behavioral sciences, they are likely to have more meaning for readers than the corresponding and roughly analogous Age of Faith, Age of Reason, and Age of Anxiety. But more important, we have followed this typology because it appears meaningful for the larger society represented by behavioral science. To characterize contemporary society as other

249

directed seems apt, if for no other reason than that society has virtually made the term its hallmark. Since other directedness has become so popular as a social slogan, one must assume that in some significant way Riesman's description does indeed resonate to the actual social experience of contemporary man.

It seems to be psychologically as well as historically necessary to label various periods of time. But like the diagnosis of an individual, this necessity often has evil consequences, such as an inevitable overgeneralization and oversimplification. The Age of Faith did not totally negate reason in its tradition-directed orientation; instead, through natural law it forged an encapsulated but highly reasoned form of truth. The Age of Reason which followed did not negate the older values of faith, even though the eighteenth century is classically an inner-directed period; it merely accepted different things on faith.

THE MORAL DEENCAPSULATION OF MODERN MAN

Even more dangerous than an attempt to label a historic period is an attempt to characterize one's own age with a quick phrase or a rapid summary. Self-understanding is even more necessary, however, than historic comprehension. When we compare ourselves with the fairly recent past, it seems fairly safe to assume that ours is a peculiarly unstructured time in both a psychological and a moral sense. The combination of doubt about the nature of final truth and skepticism about one's ability to know what is good has produced a unique psychological and sociological anomie shared with no other recent period in history.

Even though contemporary society has avidly seized upon other directedness as a self-description, little objective evidence supports the belief that the postrational individual is in fact any less free than the inner-directed individual who was uniformly beholden to what is called the Protestant ethic in countries where individualistic values dominated. Conformity and the need for approval are important values in many cultures. The fact that man is concerned about social uniformity is not necessarily a sign that he has in fact succumbed to herd instincts. Contemporary man's dislike of other directedness may be much like his fear of anxiety. Modern man also characterizes his period as the Age of Anxiety. This description is hardly an objective sign that man today is in fact more fearful than man was in the Age of Faith, when he had a physical horror of plagues and pestilences in this life and an equally intense spiritual fear of damnation in the next.

Modern man still falls rather short of the new individualism to which he aspires. Because values are transmitted socially, they are seldom completely individual. By definition, an individual who chooses socially mediated values conforms to some aspect of the culture. Conformity can hardly be a unique characteristic in our age. In every culture and in every age the individual is forced to adhere to some set of social expectations. But in a society with several standards for conduct and correspondingly different moral expectations, man has a freedom of moral action as expanded as his freedom of moral choice.

A totally different book would have to be written if the twentieth century was in fact a period of such conformity that the society pledged its allegiance to a single value. This book presents a social value orientation which often emphasizes adjustment and the need for approval by others, a popular view in contemporary society. But other values are also highly significant socially, and no general recommendation has been made for any single value. The existence of competing value orientations reveals that no single system irrationally binds man in a mass fashion. If this book's premise has any validity, it should be obvious that in fact the opposite danger threatens. Individuality is not so much endangered by a culture in which the desire to please others dominates all other values as it is threatened by a social system in which consensually validated moral standards have disintegrated, weakening man's identity.

Riesman and many others are concerned with what they believe is a loss of individual freedom of choice. These theorists have sensitively described the plight of modern man as he seeks to escape assuming individual responsibility. But while theorists are sound in their conclusions, they may have traced man's current moral difficulty to the wrong premises.

Although our society may demand as much conformity as other cultures, accelerating social change and constant proliferation of new ways of life prevent modern man from conforming to one set of mores long enough for them to be deeply engrained. Because the contemporary individual is exposed to a kaleidoscope of new experiences, his catholic viewpoint makes him less likely to be limited to the narrowly parochial.

Although Wheelis (1958) starts from premises similar to Riesman's by describing a loss of identity and of a coherent self, Wheelis arrives at the opposite conclusion. The loss of an inner-directed identity exposes the individual to a more varied social reality with a potential for choosing identifications far richer and more meaningful than those his father or grandfather had. Wheelis notes that individualism means many things, all of which have not declined. Wheelis agrees with Riesman that aspects of individuality —notably self-reliance, self-sufficiency, and immunity to social criticism—are indeed waning. But individualism also means the awareness of individuality, which Wheelis believes has increased. He concludes that "as man has lost his sense of identity he has, paradoxically, discovered more of those elements of his nature out of which identity may be formed, the raw materials with which to build" (1958, pp. 20-21).

Reality is no longer confined within human reason; now it includes a world with wider scope. Wheelis also points out that it is not reason that has failed, but "the attempt to achieve certainty, to reach an absolute, to bind the course of human events to a final end" (1958, p. 135). Being aware of those contingencies in his nature as the inner-directed man never was, the other-directed individual has expanded his consciousness by becoming newly aware of causal forces.

Man can no longer believe in that absolute freedom from natural cause which was so vital to his inner-directed forebears. His perception of the impingement of a social other has made him newly aware of external forces in social space which seek to direct his social movement. Man must now reconceptualize his freedom by allowing for the contingencies of life in a world which contains others. But this very awareness of the social forces which act upon him has given man insight to help him preserve his individuality from the threatening influence of a mass culture. Awareness of those factors which limit human freedom has given man additional control over them. Through knowledge of the causes of his behavior, man can transcend the spatiotemporal limits in a way that was not possible in the Age of Reason.

At the same time that an expanded awareness of the human condition has developed, freedom of social movement has also increased. Modern man regards other directedness as an epithet and much of his social behavior seems to be a self-conscious reaction against the conventional. The individual seems so stung by the charge that he lacks freedom that he chooses to be a rebel.

Joseph R. Royce (1964) uses the term encapsulation to describe the way a culture imposes the blinders of a limited world outlook on everyone who is enculturated within it. As a result of encapsulation, the dominant value orientation of the day determines man's perception of things. As a result of freezing his viewpoint, man's *zeitgeist* will not allow him to entertain ideas which are too alien to the existing habits of thought. In Royce's view, any way of thinking can become encapsulating. He observes encapsulation by rational and empirical attempts at knowing in our time.

Royce sees periods of important historical and social transition as periods of deencapsulation. He cites as examples the rending of the world view when Galileo challenged the feudal universe and the overturning of Victorian morality which resulted from psychoanalysis.

These crucial periods of change which Royce cites are what we noted in Chapter Ten as periods of revolution in the nature and purpose of science. Since our society is witnessing rapid changes in the physical and the behavioral sciences, it might seem that we would have a special opportunity to free ourselves from the constrictive enculturating forces of the past.

Royce seems quite hopeful that man can at least partly break through the several cocoons within which he is culturally encapsulated and find a broader reality. He notes that the first step in deencapsulation is to gain insight into the extent of one's entrapment within existing modes of thought. In other words, man must become aware of limitations in his conscious process. The unstable morality of our day, which forces us to realize contrasting and competing value orientations, has done much to dispel the illusion that the values into which we are enculturated are self-evidently ordained.

An awareness of alternative morals and values has also provided man with a broader awareness that further reduces encapsulation. For Royce, the second step in becoming unencapsulated is to "take in" reality through many levels of awareness. He notes that any epistemological approach is susceptible to encapsulation. Looking back over the historic periods surveyed in this book, we see that man was encapsulated by reason until fairly recently. During the Middle Ages man's overemphasis on reason entrapped him theologically. Reason also isolated and alienated his mind from other parts of his nature during the Enlightenment and Age of Reason. And still more recently, man encapsulated himself within that false rational scientific positivism which sought truth too exclusively through empiricism.

Modern man now seeks a New Truth which lies as much beyond science as it does beyond theology and philosophy. If he is to find it, he must have the freedom to interrelate the overlapping concerns of science and religion in new and creative ways; rigid answers can only trap him behind even higher walls of cognitive imprisonment. Man needs shifting modes of knowing among different moral concerns, or in Royce's terms, an intermingling of intuition, empiricism, and rationalism. The new freedom from older thought forms offers the other-directed individual the best chance to become the unencapsulated man.

One can easily be pessimistic about our age and believe that the changes taking place in society are the decay of old values which represent all that is true and just and proper in life. Indeed, little in the present cultural situation causes one to be optimistic. But an equal danger exists in reacting so strongly against an earlier false optimism that we assume change threatens all of the older human values.

Those who require a sense of moral certainty indeed have reason to despair. Science can not be expected to provide man with a synthesis of faith and reason similar to that which the Medieval Church provided feudal society. It is not even realistic to hope that science will provide man with an unbounded faith in his ability to plot his own destiny as the Enlightenment and Age of Reason did. In the name of truth science must prevent the use of mental-health concepts to achieve moral certainty and must destroy all the other rationalizations which man has devised to avoid making responsible decisions about the nature of good and evil.

MAN'S NEW MORAL FREEDOM

The new understanding of man which the behavioral sciences provide offers modern man a fresh opportunity for freedom. Today he has increased insight into the meaning and significance of his behavior. The repetition of human follies is one of the worst human tragedies, which man is now spared by a better understanding of his behavior. From a scientific understanding of cause and effect, man can in fact learn to change his behavior so that he may more profitably benefit from experience.

As man breaks through his encapsulation, he is able to transcend the creaturely bonds of space and time for the first time. Now he can see beyond the particularity and provincialism of his culture and gain an increased freedom. The new, broadened consciousness also frees man from that misleading reliance upon myth which occurs when he is trapped by a narrow cultural and historical perspective.

Contemporary man is in the enviable position of having been liberated from old superstitions and myths. He is no longer forced to rely upon magic to control a universe whose untamed forces would be terrifying were he not in technological control. He is no longer forced to place the blame for moral failure on witches and demons. To an increasing extent, he has even become sophisticated in his understanding of mental "illness," and does not use the concept to avoid responsibility by recourse to an impersonal disease process. Man's increasing knowledge frees him from old beliefs which demanded an unquestioning ideological allegiance of his forebears.

And as he has been liberated from the social demands of outmoded beliefs, modern man also has an opportunity to choose a less-arbitrary morality. A compulsive morality can not be easily sanctioned in the midst of the modern diversity of customs. The individual trapped in an anomic society may suffer, but he is at least spared the rigors of religious legalism. A pluralistic society which continually questions the nature of the good has a new openness and personal experiencing in social morality.

The most salient characteristic of our day may not be other directedness or conformism or a dominating desire to please, but what Harvey Cox (1965) terms secularization. Cox describes secularization as "the loosing of the world from religion and quasireligious understandings of itself, the dispelling of all closed world views, the breaking of all supernatural myths and sacred symbols" (1965, p. 2). Cox's premises are obviously opposed to Riesman's historical assumptions. Man's geographical crowding in a limited social space has not created other-directed values for Cox. Instead, it has resulted in the modern city, where cosmopolitan confrontations continually remind man of the relativity of myths and traditions men once thought unquestionable. Cox sees the newly secularized city providing man with an opportunity for freedom which previous ages have not possessed. He writes from a theological perspective which sees the secular city as enabling man to free himself from the legalism of a tightly controlled society so that he may embrace a gospel of love opposed to the law.

The same opportunity to embrace a freer morality transcending religious and legalistic certainty is obviously given to other men who are not theologically concerned. As man becomes increasingly sophisticated about himself and his works, he is given what may well be a unique opportunity to discard the myths of the past. The anonymity and depersonalization of mass society offer the individual a new freedom from social compulsions.

The destruction of old moral myths and the corresponding decline in absolute standards of conduct have produced what is commonly called the "new morality." This term has been loosely used to describe a number of different attitudes toward contemporary morality. The philosopher and historian Henry D. Aiken suggests that underlying this loose social movement is a common belief that ethical terms such as "good" and "bad" can no longer be associated with reason or with logic. Aiken describes the new moralists' primary attitude as that "moral experience is something wholly real but its reality is wholly personal" (1968, p. 60). He suggests that the new moralists base their values upon what they experience as their personal identity, rather than conventional standards.

Because the new morality seeks to destroy the old absolutes, it can be interpreted as modern man's attempt to escape from an encapsulated morality which seeks to restrict his personal freedom to determine his attitudes to good and evil. Bishop J. A. T. Robinson points out, in a sentence widely quoted in theological discussions of the new morality, that "Nothing can of itself always be labelled as 'wrong' " (1963, p. 118). Man's conduct ceases to be governed by social interpretations of absolute laws and regulations as man seeks to regulate his own conduct through a highly personal ethical code which is unique to his situation.

Naturally the new morality is controversial. Some fear that it will deteriorate into a "no morality" without an ethical responsibility to resist more primitive feelings and emotions. The equally passionate defenders of the new morality include Henry Aiken quoted here.

I cast my lot irrevocably with all the young sons of Socrates who in our time insist that the only morality worthy of the name is one which, finally, one discovers for oneself. If an unreflective life is not worth living, an unreflective morality, whatever its sanctions or authority, is not worth having. Indeed, it is not a morality at all but a form of politics and ideology (1968, p. 72).

Placed in this philosophical perspective, the new morality can be seen as the individual's attempt to grasp that promise of individual and personal freedom so long held out to him in the Western world as a highly illusive and an intangible promise.

This book attempts to distinguish between morals, described as standards of good and evil imposed from outside through sanctions, and values, highly individual perceptions of good and evil stemming from internal or psychological determinants. In terms of this distinction between social morals and personal values, the new morality can be interpreted as an attempt to secure a better balance between social demands and personal needs. The new morality does not seek to eliminate general ethical principles, but to become a middle ground between moral legalism and an existential antinominialism which seeks to abrogate all forms of external restraint (see Fletcher, 1966). If the new morality does not give the individual unbridled reign to pursue his own self-determined good, it does provide a balance of sorts between social demands for limits on individual behavior and personal needs to be free from the social expectations of others.

In terms of historical development, the new morality can be seen as the final decay of the social homogeneity that Pound (1942) describes as existing in so-called primitive societies and combining the social sanctions of undifferentiated religious, economic, and political suasion against the individual. Aiken (1958) observes that the old moralities were based upon what he terms "my stations and its duties" of the conventional political man, educator, churchgoer, family man, art lover, good citizen, and good man. He points out that "when this world breaks down, when its 'stations' fail to stay put or involve him in conflicting responsibilities which he cannot resolve, his sense of objective right and wrong becomes insecure and in some instances, disintegrates" (1968, p. 67). As we have seen, such an experience of anomie and *angst* motivates contemporary man to seek therapy. The current moral flux does, however, provide the individual with a unique opportunity to differentiate himself from the social other so that he can construct his own authentic values.

THE NEW MORALITY AS THERAPEUTIC ETHIC

Therapists differ among themselves about what values are basic to counseling and psychotherapy. Furthermore, the conceptions or constructs of the psychotherapist maintain a dynamic tension with the somewhat-parallel interpretations of moral truth by the theologian and the political theorist. One value, however, occupies such a prominent place in the Western world that it appears capable of providing a common ground for different schools of therapy as well as for professional groups: personal freedom.

Freedom has not always been clearly defined, and because it is such an elusive ideal, modern man has become embroiled in a controversy over what it is and how he is to attain it. There is increasing agreement, however, that man should be free from external authority and from myth, magic, and superstition. Dominant trends in our culture are veering sharply away from ethical principles based upon a repressive social morality toward a new morality in which the individual determines his own values. It seems appropriate, therefore, to seek in personal freedom the resolution of the ethical dilemma posed for the therapist by competing and contradictory value orientations. Therapists are still unlikely to agree among themselves about the meaning of mental health. They are more likely to agree, however, that the so-called good life is a highly personal matter, and that one should select his values without even those attempts at social suasion which are intended to be helpful.

This perspective gives new meaning to the historical development of counseling and psychotherapy. The founding of psychoanalysis can be regarded less as a scientific breakthrough and more as an attempt to strike a blow for individual freedom in the stifling atmosphere of Victorian morality. Further support for this view appears in David Bakan's (1958) suggestive interpretation of Freud's work. Bakan believed that Freud was greatly influenced by the Chasidim, a Jewish mystical sect who were antimoralistic in their opposition to the legalistic strictures of the Torah or Jewish law. The Chasidim, or Hasidim, believed that Judaism should encourage the individual to derive his own values from a mystical and therefore a highly personal experiencing of God. Bakan believes Freud saw his historical mission as that of a new Moses. If the first Moses led the Jews into moral oppression by imposing the law upon them, Freud identified himself as a latter-day Moses who would at last lead them into a promised land of individual freedom.

The nature of Freud's personal motives must remain a conjecture, but the effect of psychoanalysis upon Western morality can be publicly observed. Whether or not Freud was motivated as Bakan suggests, Freud's success in demolishing a legalistic and moralistic view of life must have exceeded his wildest imaginings, although psychoanalysis alone is hardly responsible for that general relaxation of moral restriction in such diverse social areas as sexual morality and child rearing. If psychoanalysis can be viewed as but one of a number of complexly interrelated social changes, at the very least it has provided a convenient rationalization for accepting the changes engendered by other social pressures.

Nonpsychoanalytic counselors and psychotherapists have not always been as direct or as simplistic as many analysts in seeking to overturn society's moral control over the individual. Nevertheless, therapists have rather universally conceived themselves to be the agents of their client and therefore have tried to help him achieve an identity which will more completely differentiate him from others in the so-called other-directed social mass.

Aiken notes that the phrase new morality applies to people who are in one way or another uniquely exposed to the predicaments of modern life. He suggests that "this vulnerability is usually a function of their thoughtfulness and sensitivity, their powers of imagination, and their readiness to assume personal responsibility for their choices and actions" (1968, p. 60). The new moralist whom Aiken describes appears to be someone whom the typical therapist would regard as the ideal client. Such a person certainly would be well-motivated for therapy and would carry an excellent prognosis. If, as Aiken suggests, this person's goal is to become like the "self-renewing ancients for whom today is the beginning, as well as conceivably the end of time" (1968, p. 60), then the therapist would find his goals for personal growth and maturity to be quite compatible with his own.

Various schools of therapy have sought to translate the principles of the new morality into practice in different ways. Even though opinion diverges rather broadly about how personal freedom is best attained, agreement appears common among virtually all types of counseling and psychotherapy that the purpose of therapy is to loosen the constrictive effects of a social control which uses oppressive and legalistic morality to deprive the individual of a meaningful choice of values.

The goal of increased moral freedom can be seen in a humanistic value orientation. Humanistic therapies attempt to increase the range of moral choices by promoting such inner qualities as growth, personality enhancement, and self-actualization. The purpose of therapy is to help the client develop a stronger concept of self or sense of identity by providing him with the strength to assert his independence of the demands and expectations of others. Because humanism regards the individual as the ultimate value, his right to affirm his unique experience of the highest good is the basic value underlying humanistic thought. The individual's decision to subordinate his personal values to a general social good must be a free act reflecting rational decision-making. Therapy thus becomes a process of learning to assert one's personal mastery over social moralism.

While a humanistic value orientation seeks rather gently to strengthen and develop the human will to assert itself, a naturalistic orientation uses more radical means to free man from moral bondage. The learning theorist associates the acquisition of a social morality with punishment and other aversive controls. Unlike the humanist, the behaviorist does not believe that man is in any meaningful sense free to choose his personal values and therefore he can not define the term new morality as such thinkers as Aiken, Fletcher, and Robinson do. Naturalism does appear to have its own interpretation of the new morality in its description of rewards or positive reinforcement to replace coercion as a social control. Theologians such as Fletcher and Robinson base the new morality on *agape* or Christian love, but naturalists such as Skinner subscribe to a more naturalistic love. Skinner's novel, *Walden Two* (1948), describes the Utopian ethic in a conversation between Frazier, the behavioral engineer who controls the colony, and Burris, the autobiographical protagonist.

> "These are my children, Burris," he [Frazier] said, almost in a whisper. "I *love* them . . . . What is love," he said with a shrug, "except another name for the use of positive reinforcement?"
> "Or vice versa," I said (1948, pp. 249-250).

From a moral standpoint, a social orientation is perhaps the most conservative system discussed in this book. Social-value therapies often seek to increase the client's understanding of the moral demands and expectations of various significant others and typically seek to create a moral interchange between the individual and the social other. A morality based on social mutuality is described in Buber's (1947) concept of the I-Thou dialogue. What this book describes as a social value orientation appears to be most closely related to Fletcher's (1966) interpretation of the new morality as "contextual" or "situation" ethics. Therefore certain parallels exist between therapies which attempt to make human relationships more meaningful and situation ethics which interprets moral situations in terms of personal meaning for the individuals involved.

Existentialism is the value orientation which most searchingly questions the old moral order. Historically speaking, Søren Kierkegaard seems to have been the first modern man to be concerned with a loss of individuality in an encapsulating society. Kierkegaard saw the individual completely surrounded by moral demands until he became little more than a hapless puppet who enacted the social roles demanded by others. In our century existentialists share a common concern for an individuality which can find courageous being by creating uniquely purposive values. Today some existentialists' desire for a sense of moral freedom may be carrying the principles of a new morality to the extreme which their critics often term a no morality. Joseph Fletcher (1966) regards his situation-ethics approach to the new morality as alien both to legalism, with its moral straitjacket, and to the existential thought that he regards as antinomian.

MORAL DEENCAPSULATION:
AN INTERDISCIPLINARY APPROACH

A broad interpretation of the new morality has an advantage not only of providing a meeting ground for otherwise highly divergent types of therapy but also of providing a common frame of reference for relating the therapist's professional concerns to the activities of other professionals. The therapist's roles overlap those of the clergyman, the political theorist, and the scientist in ways that are poorly understood. These professional groups devote themselves to reducing man's encapsulation within a narrowly limited cosmology or world view. As moral freedom becomes more dominant as a contemporary style of life, other professions seek to widen man's perceptual horizons.

Because different fields of knowledge are becoming more interrelated, the task of increasing man's deencapsulation must involve many professional groups. If man is to reduce his allegiance to the moral myth, the therapist must join other professionals seeking to expand man's general awareness. While it would seem appropriate for the religionist, the politician, the scientist, and the therapist to maintain their distinctive professional identities, each of them may contribute in his particular fashion to the general goal.

Religious Deencapsulation

In a primitive society, religion functions in a predominantly moralistic way. The meaning of the term religion is implied by its etymology: *re+ligare*, to tie back, to bind together; thus to unite disparate elements of the culture into a homogeneous unity. Primitive religion typically receives its cohesive force from the traditions of the society and provides a rather elaborate rationalization for beliefs which it encloses with sanctions derived from society's belief in a supernatural.

Perhaps the most obvious example of a moralistic religion is medieval Christendom. Through its elaborate synthesis of faith and reason, Roman Catholic scholasticism provided the believer with an elaborate explanation for the whole natural order. While feudalism never became a completely closed society, the Church provided an organic unity that seems unparalleled in Western history.

Feudal unity collapsed with the breakup of the Middle Ages and the advent of the Renaissance and the Reformation. To some extent the Reformation did result in religious diversity, but the new Protestantism remained entwined with the social order, providing a partial justification for a new moralism. To label the capitalistic morality which emerged during the Reformation as the Protestant ethic is not entirely fair. Certainly the new religion and the new mores were interrelated, however, even if the connection seems more complex than many sociologists have implied. Religion thus continued to provide a general justification for society to the extent that as late as the early twentieth century Émile Durkheim could describe religion as functioning as society's only effective cohesion. In his view, religious beliefs and rituals symbolized the moral power of society itself.

The last half century has witnessed an abrupt shift in the social role of religion, however. Sociologists still define religion as a social process and study its relationship to other aspects of culture, but now religion is a more personal matter and to an increasing extent, it is becoming more meaningful to describe it psychologically as man's own highly personal experiencing of what he regards as his highest good. Older religions binding the individual to traditional mores still exist; but as the forces building what Cox (1965) terms the secular city become socially more pervasive, religion will no longer be able to justify the older moralities.

Within this context of a psychological or individualistic religious style, the new morality has taken form. Aiken writes that "the younger new moralists, consciously or unconsciously taking a leap out of the writings of certain radical Christian thinkers, including St. Augustine, Pascal, and Kierkegaard, are preoccupied with possibilities of self-discovery and self-transcendance of being 'twice-born' " (1968, p. 70). While Christian new moralists limit the individual's moral freedom, these restrictions are set forth by *agape*, or love. Love in essence becomes a law unto itself. Advocates of situational morality are therefore fond of quoting Augustine's famous saying: *Dile et quod vis fac* "Love and do as you please," or as Fletcher translates it, "Love with care and *then* what you will, do" (1966, p. 79).

The type of love which guides the theological new morality is plainly a different quality from emotional feeling or desire. Robinson describes the basic value of the new morality as "the fact that persons matter and the deepest welfare of these particular persons in this particular situation matters, more than anything else in the world" (1963, p. 118). The new moralist is therefore extremely self-conscious of the danger that an abstract ideal such as *agape* can become an encapsulated or legalistic moralism when one attempts to translate it into universal principles of human conduct. The new moralist must concretely express his concern for the particular person by considering each case as a unique ethical problem. Therefore Fletcher appropriately titles his book *Situation Ethics* (1966) and James A. Pike calls his book on this topic *You and the New Morality: Seventy-four Cases* (1967). Both books would be rather meaningless without the illustrative material the authors provide to discuss the love ethic in a particular person's life.

While it may be true as David Roberts (1950) suggests that traditional types of theology have also shared a concern for an individualized morality with the contemporary psychotherapist, it is obvious that the new moralist has been able to find a new meeting ground where theological and therapeutic values may reinforce one another. It seems therefore highly significant that both have adopted the case-study approach. Because the theological new moralist regards love as a transcendent reality which he can not adequately describe in psychological terms, he depends on the therapist to illuminate the actual or psychodynamic significance of love for a particular person. Robinson points out that the new morality makes searching demands on the depth and the integrity of one's concern for another. Therapists show this concern in their attempt to respect unconditionally the unique individual that they and the theological new moralist serve.

Political Deencapsulation

Many of the same forces responsible for religious deencapsulation have also increased the individual's political freedom. The feudal political system encapsulated the individual within a tightly structured society in which everyone from the serf to the feudal lord had a social position with only a limited possibility of movement. During the High Middle Ages a limited amount of political freedom could be gained by becoming an artisan or a merchant in the nascent cities. Later, during the Renaissance and Reformation, man could consider a variety of ways to govern his political life. Political freedom came slowly, and not until the great political revolutions of the eighteenth century did political systems emerge to express the democratic ideals of freedom, liberty, and equality.

To claim that the political deencapsulation of modern man has been completed would be foolish. Indeed, political theorists representative of rightist and leftist ideologies fear that the modern individual is losing his political freedom. They perceive as the danger a political establishment or governmental bureaucracy that becomes insensitive to individual differences and must demand an increasing similarity and passivity among its citizens. Many political ideologists fear that the hard-won political freedom implied by terms such as democracy and human rights is lost when the substantive meaning of these terms is replaced by a jargon which further encapsulates political thought.

While the term new morality seems to have originated in a theological concern for individualizing religious ethics, it has entered popular usage more often as a description of the moral attitudes of individuals who feel that they are in social and political bondage. Aiken (1968) traces several social and ideological currents that contribute to what is in effect a turbulent vortex of strains providing the cultural context for the new morality. He describes a number of predicaments which have contributed to modern man's feeling that he has lost political control over his destiny: the endless nuclear crisis; the race crisis, with its suggestion that American democracy is in fact an oligarchy with a democratic front; and the educational crisis of a multiversity subservient to moral ideologies which contradict the aspirations or values of students and teachers.

Chapter One showed that as man becomes disillusioned with conventional political solutions to social problems, he turns to counselors and to psychotherapists for highly personal solutions to problems which politicians have been unable to alleviate through large-scale government programs. As politicians and jurists work more closely with therapists, government in its many forms will likely become more open to individual differences.

Counselors and psychotherapists are a morally and politically diverse group who hardly adhere to any narrow political line. Few, if indeed any, comprehensive studies have been made of the political attitudes of therapists. A probable general description of the political attitudes of social scientists by Nevitt Sanford also applies to the typical therapist: "It is a plain fact of observation, well-known to politicians, foundations, and government officials, that social scientists as a group tend to display a value orientation of a characteristic sort; they are overwhelmingly on the liberal or humanistic side of issues" (1965, p. 60). Sanford believes that his scientific training causes the social scientist to line up against what he describes as the enemies of freedom and humanity. By combining the scientist's inherent skepticism of any closed system of thought with the clinician's sensitivity to individual need, the therapist is well prepared to produce a political deencapsulation which can provide the citizen with a significant increase in his moral freedom.

Scientific Deencapsulation

Modern science has been so closely associated with man's success in freeing himself from prescientific myths, superstitions, and magic that one might assume that scientific enterprises have always produced open and flexible knowledge. However, science has often produced beliefs which became dogmatic and closed to possible revision.

The original function of science was to rationalize various aesthetic and philosophical conceptions of the world. During the classical and the medieval periods, science was an encapsulating force that justified old beliefs rather than opened man's mind to possible reinterpretations of the world through new forms of knowledge. Indeed, as time passed, scientific encapsulation became more rigid. During the High Middle Ages when the scholastic philosophers attempted to combine Aristotelian science with feudal Christian theology in a grand synthesis of faith and reason, they produced a philosophical system which, if highly unified, was also tightly enclosed.

After the Renaissance, science gradually emerged as a progressive ideological influence which helped to open man's minds to the possibility that he might construe the natural world in radically different ways from those of the Middle Ages, but there was no sudden break. If the Copernican revolution finally succeeded in opening man's eyes to a radical reconceptualization of the world and the nature of man, the process was, as Kuhn (1957) points out, a prolonged one in which truth commingled with error for a long time.

The more sophisticated mental attitudes and the more highly developed experimental methods of the post-Renaissance scientist kept man from becoming enslaved to grossly superstitious beliefs about nature. During the classical period which culminated in the work of Sir Isaac Newton, science nevertheless replaced a primitive superstition with more sophisticated encapsulation. E. A. Burtt (1932) points out that during the period between Copernicus and Newton the physical sciences developed their own metaphysical truth, which in many respects was as arbitrary as that of the pre-Renaissance philosophers.

The twentieth century is witnessing a new openness and freedom in science. This change is in part due to modern science's freedom from the metaphysical presuppositions and mechanistic theories of Newtonian physics granted by the new discoveries of relativity and quantum physics. In large measure this deencapsulation is also due to a new understanding of how man's nature intrudes into scientific exploration and discovery. Chapter Nine cited the work of such scientists as Heisenberg (1958), Bridgman (1959), and Young (1951), who describe scientific discovery in psychologically dynamic ways. The new need for scientific openness is also suggested by Kuhn's (1962) description of scientific discovery as the discoverer's ability to accept the incongruity of scientific anomaly. New discoveries can, in his view, occur only when the scientist possesses the cognitive flexibility to overcome the response set imposed upon him by the entrenched scientific status quo.

Because counselors and psychotherapists are rather self-consciously aware that they lack prestige in the scientific community, they too often have been willing to accept secondhand theories which are already timeworn in the scientific disciplines which developed them. Borrowed theories are even more likely to become encapsulating than other types. When therapists tacitly accept a bottom position in the scientific hierarchy, they become the unwilling slaves of authoritarian dogma which they do not dare question.

When the therapist deencapsulates himself from inappropriate scientific models, he creates a new spirit of questioning which may spread to older, closed types of scientific knowledge. Michael Polanyi (1964) suggests that qualities of passion, commitment, and conviviality are vital qualities of what he calls personal knowledge. The therapist can develop these qualities in the scientific investigator by helping him create an openness which, in turn, can invite new types of discovery.

THE DANGER OF A NEW MYTHOLOGY

As man renews his quest for moral certainty, he inevitably turns to the one moral source whose authority he can now accept: the therapist. Since man regards older moral standards as but the relics of the past, science has become a bright hope in what some despair to be an enveloping moral darkness. Through necessity, modern man who can find no other certainty turns to the therapist as a secular priest and the giver of a new psychological law. In these new social roles the therapist must provide a growing number of individuals with their only certainty.

In this new role of replacing older moral myths with newer, more subjectively real beliefs the therapist experiences ethical and moral dilemmas. He can not be certain of the truth himself. Even though they have a basic commitment to an objectivity which produces consensual agreement, counselors and psychotherapists find their collective efforts create a cacaphony of competing and conflicting claims of the nature of good and evil.

While the therapist as a behavioral scientist has traditionally been regarded as a purveyor of objective truth, his social role must now change. The new scientist, who can not provide certainty, can offer man a broader understanding of his behavior. Today part of the behavioral scientist's role must be to transcend his encapsulation by space and time. He has already helped man to outgrow narrow, nineteenth-century bourgeois individualism by exposing man to a broader reality. By placing human behavior in a causal matrix, the psychologist enables man to enrich his understanding of past history and of man's behavior in terms of its causal antecedents. At the same time, the anthropologist has extended the new significant awareness of behavior into space by enabling man to transcend cultural limits.

While science has erected a cognitive platform from which man may view the past and surrounding cultural space, it can not forecast future behavior with the same confidence. In our culture man is highly jealous of his moral freedom, however, and will rebel whenever science predicts a new world in which man sees himself deprived of moral choice.

As tempted as the scientist may be to use his powers of prediction and control to project into the future, he must not become a seer. Setting distant goals is not part of the scientific enterprise. While the therapist as a behavioral scientist must make his own commitment to an ever-improving good life, little in either his training or his professional role gives him the right to proclaim the best of all possible worlds to which man must be beholden.

In man's present state of historical evolution, he can not know the final Truth any more than he can feel absolutely free from natural contingencies. Man is now more aware of his limited knowledge than he has been for many centuries, a state that science has done much to create. Fortunately science has made unreal those older values which were relative to historical circumstances, and has liberated man from a destructive reliance upon myths which create a false certainty.

If it has been good for science to liberate man from the false certainty of moral superstition, it would be wrong for the scientifically oriented therapist to forego his quest of objectivity in order to heed the importunate seeking for the moral guidance of an other-directed culture. No matter how much man may fear the uncertainties of an age of relativities and may seek a new absolute to free him from moral ambiguity, the therapist can not allow science to become a placebo or a psychological aspirin pill. While contemporary man may seek some new authority to provide a renewal of moral certainty, the therapist's scientific commitment to truth will not let him accept these new social demands.

The therapist as a man of science is properly a destroyer of myths. His social role causes man piquantly to question the significance and meaning of even those beliefs which he most cherishes. His task is to provide the inquiring and objective attitude which enables man to correct the irrelevancies and inconsistencies of old beliefs which are no longer useful.

If one combines a historical interest with an inquiring mind, it is not too hard to refute past myths. The foibles of cultures alien to our own are easily exposed by the anthropologist. Even a second-rate philosopher or semanticist can expose past conceptual fallacies once glorified as philosophical absolutes even in our culture. The ease with which one exposes the inappropriateness of other ways of life is directly proportional to one's psychological distance from them. When contemporary values are at stake, it is manifestly more difficult to deny the assumptions upon which our ideological beliefs must rest.

Our generation would be exceedingly presumptuous to claim that it is immune to mythmaking. Contrary proof can be seen in the appearance of so many different value systems seeking to replace the myth of mental health. Each of these value orientations presents itself as the ideological successor to the mental-health myth and, in a certain sense, each claims the other systems are part of modern mythmaking. One value system claims ideological correctness by branding all competitors as false.

To resist new mythmaking is somewhat painful; man must pay for his new moral freedom. As he bears the full weight of his new responsibility, he experiences that experience of personal crisis which the existentialist terms dread, or *angst*. Modern man's anxiety no longer seems due to threats to his physical survival but to an increasing lack of social structure. Old values are disappearing and no new ones replace them. Man despairs and often is angry because old beliefs can no longer be accepted, and society seems incapable of providing a new morality that can claim his allegiance. Moral structure is lacking, and man faces painful ambiguity. Alienated from traditional Western values, he experiences anomie at the lack of meaningful social goals with which he can identify.

Life has always had painful ambiguities. Man feels anxious when he can not maintain psychological control over certain areas of life. The therapist as a human being also dreads the ambiguous. Indeed, the very intensity of his need for clarity has driven him to become a behavioral scientist in order conceptually to tame the realm of human behavior. The scientist who sought for certainty in the physical realm has been startlingly successful in creating a technology which has tamed nature. But while the natural sciences have found their subject matter readily cooperative, the reality pursued by the behavior scientist is much more elusive. Although the physical scientist must make certain metaphysical assumptions, the behavioral scientist confronts a much less structured reality and must project more of his own values upon the amorphous phenomenon of human behavior.

Ironically the same quest for certainty that seems so desirable in the study of the physical universe becomes the therapist's nemesis when his intense need to be objective is directed by social necessity to morality. In the physical sciences, the scientist can ground his search for meaning on mathematical absolutes. The behavioral sciences can create order only from central tendencies and deviations based on norms that are entirely relative to his social times. Lacking mathematical absolutes, the behavioral scientist must project a more highly personal intellectual order onto his field of study. The very intolerance for uncertainty which motivates the scientist's search for truth can totally undo the therapist when it leads him to postulate simple answers for highly complex moral problems. His intense need for objectivity may lead him to replace old falsehoods with a newer mythology made even more insidious by its very claim to scientific impartiality.

Man is never so wrong, it seems, as when he is falsely certain. Perhaps science's greatest gift to man is an inquiring mind, constantly searching for an elusive truth which has refused to take tangible form. Among these things which must still be accepted on faith are the goals toward which behavior is directed. These goals are determined by man's views of good and evil, and not by scientific method. The therapist's role is to destroy myths. He is not allowed to create new ones.

SUMMARY

Contemporary man's bewilderment over personal values and social morals is a problem crying for a solution. No consensually validated answer can be given to the perplexed individual seeking moral direction. Contemporary value orientations are all controversial. The proverbial dark cloud does, however, have a silver lining. While contemporary moral ambiguity makes many individuals acutely uncomfortable, the presence of competing and contrasting value orientations provides modern man with a wider range of moral choice than probably ever existed before.

Modern man has been concerned lest he lose his freedom to choose personal values. The popularity of the epithet "other directedness" symbolizes modern man's fear of becoming a moral conformist. Man's awareness of alternative values, however, has produced an open-mindedness which helps him avoid moral encapsulation.

The open moral style of a culture which has learned to tolerate the individual's choice of his own values has been termed the new morality. The new moralists advocate reducing the amount of social control over the individual and increasing his freedom to select personally meaningful values. While therapists disagree about virtually everything else, almost all counselors and psychotherapists would agree with the new morality. Other new moralists can be found in professions with whom counselors and psychotherapists share moral leadership, and the value these professions place upon the new morality provides a common social bond among them.

Therapists have traditionally identified with science in their attempt to increase man's moral deencapsulation. While the spirit and method of science have helped man become more open, the danger always exists that scientific orthodoxies will produce new forms of encapsulation. The therapist must beware lest he destroy the client's moral freedom by imposing a new scientific encapsulation upon him.

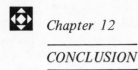

Chapter 12

CONCLUSION

Do not be conformed to this world but be transformed by the renewal of your mind . . . . PAUL'S LETTER TO THE ROMANS

❖❖❖

This book has discussed the moral significance of a relationship between a client who is typically anxious and uncertain about his system of personal values and a counselor or psychotherapist who faces an ethical dilemma of what value orientation is to determine the moral guidance he provides the client. Clients seldom describe their need for therapy in terms of problems involving values, just as therapists seldom describe themselves as moralists. On one hand, if we define values as the psychological process of constructing a general outlook on life, then values logically color every decision-making process. On the other hand, if morals are related to the social process through which society imposes sanctions to influence the individual to follow socially defined standards of conduct, then therapy can be regarded as a process in which the client searches for significant values while the therapist responds either actively or passively by providing moral direction.

Certain general themes recur throughout the book. The first theme is that problems involving values and morals have become intensified because our period in history considers itself post-rational. Previously values and morals were determined by tradition or by reason. These guidelines are particularly apt to be unavailable to those seeking guidance from the counselor or psychotherapist.

The second general theme is that the therapist combines science with morality in his relationship with clients. The inter-relationships between these two roles are highly complex. Therapists disagree as to how they should integrate morals and science, or even whether they should try to do so. Because controversial issues are involved, counselors and psychotherapists find themselves faced with a professional or an ethical dilemma.

The third general theme of this book is that typically therapists attempt to disguise their professional moral dilemmas by using a professional terminology that connotes scientific objectivity. A serious example is the use of psychiatric terminology derived from concepts of mental illness to rationalize the psychiatrist's moralistic biases. While the concept of mental illness has been morally very meaningful for a rational or an inner-oriented culture, it has only limited relevance for a post-rational society.

A fourth recurring theme is that as mental illness is exposed as moral myth, counselors and psychotherapists must discover alternative theoretical value orientations to provide moral meaning for the client. Although theories of personality or therapeutic orientations are not lacking, these terms are as heavily laden with implicit value judgments as the psychiatric concepts which they have replaced.

The first part of the book was a general consideration of the relevance of morals and values for counseling and psychotherapy. The modern individual who finds the older moral guidelines to be wanting experiences a general moral bewilderment. He seeks guidance from a therapist, who finds that he has become a moralist, expected to function as the clergyman and the social philosopher have in the past. But while the therapist describes the various aspects of the therapeutic relationship in nonmoral terms, his personal values subtly and inevitably intrude. If he is somewhat of a traditionalist, he may still seek to disguise the moral nature of his task by saying that he is merely curing a mental illness. He is more likely to be psychodynamic in his outlook, however, and attempt to disguise the intrusion of his values with personality concepts. He therefore describes therapy in terms of the seemingly objective concepts of needs, frustrations, and goals.

Part Two discussed what currently appear to be the most important moral alternatives to mental health: the humanistic, the naturalistic, the social, and the existential alternative. Each of these four replaces the inner-oriented mental-illness myth with a new, other-oriented reality based on concepts implying causation, antecedent conditions, intervening variables, and similar terms. These alternative mental-health meanings were discussed in a causal or psychodynamic framework involving needs, frustrations, therapeutic intervention, and goals. Each orientation is as moral as the mental-illness model which it replaces, however, because each system starts with a subjective and personal judgment of which human motives are the most highly valued aspects of human experience. These four basic value orientations have a significant number of adherents and of critics who raise serious objections to them.

Part Three considered the issues raised in the first part at greater depth. The counselor and the psychotherapist face a professional or an ethical dilemma because the value orientations discussed previously conflict with one another. The therapist is clearly required to declare his allegiance to some basic system of values, yet the choice of values is not only doubtful, but the justification for it is also problematical. While the therapist can justify his choice either scientifically or morally, he faces an ethical dilemma in either event. No resolution exists for the dilemma of competing and conflicting value orientations. The therapist should perhaps relate his role as social moralist to the professional efforts of others with whom he shares contemporary moral leadership. Modern theology and political theory share much of the therapist's moral confusion. One common value therapists share with each other and with kindred minds in other professions is the new morality, which encourages each individual to construct his own interpretation of good from uniquely meaningful experiences.

THE NEW MORAL ORDER

One can come to different conclusions about the contemporary social situation. For some, the disintegration of moral standards symbolizes the incipient decay of Western civilization. They believe that the preservation of Western culture depends upon sharing certain basic values. They fear that civilization will be sorely threatened by the disintegration of what they regard as morals basic to Western culture during the last five hundred years of rapid growth and expansion. They fear a world which lacks effective social sanctions because they see an urban, industrial society as uniquely dependent upon a high degree of social structure. They believe that in a world which is increasingly interdependent, individuals anticipate and predict each other's actions with reasonable precision. They perceive signs of social disorganization in moral changes and dread the approaching tragic fulfillment of Hobbes' classic prediction that life in a world without social control is nasty, brutish, and short.

Others, however, have reached an opposite conclusion. They regard the current moral flux as the final flowering of certain values which have long remained dormant. They believe that man finally is to witness the triumph of an individualism he has been struggling to realize ever since the Hebrew prophet and the Greek philosopher challenged the social provincialism and moral conformity of the primitive tribe. They see the increased moral freedom as an opportunity for the individual to develop a new experience of personal responsibility. Contemporary society offers man a new challenge to control his own destiny and to advance a culture whose moral orientation is based on individual freedom and equality.

Many long nostalgically for historic periods which have been morally serene. Some want to return to an organic unity such as that existing during the Age of Faith and unknown in later periods. Others choose that spirit of rationalism dominant during the Age of Reason as their highest value. Both groups therefore would actively resist the social forces helping to produce a postrational society.

To approve a new moral freedom which gives the individual greater freedom to choose personally meaningful values is itself a value judgment, possibly one that a majority of people in our society would not care to make. Value judgments are also required, however, in the vocational choice to be a counselor or a psychotherapist. Since the therapist is still a minority in our society, many of his attitudes and his biases must also represent a minority viewpoint.

The personal value that most characteristically seems to lead one to become a therapist is that other individuals should be helped to become more free. The therapist must therefore oppose the counterclaims of moral conservatives who believe that individuals should conform to existing conventions. Since he has chosen to become the agent of a client, he must seek to remove the constrictions imposed on his client by an outside society. In this way he can help the client to develop the completeness of individuality which he regards as an unqualified good.

Because he has chosen to be the advocate of the individual, the counselor and the psychotherapist must join hands with those optimists who see in the new moral freedom opportunities for personal fulfillment which could not exist in a society that tolerates only minimal individual differences. The therapist need not assume that all changes are for the best, but certainly he is not required to assume that all social morals are bad and he must regard the present moral deencapsulation as good.

If the therapist is thoughtful, he will often be dismayed and even shocked at the immature client who recklessly, impetuously discards values which provide the therapist with profound personal satisfactions. The counselor and the psychotherapist is hardly required, however, to embrace an audacious moral activism which seeks to confront and to surmount all of the basic limits which society seeks to place upon individual conduct.

The counselor and the psychotherapist must be accepting of clients who experience a confused and chaotic inner world in which older values, which may include those the therapist still embraces, are no longer meaningful. The therapist need not approve of every choice his client may make, but he must stand behind the client as he wrestles against the social pressures that would force him into an encapsulating mold of moral demands and expectations.

The client needs help. He seeks treatment because his individuality is a tender plant requiring careful nurturance. An individualized self can not grow by itself in a world which is insensitive to individual differences. The client needs the counselor's help in differentiating himself from the surrounding social other to experience a distinct personal identity. The values which the client discovers in therapy must be expressive of his unique personality.

In providing support and shelter from the moral demands of the outside world, the therapist must be on guard lest he inadvertently impose his own demands and expectations upon the client. He must shelter the client but never smother him with his own morality. The therapist must be careful not to pry the client loose from an unthinking adherence to one morality merely to affix him to the therapist's moral standards.

The therapist may be guided ethically by the principles of a new morality, which seeks to free the individual from conforming to the demands and expectations of others so that he can fashion personal values for himself. The new morality can, however, soon become an old morality if therapists impose it as their moral structure upon the client. No matter how well intentioned the counselor or psychotherapist may be, he inevitably destroys the client's freedom when he seeks to impose his own cognitive forms upon wiggling and twisting individuals who are seeking to free themselves from a pigeonhole. Clients who are attempting to become morally free must therefore seek to resist being categorized by mental-health and mental-illness terminology or by other concepts which reduce subjective personal concern to the realm of objective fact.

Carkhuff and Berenson (1967) have suggested that most practiced forms of traditional psychotherapy should instead be considered merely as formal structures within which individuals seek to resolve their personal crises. They believe that counselors and psychotherapists should be broadly concerned with this crisis and not narrowly interested in the therapeutic. Carkhuff and Berenson suggest that only when the therapist can transcend his concepts and theories can he arrest a downward trend that otherwise leads only to the client's psychological death. Therefore they conclude that "the only person who can be an effective therapist is the one who will not be counseled by any of the existing approaches" (1967, p. 233).

Mental health becomes an old morality whenever it becomes encapsulated within a system. While therapists properly seek guidance from different theoretical orientations, they should never become unquestioningly beholden to any therapeutic virtues, even if they are such seemingly noncontroversial values as flexibility, eclecticism, or nonjudgmentalism. The challenge of the therapeutic is the possibility of establishing an open encounter between two people who are both learning to be free. Within this encounter, the most serious obstacle to the client's search for moral freedom is often the therapist's subservience to the moral meanings he has given to mental-health concepts and to other psychological terms with which he categorizes the client. The meaning of personal experience is to be the client's: It can never be totally possessed by the therapist's value orientation.

REFERENCES

Abrahamsen, D. Who are the guilty? New York: Rinehart, 1952.

Ackerman, N. W. The psychodynamics of family life. New York: Basic Books, 1958.

Aiken, H. D. The new morals. Harpers 1968, 236 (1413), 58-72.

Alexander, F., and H. Staub. The criminal, the judge, and the public. New York: Macmillan, 1931.

Andrews, J. D. W. Psychotherapy of phobias. Psychological Bulletin, 1966, 66, 455-480.

Ansbacher, H. L., and R. R. Ansbacher, eds. The individual psychology of Alfred Adler. New York: Basic Books, 1956.

Bakan, D. Sigmund Freud and the Jewish mystical tradition. Princeton: Van Nostrand, 1958.

Barrett, W. Irrational man. New York: Doubleday, 1958.

Benedict, R. Anthropology and the abnormal. Journal of General Psychology, 1934, 10, 59-80.

Benne, K. D. The uses of fraternity. Daedalus, 1961, 90, 233-246.

Berg, C. The problem of homosexuality. New York: Citadel, 1958.

Berg, I. A. Deviant responses and deviant people: The formulation of the deviation hypothesis. Journal of Counseling Psychology, 1957, 4, 154-161.

Berg, I. A., and H. E. Adams. Differentiating mental defectives from schizophrenics on the basis of deviant response sets. American Journal of Mental Deficiency, 1965, 70, 16-20.

Bijou, S. W. Implications of behavioral science for counseling and guidance. In J. D. Krumboltz, ed., Revolution in counseling. Boston: Houghton Mifflin, 1966.

Binswanger, L. The case of Ellen West. In R. May, E. Angel, and H. F. Ellenberger, eds., Existence: A New Dimension in Psychiatry and Psychology. New York: Basic Books, 1958.

Bisch, L. E. Be glad you're neurotic. New York: McGraw-Hill, 1936.

Boisen, A. T. Out of the depths. New York: Harper, 1960.

Bonney, M. E. Some correlates of a social definition of a normal personality. Journal of Clinical Psychology, 1964, 20, 415-422.

Boorstin, D. J. The mysterious science of the law. Cambridge, Mass: Harvard University Press, 1941.

Boring, E. G. A history of experimental psychology, 2nd ed. New York: Appleton-Century-Crofts, 1950.

Boss, M. Psychoanalysis and daseinsanalysis. New York: Basic Books, 1963.

Bradburn, N. M., and D. Caplovitz. Reports on happiness. Chicago: Aldine, 1965.

Bradfield, L. P., J. R. Gibb, and K. P. Benne. T-group theory and laboratory method. New York: Wiley, 1964.

Branden, N. Who is Ayn Rand? New York: Randon House, 1962.

Branden, N. Mental health versus mysticism and self-sacrifice. In Ayn Rand, The virtue of selfishness. New York: New American Library, 1964.

Branden, N. Psychotherapy and the objectivist ethics. Paper read at Michigan Society of Consulting Psychologists, November 24, 1965.

Breger, L., and J. L. McGaugh. Critique and reformulation of "learning theory" approaches to psychotherapy and neurosis. Psychological Bulletin, 1965, 63, 338-358.

Brewer, J. M. History of vocational guidance. New York: Harper, 1942.

Bridgman, P. W. The way things are. Cambridge, Mass: Harvard University Press, 1959.

Bronowski, J. Science and human values. New York: Messner, 1956.

Brown, J. S. Problems presented by the concept of acquired drives. In Current Theory and Research in Motivation, Vol. I. Lincoln: University of Nebraska Press, 1953.

Bruner, J. On knowing. Cambridge, Mass.: Harvard University Press, 1962.

Bruner, J. S., and C. Goodman. Value and need as organizing factors in perception. Journal of Abnormal and Social Psychology, 1947, 42, 33-44.

Buber, M. Between man and man. London: Routledge and Kegan Paul, 1947.

Bugental, J. F. T. The third force in psychology. Journal of Humanistic Psychology, 1964, 4, 19-26.

Bugental, J. F. T. The search for authenticity. New York: Holt, Rinehart and Winston, 1965.

Buhler, Charlotte. Values in psychotherapy. New York: Free Press, 1962.

Burton, A. The clinician as moralist. Journal of Existential Psychiatry, 1960a, 2, 207-218.

Burton, A. Schizophrenia and existence. Psychiatry, 1960b, 23, 385-394.

Burtt, E. A. The metaphysical foundations of modern science. London: Routledge and Kegan Paul, 1932.

Buttrick, G. A. The parables of Jesus. New York: Harper, 1928.

Camus, A. The stranger. New York: Random House, 1946.

Camus, A. The myth of Sisyphus. New York: Random House, 1955.

Cantril, H. The "why" of man's experience. New York: Macmillan, 1950.

Cardno, J. A. Psychology: human, humanistic, humane. Journal of Humanistic Psychology, 1966, 6, 170-177.

Carkhuff, R. R., and B. G. Berenson. Beyond counseling and therapy. New York: Holt, Rinehart and Winston, 1967.

Cleckley, H. M. The mask of sanity, 4th ed. St. Louis: Mosby, 1964.

Combs, A. W., and D. Snygg. Individual behavior. New York: Harper, 1959.

Cook, J. O. "Superstition" in the Skinnerian. American Psychologist, 1963, 18, 516-521.

Cook, T. E. The influence of client-counselor values similarity on change in meaning during brief counseling. Journal of Counseling Psychology, 1966, 13, 77-81.

Cox, H. The secular city. New York: Macmillan, 1965.

Davis, K. Mental hygiene and the class structure. Psychiatry, 1938, 1, 55-65.

Dicks, H. V. In search of our proper ethic. British Journal of Medical Psychology, 1950, 23, 1-14.

Dollard, J., and N. E. Miller. Personality and psychotherapy. New York: McGraw-Hill, 1950.

Douglas, W. Psychology in theological education. In H. Hofmann, ed., The ministry and mental health. New York: Association Press, 1960.

Ehrenwald, J. Psychotherapy: myth and method. New York: Grune and Stratton, 1966.

Ellis, A. Reason and emotion in psychotherapy. New York: Stuart, 1962.

Ellis, A. Sex without guilt, rev. ed. New York: Stuart Lyle, 1966.

Ellis, A. Should some people be labeled mentally ill? Journal of Consulting Psychology, 1967, 31, 435-446.

Ellis, A. John Jones (tape recording with script). Philadelphia: American Academy of Psychotherapists, no date.

Emerson, R. W. The transcendentalist. In B. A. Atkinson, ed., The complete essays and other writings of Ralph Waldo Emerson. New York: Random House, 1940. (Originally published 1843.)

Eysenck, H. J., and S. Rachman. Causes and cures of neurosis. San Diego: Knapp, 1965.

Farson, R. E. Introjection in the psychotherapeutic relationship. Journal of Counseling Psychology, 1961, 8, 337-343.

Festinger, L. A theory of cognitive dissonance. Stanford: Stanford University Press, 1957.

Feuer, L. S. Psychoanalysis and ethics. Springfield, Ill.: Thomas, 1955.

Fletcher, J. Situation ethics: the new morality. Philadelphia: Westminster, 1966.

Flugel, J. C. Man, morals, and society. New York: International Universities Press, 1945.

Foucault, M. Madness and civilization: a history of insanity in the age of reason. New York: Pantheon, 1965.

Frank, J. D. Persuasion and healing. Baltimore: Johns Hopkins University Press, 1961.

Frankl, V. The doctor and the soul. New York: Knopf, 1955.

Frankl, V. Man's search for meaning. New York: Washington Square, 1963.

Freud, S. Beyond the pleasure principle. New York: Liveright, 1922.

Freud, S. Civilization and its discontents. London: Hogarth, 1930.

Freud, S. New introductory lectures on psychoanalysis. New York: Carlton House, 1933.

Freud, S. Totem and taboo. In Basic writings of Sigmund Freud. New York: Random House, 1938.

Fromm, E. Escape from freedom. New York: Rinehart, 1941.

Fromm, E. Man for himself. New York: Rinehart, 1947.

Fromm, E. Psychoanalysis and religion. New Haven: Yale University Press, 1950.

Fromm, E. The sane society. New York: Rinehart, 1955.

Fromm, E. The art of loving. New York: Harper and Row, 1956.

Fromm, E. Sigmund Freud's mission. New York: Harper and Row, 1959.

Gaster, T. H. Demon, demonology. In Interpreter's dictionary of the Bible. Nashville: Abingdon, 1962.

Gendlin, E. T. Values and the process of experiencing. In A. H. Mahrer, ed., The goals of psychotherapy. New York: Appleton-Century-Crofts, 1967.

Ginsberg, S. W., and J. L. Herma. Values and their relationship to psychiatric principles and practices. American Journal of Psychotherapy, 1953, 7, 546-565.

Glad, D. D. Operational values in psychotherapy. New York: Oxford University Press, 1959.

Goldstein, K. The organism. New York: American Book Co., 1939.

Green, A. W. Social values and psychotherapy. Journal of Personality, 1946, 14, 199-228.

Group for the Advancement of Psychiatry. Sex and the college student. New York: Atheneum, 1965.

Halmos, P. The faith of the counsellors. New York: Schocken, 1966.

Harper, R. A. Psychoanalysis and psychotherapy: thirty-six systems. Englewood Cliffs, N. J.: Prentice-Hall, 1959.

Heisenberg, W. Physics and philosophy. New York: Harper, 1958.

Hilgard, E. R., and G. H. Bower. Theories of learning. New York: Appleton-Century-Crofts, 1966.

Hiltner, S. Preface to pastoral theology. Nashville: Abingdon, 1958.

Hobbs, N. Science and ethical behavior. American Psychologist, 1959, 14, 217-225.

Hobbs, N. Sources of gain in psychotherapy. American Psychologist, 1962, 17, 741-747.

Hobbs, N. Mental health's third revolution. American Journal of Orthopsychiatry, 1964, 34, 822-833.

Hollingshead, A. B., and F. C. Redlich. Social class and mental illness. New York: Wiley, 1958.

Horney, Karen. The neurotic personality of our time. New York: Norton, 1937.

Horney, Karen. Self-analysis. New York: Norton, 1942.

Huxley, A. L. Brave new world. New York: Harper, 1946.

Huxley, J. New bottles for new wine. New York: Harper, 1957.

Jahoda, Marie. Current concepts of positive mental health. New York: Basic Books, 1958.

James, W. Principles of psychology. New York: Holt, 1890.

Johnson, W. People in quandries. New York: Harper, 1946.

Johnston, T. Freud and political thought. New York: Citadel, 1965.

Jones, H. M. The pursuit of happiness. Cambridge, Mass.: Harvard University Press, 1953.

Jones, M. The therapeutic community. New York: Basic Books, 1953.

Jung, C. Modern man in search of his soul. New York: Harcourt and Brace, 1933.

Kelly, G. A. The psychology of personal constructs. New York: Norton, 1955.

Kierkegaard, S. The sickness unto death. Princeton: Princeton University Press, 1941.

Kiesler, D. J. Some myths of psychotherapy research and the search for a paradigm. Psychological Bulletin, 1966, 65, 110-136.

Koch, S. Psychological science versus the science-humanism antinomy: intimations of a significant science of man. American Psychologist, 1961, 16, 629-639.

Krasner, L. Behavior control and social responsibility. American Psychologist, 1962a, 17, 199-203.

Krasner, L. The therapist as a social reinforcement machine. In Research in psychotherapy, Vol. II. Washington, D.C.: American Psychological Association, 1962b.

Krasner, L. The behavioral scientist and social responsibility: no place to hide. Journal of Social Issues, 1965, 21 (2), 9-30.

Krutch, J. W. The measure of man. Indianapolis: Bobbs-Merrill, 1953.

Kuhn, T. S. The Copernican revolution. Cambridge: Harvard University Press, 1957.

Kuhn, T. S. The structure of scientific revolutions. Chicago: University of Chicago Press, 1962.

Landfield, A. W., and M. N. Nawas. Psychotherapeutic improvement as a function of communication and adoption of therapist's values. Journal of Counseling Psychology, 1964, 11, 336-341.

Langner, T. S., and S. T. Michael. Life stress and mental health. New York: Free Press, 1963.

Lecky, P. Self-consistency. New York: Island Press, 1951.

Lee, A. M. Social pressures and the values of psychologists. American Psychologist, 1954, 9, 516-522.

Lindner, R. Prescription for rebellion. New York: Rinehart, 1952.

Lippmann, W. A preface to morals. New York: Macmillan, 1929.

London, P. Modes and morals of psychotherapy. New York: Holt, Rinehart and Winston, 1964.

Lowe, C. M. Value-orientations: an ethical dilemma. American Psychologist, 1959, 14, 687-693.

Lowe, C. M. The self-concept: fact or artifact? Psychological Bulletin, 1961, 58, 325-336.

Lowe, C. M. The rediscovery of man. Religion in Life, 1963, 32, 621-628.

Lowe, C. M. Values versus sickness in the mental health field. Journal of Individual Psychology, 1964, 20, 196-201.

Lowe, C. M. The healing community: church and mental hospital. Pastoral Psychology, in press.

Lowe, C. M., and R. O. Braaten. Differences in religious attitudes in mental illness. Journal for the Scientific Study of Religion, 1966, 5, 435-445.

McClelland, D. C. The use of measures of human motivation in the study of society. In J. W. Atkinson, ed., Motives in fantasy, action, and society. Princeton: Van Nostrand, 1958.

McClelland, D. C. The achieving society. Princeton: Van Nostrand, 1961.

McNeill, J. T. A history of the cure of souls. New York: Harper, 1951.

Magaret, Ann. Generalization in successful psychotherapy. Journal of Consulting Psychology, 1950, 14, 64-70.

Maguire, J. D. The theological uses of psychoanalysis: patterns, problems, and proposals. Religion in Life, 1962, 31, 169-184.

Malinowski, B. Magic, science, and religion. New York: Doubleday, 1948.

Margolis, J. Psychotherapy and morality. New York: Random House, 1966.

Maslow, A. H. Motivation and personality. New York: Harper, 1954.

Maslow, A. H. Toward a psychology of being. Princeton: Van Nostrand, 1962.

Maslow, A. H. The psychology of science. New York: Harper and Row, 1966.

May, R. Historical and philosophical presuppositions for understanding therapy. In O. H. Mowrer, ed., Psychotherapy: theory and research. New York: Ronald, 1953.

May, R. Origins and significance of the existential movement in psychology. In R. May, E. Angel, and H. Ellenberger, eds., Existence: a new dimension in psychiatry and psychology. New York: Basic Books, 1958.

May, R. Dangers in the relation of existentialism to psychotherapy. In H. M. Ruitenbeek, ed., Psychoanalysis and existential philosophy. New York: Dutton, 1962a.

May, R. Freedom and responsibility reexamined. Paper read at American College Personnel Association, Chicago, April 18, 1962b.

Mead, G. H. Mind, self, and society. Chicago: University of Chicago Press, 1934.

Mednick, S. A. A learning theory approach to research in schizophrenia. Psychological Bulletin, 1958, 55, 316-327.

Mendelsohn, G. A. Effects of client personality and client-counselor similarity on the duration of counseling: a replication and extension. Journal of Counseling Psychology, 1966, 13, 228-234.

Mendelsohn, G. A., and M. H. Geller. Effects of counselor-client similarity on outcome of counseling. Journal of Counseling Psychology, 1963, 10, 71-77.

Mendelsohn, G. A., and M. H. Geller. Structure of client attitudes toward counseling and their relation to client-counselor similarity. Journal of Consulting Psychology, 1965, 29, 63-72.

Mendelsohn, G. A., and M. H. Geller. Similarity, missed sessions, and early termination. Journal of Counseling Psychology, 1967, 14, 210-215.

Miller, N. E. Some reflections on the law of effect. In Current Theory and Research in Motivation, Vol. XI. Lincoln: University of Nebraska Press, 1963.

Moreno, J. L. Sociodrama, a method for the analysis of social conflicts. Psychodrama Monograph No. 1. New York: Beacon House, 1944.

Moreno, J. L. Psychodrama, Vol. I. New York: Beacon House, 1946.

Morgan, C. Physiological theory of drives. In S. Koch, ed., Psychology: a study of a science, Vol. I. New York: McGraw-Hill, 1959.

Mowrer, O. H. Crisis in psychiatry and religion. Princeton: Van Nostrand, 1961.

Mowrer, O. H. Psychotherapy: theory and research. New York: Ronald, 1953.

Mowrer, O. H. The new group therapy. Princeton: Van Nostrand, 1964.

Murphy, G. Personality. New York: Harper, 1947.

Murphy, G. The cultural context of guidance. Personnel and Guidance Journal, 1955, 34, 4-9.

Murray, E. J. Learning theory and psychotherapy: biotropic versus sociotropic approaches. Journal of Counseling Psychology, 1963, 10, 250-255.

Nawas, M. M., and A. W. Landfield. Improvement in psychotherapy and adoption of the therapists' meaning system. Psychological Reports, 1963, 13, 97-98.

Neibuhr, R. The nature of man. New York: Scribner, 1941.

Niebuhr, R. The irony of American history. New York: Scribner, 1952.

Niebuhr, R. The self and the dramas of history. New York: Scribner, 1955.

O'Connell, W. E. Humanistic identification: a new translation for gemeinschaftsgefühl. Journal of Individual Psychology, 1965, 21, 44-47.

Patterson, C. H. Counseling and psychotherapy: theory and practice. New York: Harper, 1959.

Patterson, C. H. Theories of counseling and psychotherapy. New York: Harper and Row, 1966.

Pavlov, I. P. Conditioned reflexes and psychiatry, Vol. II. New York: International Publishers, 1941.

Pepinsky, H. B., and T. O. Karst. Convergence: a phenomenon in counseling and psychotherapy. American Psychologist, 1964, 19, 333-338.

Pike, J. A. You and the new morality: seventy-four cases. New York: Harper and Row, 1967.

Polanyi, M. Personal knowledge. New York: Harper and Row, 1964.

Postman, L. J., J. S. Bruner, and E. M. McGinnies. Personal values as selective factors in perception. Journal of Abnormal and Social Psychology, 1948, 43, 142-154.

Pound, R. Spirit of the common law. Boston: Marshall Jones, 1921.

Pound, R. Law and morals. Chapel Hill: University of North Carolina Press, 1926.

Pound, R. Social control through law. New Haven: Yale University Press, 1942.

Rand, Ayn. The fountainhead. New York: Bobbs-Merill, 1943.

Rand, Ayn. Atlas shrugged. New York: Random House, 1957.

Rand, Ayn. The virtue of selfishness. New York: New American Library, 1964.

Raushenbusch, W. Christianizing the social order. New York: Macmillan, 1912.

Ribble, Margaret. The rights of infants, 2nd ed. New York: Columbia University Press, 1965.

Reisman, D. The lonely crowd. New Haven: Yale University Press, 1961.

Roberts, D. E. Psychotherapy and a Christian view of man. New York: Scribners, 1953.

Robinson, J. A. T. Honest to God. Philadelphia: Westminster, 1963.

Rogers, C. R. Divergent trends in methods of improving adjustment. Harvard Educational Review, 1948, 18, 209-219.

Rogers, C. R. Client-centered therapy. Boston: Houghton Mifflin, 1951.

Rogers, C. R. Persons or science? a philosophical question. American Psychologist, 1955, 10, 267-278.

Rogers, C. R. Review of Reinhold Niebuhr's The self and the dramas of history. Chicago Theological Seminary Register, 1956, 46, 13-14. (Reprinted in Pastoral Psychology, 1958, 9 (85), 15-17.)

Rogers, C. R. The necessary and sufficient conditions of therapeutic personality change. Journal of Consulting Psychology, 1957a, 21, 95-103.

Rogers, C. R. A therapist's view of the good life. The Humanist, 1957b, 17, 291-300.

Rogers, C. R. The characteristics of a helping relationship. Personnel and Guidance Journal, 1958a, 37, 6-16.

Rogers, C. R. A process conception of psychotherapy. American Psychologist, 1958b, 13, 142-149.

Rogers, C. R. On becoming a person. Boston: Houghton Mifflin, 1961.

Rogers, C. R. Some questions and challenges facing a humanistic psychology. Journal of Humanistic Psychology, 1965, 5, 1-5.

Rogers, C. R. Mr. Lin (tape recording). Philadelphia: American Academy of Psychotherapists, no date.

Rogers, C. R., and B. F. Skinner. Some issues concerning the control of human behavior. Science, 1956, 124, 1057-1065.

Rogers, C. R., and B. F. Skinner. Dialogue, University of Minnesota, Duluth, June 11 and 12, 1962 (tape recording and typescript). Philadelphia: American Academy of Psychotherapists.

Rome, H. P. Psychiatry and changing social values. Mental Hospitals, 1965, 16, 295-300.

Rosenthal, D. Changes in some moral values following psychotherapy. Journal of Consulting Psychology, 1955, 19, 431-436.

Rostow, E. V. The sovereign prerogative: the Supreme Court and the quest for law. New Haven: Yale University Press, 1962.

Royce, J. R. The encapsulated man. Princeton: Van Nostrand, 1964.

Salter, A. Conditioned reflex therapy. New York: Creative Age Press, 1949.

Samler, J. Change in values: a goal in counseling. Journal of Counseling Psychology, 1960, 7, 32-39.

Sanford, N. Social science and social reform. Journal of Social Issues, 1965, 21, (2), 54-70.

Sarbin, T. R. On the futility of the proposition that some people be labeled "mentally ill." Journal of Consulting Psychology, 1967, 31, 447-453.

Sartre, J. Being and nothingness. New York: Philosophical Library, 1956.

Satir, Virginia. Conjoint family therapy. Palo Alto: Science and Behavior Books, 1964.

Schofield, W. Psychotherapy: The purchase of friendship. Englewood Cliffs, N.J.: Prentice-Hall, 1964.

Shaffer, L. F., and E. J. Shoben. The psychology of adjustment. Cambridge, Mass.: Riverside, 1956.

Shoben, E. J. Some observations on psychotherapy and the learning process. In O. H. Mowrer, ed., Psychotherapy: Theory and Research. New York: Ronald, 1953.

Shoben, E. J. Work, love and maturity. Personnel and Guidance Journal, 1956, 34, 326-332.

Shoben, E. J. Toward a concept of the normal personality. American Psychologist, 1957, 12, 183-189.

Shoben, E. J. Love, loneliness, and logic. Journal of Individual Psychology, 1960, 16, 11-24.

Shoben, E. J. Culture, ego psychology, and an image of man. American Journal of Psychotherapy, 1961, 15, 395-408.

Shoben, E. J. Psychology: natural science or humanistic discipline? Journal of Humanistic Psychology, 1965, 2, 210-218.

Simpson, G. G. The meaning of evolution. New Haven: Yale University Press, 1949.

Simpson, G. G. Naturalistic ethics and the social sciences. American Psychologist, 1966, 21, 27-36.

Skinner, B. F. Walden two. New York: Macmillan, 1948.

Skinner, B. F. Science and human behavior. New York: Macmillan, 1953.

Smith, M. B. "Mental health" reconsidered: a special case of the problem of values in psychology. American Psychologist, 1961, 16, 299-306.

Snow, C. P. The two cultures and the scientific revolution. New York: Cambridge University Press, 1959.

Snow, C. P. The two cultures: and a second look. New York: Cambridge University Press, 1963.

Srole, L., T. S. Langner, S. T. Michael, M. K. Opler, and T. A. C. Rennie. Mental health in the metropolis. New York: McGraw-Hill, 1962

Stewart, L. H., and C. J. Warnath. The counselor and society. Boston: Houghton Mifflin, 1965.

Sullivan, H. S. The interpersonal theory of psychiatry. New York: Norton, 1953.

Sullivan, H. S. The psychiatric interview. New York: Norton, 1954.

Sullivan, H. S. Clinical studies in psychiatry. New York: Norton, 1956.

Szasz, T. S. The myth of mental illness. American Psychologist, 1960, 15, 113-118.

Szasz, T. S. The myth of mental illness. New York: Hoeber-Harper, 1961.

Szasz, T. S. Law, liberty, and psychiatry. New York: Macmillan, 1963.

Tillich, P. The courage to be. New Haven: Yale University Press, 1952.

Tillich, P. The Protestant era. Chicago: University of Chicago Press, 1957.

Tillich, P. Dynamics of faith. New York: Harper, 1957.

Truax, C. B. Reinforcement and non-reinforcement in Rogerian psychotherapy. Journal of Abnormal Psychology, 1966, 71, 1-9.

Truax, C. B., and R. R. Carkhuff. Toward effective counseling and psychotherapy. Chicago: Aldine, 1967.

van den Berg, J. H. The changing nature of man. New York: Norton, 1961.

Watson, J. B. Behavior. New York: Holt, 1914.

Watts, A. W. Psychotherapy east and west. New York: Pantheon, 1961.

Weisskopf, Edith. Some suggestions concerning Weltanschauung and psychotherapy. Journal of Abnormal and Social Psychology, 1953, 48, 601-604.

Welkowitz, Joan, J. Cohen, and D. Ortmeyer, Value-system similarity: investigation of patient-therapist dyads. Journal of Consulting Psychology, 1967, 31, 48-55.

Wheelis, A. The quest for identity. New York: Norton, 1958.

Whitaker, C. A., and T. P. Malone. The roots of psychotherapy. New York: McGraw-Hill, 1953.

White, R. W. Motivation reconsidered: the concept of competence. Psychological Review, 1959, 66, 297-333.

White, R. W. Competence and the psychosexual stages of development. In Current Theory and Research in Motivation, Vol. VIII. Lincoln: University of Nebraska Press, 1960.

Whyte, L. L. The unconscious before Freud. New York: Basic Books, 1960.

Whyte, W. H. The organization man. New York: Simon and Schuster, 1956.

Williamson, E. G. Value-orientation in counseling. Personnel and Guidance Journal, 1958, 36, 520-528.

Wolpe, J. Psychotherapy by reciprocal inhibition. Stanford: Stanford University Press, 1958.

Wolstein, B. Irrational despair. New York: Free Press, 1962.

Young, J. Z. Doubt and certainy in science. Oxford: Clarendon, 1951.

Zigler, E., and L. Phillips. Social effectiveness and symptomatic behaviors. Journal of Abnormal and Social Psychology, 1960, 61, 231-238.

Zigler, E., and L. Phillips. Social competence and the process-reactive distinction in psychopathology. Journal of Abnormal and Social Psychology, 1962, 65, 215-222.

Zilboorg, G. History of medical psychology. New York: Norton, 1941.

INDEX OF NAMES

INDEX OF TOPICS

297